Waging War to Make Peace

Waging War to Make Peace

U.S. Intervention in Global Conflicts

SUSAN YOSHIHARA

PRAEGER SECURITY INTERNATIONAL

PRAEGER

AN IMPRINT OF ABC-CLIO, LLC
Santa Barbara, California • Denver, Colorado • Oxford, England

Copyright 2010 by Susan Yoshihara

Library of Congress Cataloging-in-Publication Data

Yoshihara, Susan.
  Waging war to make peace: U.S. intervention in global conflicts / Susan
Yoshihara.
    p. cm.
  Includes bibliographical references and index.
  ISBN 978-0-275-99991-9 (alk. paper)—ISBN 978-0-275-99992-6 (e-book)
1. United States—Foreign relations—2001–2009. 2. United States—Foreign
relations—2009– 3. United States—Military policy. 4. Intervention
(International law) 5. Intervention (International law)—Government policy—
United States   I. Title.
  JZ1480.Y67   2010
  327.1'170973—dc22   2010002199

ISBN: 978-0-275-99991-9
EISBN: 978-0-275-99992-6

14 13 12 11 10 1 2 3 4 5

This book is also available on the World Wide Web as an eBook.
Visit www.abc-clio.com for details.

Praeger
An Imprint of ABC-CLIO, LLC

ABC-CLIO, LLC
130 Cremona Drive, P.O. Box 1911
Santa Barbara, California 93116-1911

This book is printed on acid-free paper ∞

Manufactured in the United States of America

Copyright Acknowledgments

Portions of chapter 2 are taken from "How to Think about the Responsibility to
Protect" by Susan Yoshihara, *First Things,* June 16, 2008. http://www.firstthings.com/
onthesquare/2008/06/how-to-think-about-the-respons. Reprinted with permission.

Portions of chapter 7 are taken from "The Trouble with Mixed Motives" by Susan D. Fink,
Naval War College Review, Autumn 2004. Reprinted with permission.

+
AMDG

for Toshi

Contents

Preface and Acknowledgments

I began thinking seriously about humanitarianism on a day some 20 years ago while steaming in the South China Sea. It was early in my first deployment as a Navy helicopter pilot in a combat logistics unit. My ship, part of the USS Midway carrier battle group, was transiting north from the Philippines to Hong Kong when someone onboard sighted a boat. It was laden with more than a hundred civilians who were, we later determined, severely dehydrated and in need of food and medical attention. After deliberating the rules about interference with refugees at sea, the captain ordered a helicopter rescue. Since I was one of only two women in the carrier battle group I was tasked with helping the women. This turned out to be a privilege, but I confess my feminist sensibilities bristled when I was denied the chance to fly the mission. As it turned out, the experience of physically helping those who had exhausted every other remedy moved me deeply. In the laborious hours of bathing and clothing the women I witnessed fear and exhaustion turn to relief—after enduring some weeks on the high seas and selling all they had to escape a repressive regime. That day made me believe how achievable, how very possible humanitarian action can be for a military so well trained and equipped and with personnel so ready to lend a hand.

In the following years, my colleagues and I would fly more humanitarian relief missions of opportunity throughout Asia and Africa, delivering aid, setting up clinics, evacuating civilians. But then came the

Somalia intervention, then Haiti, and finally the Kosovo campaign, and those missions were quite different. From a military perspective, these were simply combat operations with a humanitarian purpose. What seemed to be straightforward missions, however, were embroiled in political debates about mission creep, exit strategies, vital vs. peripheral interests, and a host of legal and ethical questions. How was it possible to wage a war and save lives? Did not dropping bombs belie any moral high ground we might claim? Even if war with a moral purpose was legal and politically possible—was it prudent? I was eager to wrestle with these dilemmas to understand how humanitarian military intervention could be as achievable as our rescue that day on the high seas.

Resolution would elude me, however, as it has escaped much brighter minds in the men and women pondering this question from the trenches of humanitarian action, at the highest levels of government, and in the quiet of academic reflection. In my present work as part of a nongovernmental organization at the United Nations, I have witnessed the intractable policy debates rage on. Angry delegates, whose compatriots are most likely to need humanitarian relief, resist the notion that other countries might have a responsibility to deliver it. The heated debates are not so much about humanitarianism as they are about sovereignty and power. There is real fear that protecting human rights and delivering aid is just a pretext for sinister designs.

Not everyone is displeased with humanitarian war. When I met with Kosovo's president, Fatmir Sejdiu, in his office in Pristina just days after that former Serbian province had adopted its constitution in 2008, he expressed gratitude for the Western intervention that led to political independence for his people. In hindsight, the 1999 Kosovo intervention is still contested. It was largely seen as a success for NATO allies, who united after overcoming their respective misgivings about violating Serbian sovereignty to rescue Kosovar Albanians. It was criticized by those who saw it as part of an unduly interventionist American foreign policy. Just two years later, the allies would unite again to protect the skies of the United States after the terrorist attacks of September 11, 2001. But when it came time to debate the prospect of war with Iraq in 2002, invective tore that unity apart, leaving bitterness that remains today.

What was striking to me at the time, as I was examining the Kosovo debates, was how similar the arguments made by the Americans, British, French, and Germans in 2003 were to those they had made in 1999 about war with Serbia. The most contentious aspects were again the desire for, but elusiveness of, a UN Security Council resolution authorizing force, the need for some legal or acceptable alternative form of legitimate justification for the war, and perhaps most importantly, the competing moral imperatives that charged the debates with impassioned rhetoric for and against war. This book represents an attempt to show that the fallout among the allies in 2003, and what threatens to cause fractious disputes in the future, are those unresolved but fundamental questions. The humanitarian intervention debates of the 1990s exposed but did not resolve these problems. The Iraq war debates aggravated them further. In both cases, the role of moral imperative was pivotal.

When I looked for a framework by which to examine the role of values in these debates, I came up against the limitations of international relations theories. Examining the competitive role of the great powers in these cases was best explained by realist theories, but liberal institutionalism best accounted for their quest for legitimacy through the United Nations (UN); meanwhile, the constructivist school had paid the most attention to the role of ideas and values in politics. These schools of thought are often presented as competitive, and inevitably an emphasis on any one aspect led to policy prescriptions with a similar emphasis. Thus, realists proposed more attention to national interests and eschewed humanitarianism, liberalists called for stricter adherence to the UN Charter, and constructivists advocated developing and enforcing of new transnational norms to encompass human rights and humanitarian principles.

With the help of David Yost I found the work of Martin Wight and his alternative way of comparing the apples and oranges of international relations by tracing traditions of international thought in the war debates, which took account of all three influences—political, legal, and moral—in practice. The result is the story told in the following pages about how world leaders grappled personally and publicly with the practical challenge of trying to rescue, to liberate, to relieve human suffering by force of arms. In the end, I hope that exposing these debates in this manner will help policy makers and practitioners to recognize the way genuine shared values can unite the allies, while making moral issues out of what are really political and legal concerns can divide them.

I am grateful for the patience and thoroughness of many people who have commented on this work at various stages: Robert L. Pfaltzgraff and Ian Johnstone at the Fletcher School at Tufts University and David Yost at the Naval Postgraduate School, as well as Jon Rosenwasser and Karen Coppock who, along with my husband Toshi Yoshihara, read this work in its initial drafts. My research was made possible through the generosity of the U.S. Navy's Admiral Arthur S. Moreau fellowship and Admiral Samuel Eliot Morison Naval history scholarship, as well as the Eisenhower Institute's Dwight D. Eisenhower/Thomas Pappas graduate fellowship. I thank my students and colleagues at the Naval War College who offered feedback as I attempted to apply the lessons I gleaned from research in the classroom. My thanks to Catherine Kelleher, who published, and Pell Boyer, who edited parts of this work and inspired the comparison of the Kosovo and Iraq cases for the pages of the *Naval War College Review.* Thanks also to my fellow panelists at the International Studies Association annual convention in 2006, Terry Nardin, David Mapel, Tony Lang, and Peter Digeser, who offered a much-needed critique of the ethical dimensions of the work. I am grateful to Robert George and his team at the James Madison Program in American Ideals and Institutions at Princeton for the opportunity to test some of these ideas about "the responsibility to protect" at their 2008 annual conference, which commemorated the 150th anniversary of the Lincoln–Douglas debates, and to my fellow panelist J. Daryl Charles for his comments. Thanks to the late Fr. Richard John Neuhaus and the editors at *First Things,* who improved that work for publication. I am also grateful for the comments of the anonymous reviewers of the original manuscript, and for the editors at Praeger who saw the book through to publication. While many people helped improve the final product, the many shortcomings of the work are mine alone.

This book would not have made it to publication without the inspiration of my newborn baby girl. It was Teresa's good nature and regularity in her three A.M. feedings that afforded me many quiet hours of writing before she and the sun rose again. I thank my father and mother, George and Joyce Fink, my sister Patricia for helping out at home, and my brothers Tom and Dan for their encouragement over the years. My husband stands out as the most constant companion and truest friend one could ever have. It is to him and to our mutual Benefactor that this book is dedicated. I am grateful for the men and women with whom I served throughout my military career, and for those who now stand the watch. I salute my professional colleagues, who dedicate their time and talent to making sure that the dignity of the human person is not forgotten in UN policy debates. I admire and appreciate all those in government who take the personal and political risks and work the long hours to do the same.

CHAPTER 1

Introduction

That is the real issue. That is the issue that will continue in this country when these poor tongues of Judge Douglas and myself shall be silent. It is the eternal struggle between these two principles—right and wrong—throughout the world. They are the two principles that have stood face to face from the beginning of time; and will ever continue to struggle. The one is the common right of humanity and the other is the divine right of kings.

—Abraham Lincoln, 1858

Debates about humanitarian intervention endure because they pose some of the most important political, legal, and moral questions of our time: about the meaning of sovereignty, the nature of international law, the just use of force, and the nature of international order. Humanitarian intervention in practice remains highly contentious because of the irreconcilable tension between the hope of achieving liberal internationalist aims using the ultimate realist means, military force.

This tension has made for odd bedfellows in U.S. foreign policy. Liberated by the end of the cold war during the 1990s, hopes ran high for putting troops to use for humanitarian ends. By the turn of the century, many scholars and practitioners hailed a new international norm of humanitarian intervention—war for primarily humanitarian purposes.[1] Some saw the powerful combination of human rights and their enforcement through intervention as a means of transforming the world.[2] It was for some the sign of the collective enlightenment of the international community. Finishing what they started after

World War II by banning wars of aggression in the UN Charter, world leaders now seemed to agree that the proper use of armed force was to rescue suffering populations from grave human rights abuses.

Euphoria was fleeting. Fallout from the contentious decision making that led up to the Iraq war changed the alliances among advocates and opponents of humanitarian war. So polarized was the debate over the justness of the war that it created an abyss where once there was robust discussion of humanitarianism. Once-passionate proponents, most notably former UN secretary general Kofi Annan and many in the liberal academic field, suddenly grew disillusioned and turned to ponder other questions.[3] By reverting to a traditional notion of war in the national interest, the critics claimed, the Bush administration had reversed a decade of momentum in the establishment of a new norm of humanitarian intervention. Madeleine Albright, who roused European support for the Kosovo intervention as President Clinton's secretary of state, blamed President Bush on the pages of the *New York Times* for causing a global relapse into traditional notions of sovereignty. She claimed that the Iraq war "generated a negative reaction that has weakened support for cross-border interventions even for worthy purposes."[4] George Bush had ruined everything, and all the hard work of crafting new rules about the use of force and a new international order was in vain.

That is not to say that substantive disagreement with the Bush doctrine of limited preemption was not real. Much antipathy about the Iraq war is due to ongoing disagreement about the adequacy of the evidence regarding Iraq's weapons of mass destruction, perceptions that the war was therefore unjustified, concerns that it did not have the support of North American Treaty Organization (NATO) allies, particularly France and Germany, and regret over the thousands of men, women, and children who have lost life and limb in the conflict. Yet it is also recognized that much of the outrage is based upon general distaste for the Bush administration from the mostly left-leaning academy, which remained ideologically opposed to President Bush's politics on a host of international and domestic issues.

Dislodged from their perches of expertise for whatever reason, then, many of the new interventionists went into a sort of self-exile; others ignored the humanitarian question in their analysis of the Iraq and Afghanistan wars, as the just war scholar James Turner Johnson has noted;[5] and the intense debates about codifying the practice of humanitarian war seemed to disappear for a while. Perennial humanitarian and human rights tragedies in places such as Darfur, Congo, and Burma never relented, however, and kept the unfinished business percolating. Some former enthusiasts, such as David Rieff, turned into skeptics and wrote their confessions, while others used the Iraq war to define all that "good" humanitarian intervention is not. Still others tried to redeem the unpopular notion of a "right of humanitarian intervention" by recasting it as a "responsibility to protect." But that refinement, too, has met fierce resistance from all sides.

How could experts after the 1999 Kosovo intervention have been so sure that the world was witnessing the creation of a new international legal norm of humanitarian intervention—along with a new definition of sovereignty, and indeed a new transnational world order—only to recoil from the idea four years later in the wake of the Iraq war? Why does the idea of a "responsibility to protect," still championed by ardent liberal internationalists, now languish in UN conference rooms, condemned by the world's weakest nations, who would be its target, and by the world's most powerful nation, who would be its executor?

The reason is that the "good" Kosovo campaign and the "bad" war in Iraq have been characterized mainly by their outcomes, while the two wars have far more in common than experts care to admit. Though some insist that Kosovo was somehow different, since it was waged principally for humanitarian aims, the fact is that the justifications the four major NATO nations used in both wars were strikingly similar. Without acknowledging this, there is a danger that the unity of the NATO alliance, strained by the disputes over Iraq, will not heal well enough or in time to face tomorrow's most challenging threats. That is what this book is about. Many have interpreted the standoff on the Iraq war as a clear disagreement about the meaning of multilateralism pitting the United States, and to some degree Britain, on one side, and France and Germany on the other. While American and European public opinions diverge on these issues, most accounts obscure the fact that the decision making among the four allies on both the Kosovo and Iraq decisions had a lot in common on this point.

By examining the Kosovo decision in context and then comparing it to the Iraq case, it becomes evident that the Bush administration, whatever its weaknesses, inherited a debate about war that was ongoing and unfinished since the Kosovo campaign. Left unresolved in the heady days of humanitarian war in the 1990s were fundamental questions about world order and the waging of humanitarian war. Namely, what do sovereign states really believe about who has the authority to wage it? When is it justified? And are states ever obligated to intervene militarily? These are the three questions this book seeks to answer.

In the Kosovo case, consensus was achieved only after overcoming sharp differences about proper authority for the use of force and reconciling a moral justification with the limits of international law. The Iraq controversy also centered on justification, but to an even greater extent than the Kosovo case, the controversy was most heated over proper authorization. In 2003 NATO leaders were unable to reconcile their various national interests, and the bitterness of the dispute was heightened by two competing moral imperatives: "liberation" of the Iraqi people on one hand, and the belief that only the UN offered legitimate authority to wage the war on the other.

The unfinished business about international authority, prominent in the academy in Europe and the United States, is the idea that the world is evolving beyond a strict notion of national sovereignty. Proponents of liberal internationalism point to the Kosovo case, among other developments in the post–World War II and post–cold war era, such as "universal jurisdiction," the International Criminal Tribunals for Yugoslavia and Rwanda, the International Criminal Court, and even the increasing activism of on the part of UN human rights treaty bodies and special rapporteurs to prove that law, morality, and politics are becoming more homogenous, more cosmopolitan. Sovereignty, to these minds, is an elastic idea that must change with prevailing thinking, including the ever-expanding notion of what constitutes human rights and how they are to be enforced.

Ongoing disagreement throughout these two decisions also centered on whether the world was witnessing a collective change of attitudes about rules, specifically where values entered in. Those who perceived the emergence of a new norm of humanitarian intervention seemed to base it on a belief that leaders were obeying a common idea commonly understood. But as the following chapters reveal, this was not what was going on during the interventions of the 1990s. What was happening was not a top-down imposition, or collective enlightenment based on an elite-inspired new norm that trumped sovereignty. Rather, values influenced decision making by rising from the people and from individual decision makers in a way that was unique to each nation and based upon its shared history, culture, and political and legal traditions. Collective action, or lack of it in the case of Iraq, was influenced in both cases by each nation's interpretation of their moral obligations.

If the Iraq war heightened the differences between war waged to defeat an enemy and war waged to make peace by solving intractable humanitarian emergencies, it also showed how inchoate the prescriptions of the new interventionists really were. Practical matters, unresolved in the theoretical debates, were thrust by the wars in Afghanistan and Iraq into the front pages of popular discourse: how to resolve tensions between upholding the UN Charter based upon national sovereignty while honoring emerging consensus around the imperative of human rights; how to create new international norms while fostering respect for and enforcement of negotiated international treaty law; how to promote universal norms garnering political will while striving for multilateral action.

And so when the allies agreed in 1999 to intervene in Kosovo, they left unresolved many of these fundamental questions. And when they disagreed in 2003, each country did so with similar reasoning, whether or not consensus was reached. The mixed motives in each case used to justify going to war or opposing it consisted of political, legal, and moral imperatives. But the role of the moral imperative was not isolated to humanitarian ideals, and it was not tacked on or used as window dressing. In fact the moral component ran throughout the legal and political arguments on both sides of the war debates, allowing consensus in 1999 and leading to vitriol in 2003.

Why were moral arguments so important? The reason is that deliberations about who is authorized to wage war and when it is justified are essentially quests for legitimacy. In an era in which international law and institutions are increasingly expected to lend that legitimacy, they proved inadequate. As a result there is a gap between expectations and capabilities of international legal regimes. This was the reason the Bush administration gave for its doctrine of limited preemption. According to the 2002 National Security Strategy, "Legal scholars and international jurists often conditioned the legitimacy of preemption on the existence of an imminent threat.... We must adapt the concept of imminent threat to the capabilities and objectives of today's adversaries."[6] When the Obama administration announced in 2009 it would review the doctrine, analysts argued it did so not because it was outmoded. In fact the doctrine was still considered an important foreign policy tool. Rather, it needed review because it caused "consternation" among many who believed it contravened international legal norms.[7]

Some believe that moral arguments were thus used to "fill in" where political and legal regimes failed. This is true as far as it goes, but it is also true that nations acted on motives of humanitarianism based upon much older norms based in the natural law, primarily in the form of the just war doctrine. For all the deepening and widening of international law institutions on a host of economic, social, and even political matters, none of the allies found them adequate to reconcile the choice of whether or not to go to war, what remains perhaps the most important decision a nation can make.

First of all, legal regimes failed to reconcile conflicting national interests. This is obvious when examining Security Council debates and the way Russia and China thwarted the allies' attempt to get a UN mandate in the case of Kosovo, the way France threatened a veto in the Iraq case, and the way Germany considered war with Iraq illegitimate even with a Security Council resolution specifically authorizing the use of force.

The way moral arguments filled in where the law failed was also was evident when secretary of state Colin Powell called the situation in Darfur "genocide." Using the term overcame bureaucratic inertia within the Bush administration and made the crisis headline news, allowing activists and national leaders to put more pressure on Khartoum. Since Sudan was not a state party to the genocide convention, invocation of the term could not be construed as putting pressure on Khartoum to fulfill its own international legal obligations. Rather, it made it harder for European state parties to leave it off their respective foreign policy agendas. Hence, there was an implicit assertion that the convention was somehow applicable, even though nations maintained that the convention did not legally bind them to intervene. Just as with the need for a United Nations Security Council (UNSC) mandate, the treaty arguably offered more power as a moral tool than a legal device.

Does this mean that states are never obligated to relieve suffering of the victims of humanitarian and human rights tragedies outside their borders? No nation has claimed there is a legal duty, but as these cases show, they were very willing to acknowledge a moral obligation. This was most notable in the example of British prime minister Tony Blair. Due to changes in domestic and international context, moral arguments have been holding more sway in the last decade, helping states overcome resistance when authority and justification are disputed, such as when German sentiment for protecting the human rights of Kosovar Albanians overcame their pacifist tradition and allowed them to participate in the NATO campaign against Serbia. The moral argument in the Kosovo case allowed the allies to overcome the controversial question of unilateralism, defined by some of them as the use of force without a Security Council mandate. Even so, these same countries balked when George Bush and Tony Blair used the moral imperative of liberating the Iraqis from Saddam Hussein as one reason why they could not be bound by the lack of a UN mandate. French leaders countered with moral rhetoric, calling the need for a UN Security Council resolution a moral, and not just a legal, imperative. The dispute, fueled by moral outrage and not just differing political interests, was a historic low point in NATO politics.

Thus the moral argument can have perverse effects, too, causing more contention when used by giving states a stronger hand to argue that it is not legitimate, even though it may be legal. This hypermoralization of arguments for and against war has the unfortunate effect of leaving lasting bitterness with a host of negative side effects on the attempt to resolve other important international political and economic problems.

PLAN OF THE BOOK

Numerous books have addressed humanitarian intervention using various lenses, including ethics, international law, philosophy, geopolitics, theology, and historical critique.[8] This volume uses a contextual reading of decision making by examining what leaders and publics said, did, and believed. It examines the way bureaucratic forces and party politics within countries, and posturing and negotiating at the international level, affected rationales for the uses of force. In this way it traces three distinct ways of thinking, or world views, that shaped policy. It then draws conclusions based upon the contradictions and confluences of those three diverse schools of thought in action.

One important lesson of the humanitarian war debates is the identification of an upswing in moralization about war, and foreign policy in general. Thus, rather than a new moral imperative about humanitarian war emerging in the 1990s, the world witnessed a rise in ideological arguments about political and legal aspects of decision making, challenging the concepts of national sovereignty and power politics on one hand, and informing understandings of international law and obligation on the other.

The book begins by looking at the most contemporary conundrum in the debate about humanitarian war: the concept of the "responsibility to protect" civilians in other countries from grave human rights abuses, even by resort to force. The topic of general debate in the 2009 64th UN General Assembly, the concept is contentious because it uncovers the worst fears of nations big and small, concerns about losing sovereignty and becoming bound by ill-defined norms defined by anonymous elite academics and UN committees and then imposed selectively by powerful states. The promise of the concept, and the reason humanitarian intervention is still such a perennial point of debate, is because it embodies the hope of injecting into a seemingly soulless realpolitik compelling moral norms common to all humanity, the basic principle of helping a neighbor in need.

The book traces the debate at three levels. First, it shows how decision makers grappled with three main aspects of decisions to use force: authorization, justification, and obligation. Second, the unique contexts of four NATO nations—Britain, France, Germany, and the United States—are examined in light of how they influenced national decisions about war. Third, the analysis traces three distinct currents of thought, or worldviews, introduced in chapter 2. It brings to light the conversation among these ways of thinking and shows how that dynamic affected the ultimate choices decision makers made in 1999 and 2003. In the contemporary context, these worldviews emphasize different aspects of the international order: national sovereignty, international law, and moral imperative. As this analysis demonstrates, decisions about the use of force are influenced by the tensions and confluences among the three ways of thinking. The building blocks of the debates—context and concepts—are set forth in chapter 3. These include, among other contemporary issues, the relationship between NATO and the UN, debates about the nature of sovereignty, the evolution of human rights, and the militarization of humanitarianism.

The Kosovo decision is the focus of the study and is examined in some depth in chapters 4 through 6. That campaign is generally seen as the culmination of the humanitarian wars of the 1990s, the "most striking example" of humanitarian intervention of our time,[9] and a turning point in international politics. The Iraq case, examined in chapter 7, tests the model presented in the Kosovo case and reveals the mixed motives present in both cases, whether or not nations agreed on the use of force.

The conclusions in chapter 8 offer implications and policy recommendations for decision makers as they grapple with how to address strategic threats, such as those from Iran and North Korea, as humanitarian and human rights emergencies in the decades ahead.

CHAPTER 2

Origins of Intervention:
Power, Principle, and Law

Humanitarian intervention may be defined as the reliance upon force for the justifiable purpose of protecting the inhabitants of another state from treatment which is so arbitrary and persistently abusive as to exceed the limits of that authority within which the sovereign is presumed to act with reason and justice.

—Ellery Stowell, *Intervention in International Law*, 1921

When Cyclone Nargis hit Burma in May 2008, killing as many as a hundred thousand people, the French foreign minister, Bernard Kouchner, invoked the concept of the "responsibility to protect" as a way to override the Burmese government's intransigence and thus deliver lifesaving aid. The U.S. Senate passed a resolution demanding the Burmese give way. Planeloads of UN aid sat on runways for weeks rather than risk having it seized by the repressive regime in Yangon. Aid barely trickled in as ships sat offshore. Tragically, more than a million survivors waited in vain for aid, and this after suffering decades of abuse from their government.

The case showed how contentious humanitarian intervention remains in the post–September 11, 2001 world, even when the use of force is only timidly on the table. The Burmese regime claimed their sovereign right to deny visas, fearing interference in their domestic affairs. The French argued that saving lives trumped sovereignty.

The Burmese position ultimately prevailed, but American policy makers had to scramble to craft a U.S. position that justified staying above the fray while condemning the junta's brutality. The United States had U.S. Navy and Marine Corps forces in nearby Thailand for the yearly Cobra Gold multinational exercise, but policy advisors urged caution to avoid "unintended diplomatic consequences."[1] They predicted correctly that India would take a hands-off approach to the crisis and would resent prolonged U.S. involvement due to its own "Monroe Doctrine" in the Indian Ocean.

On the other side of the debate, Madeleine Albright blamed the Bush administration's decision to wage war in Iraq as the cause of American negligence toward the suffering Burmese people, alleging that it was due to the "negative reaction that has weakened support for cross-border interventions even for worthy purposes." Albright said, "Governments, especially in the developing world, are now determined to preserve the principle of sovereignty, even when the human costs of doing so are high. Thus, Myanmar's leaders have been shielded from the repercussions of their outrageous actions."[2] At the same time, American policy makers under the Bush administration had decided to virtually ignore "responsibility to protect" or "R2P" debates at the UN. But in so doing, they admittedly missed an opportunity to shape the rules in play to suit U.S. interests.

Thus it was the nature of sovereignty that proved to be the sticking point in the world's collective failure to deliver relief. In that respect, the case is emblematic of the intractable contradictions of R2P and humanitarian intervention in general. The R2P debates are closely tied to deep divisions on the three fundamental questions this book examines in depth: Who may authorize intervention? When is it justified? Are states ever obligated to intervene? Likewise, diverging positions about R2P, and contemporary debates about the use of force more broadly, are staked out along the lines of thinking about the corresponding concepts of sovereignty, international law, and human rights.

Proponents such as the UN secretary-general's special assistant for R2P, Edward Luck, call it an emerging international political norm.[3] Pope Benedict recently called it a fundamental principle of the international order based on the natural law. Critics have called it everything from a license for Western imperial aggression to a ruse for curtailing American power.

The actual meaning is not so straightforward. As accepted by all world leaders in the 2005 World Summit Outcome Document, it sounds less controversial:

Each individual state has the responsibility to protect its populations from genocide, war crimes, ethnic cleansing and crimes against humanity.... The international community, through the United Nations, also has the responsibility to use appropriate diplomatic, humanitarian and other peaceful means, in accordance with Chapters VI and VIII of the Charter.... we are prepared to take collective action...including Chapter VII...should peaceful means be inadequate and national authorities manifestly fail to protect their populations.

There is room in the negotiated text to allow disagreement as well as consensus on the question of who may legitimately authorize intervention. The French and the Germans brought this to fever pitch during the 2003 Iraq War debate. As chapter 7 shows, some French officials went so far as to say that a Security Council resolution was both a legal and a moral necessity. American and British leaders maintained the traditional view that this right is reserved to sovereign states.

In a way, dispute between those who see the prerogatives of U.S. political military dominance as a force for good, and those who fear the "hyper-power" and would balance or contain it. The latter would rule out U.S. unilateralism, while putting the Global Sheriff at the service of the international community.[4] It is telling that the man who championed R2P after the failed interventions of the 1990s, former secretary-general Kofi Annan, rejected his progeny in the wake of the Iraq War. His successor, Ban Ki-moon, refers to the principle in highly moralized, almost religious terms:

Preventing mass atrocities is among the international community's, and the United Nations', most sacred callings. Regrettably, it is a duty we have not always acquitted well. The killing fields of Rwanda, Cambodia and the Balkans stand silent witness to the brutality that passed unchecked by an international system lacking both the will and the vision to act. I believe that we can, and we must, do better.... That is why, from my very first day in office, I have made Darfur my highest priority.[5]

Opposition is widespread and eclectic. At a recent briefing at UN headquarters, the lines were clearly drawn, with the Sudanese ambassador front and center to denounce any claim that Darfur might be ripe for asserting the principle. Egypt had just led a failed campaign in the General Assembly fifth committee to get rid of the special assistant's job all together. At the Security Council, China and Russia remain skeptical of anything that may bring interference in their domestic affairs.

At the General Assembly, the president of the 64th session, Miguel d'Escoto Brockmann from Nicaragua, convened a special meeting in the otherwise sleepy summer of 2009 to consolidate opposition to the concept preceding the General Debate on R2P. Some called it a "sneak attack."[6] During the debate, d'Escoto couched his opposition as a question of whether nations are "ready" for R2P. In a world where the prerogatives of power prevail, he said, it would be applied selectively, "in cases where public opinion in P5 Member States supports intervention, as in Darfur, and not where it is opposed, as in Gaza."[7] Giving voice to the still-current anti-Western sentiment of the Group of 77 (G-77), he argued that a UN stamp of approval on R2P would "generate new 'coalitions of the willing,' crusades such as the intervention in Iraq led by self-appointed saviors."[8]

Making for an odd alliance, conservatives in Washington similarly condemned the concept by arguing that it is a challenge to sovereignty, that is, American sovereignty:

U.S. independence—hard won by the Founders and successive generations of Americans—would be compromised if the United States consented to be legally bound by the R2P doctrine. The United States needs to preserve its national sovereignty by maintaining a monopoly on the decision to deploy diplomatic pressure, economic sanctions, political coercion, and especially its military forces.[9]

Much of the resistance seems puzzling to proponents, considering that the list of four egregious crimes (and therefore reasons for possible intervention) is short—some say too short. Given that it includes only genocide, war crimes, ethnic cleansing, and crimes against humanity, there is reason to believe that the notion could be popular among Americans.

One could argue that the World Summit definition enshrines the very idea that every person, no matter his origin, is endowed with *inalienable* rights. That means, chiefly, the right to life and to liberty, or freedom from grievous assaults on human dignity, such as slavery or crimes that otherwise shock the conscience of mankind. It can also be argued that Americans have a track record of deciding that such moral principle is worth protecting, even to the point of laying down American lives.

A reason for resistance, however, is that a fair amount of the debate in the United States centers on the third question this study examines, that is, the question of whether Americans should be obligated to intervene. Jean-Marc Coicaud of UN University says yes, arguing that rights and obligations need laws and cannot be left to mere "moral judgment." Coicaud holds out great hope that international legal regimes, if only they are given more power, can resolve this intractable problem:

Intervention based simply on moral considerations does not offer the benefits of the institutionalization and socialization that a right and obligation enjoy when they are a matter of law. . . . When doing the right thing is more or less a matter of moral judgment, and one somewhat at odds with standard law, it is destined to be problematic.

From Coicaud's perspective, codification of moral values makes them enforceable. It shores up the gap between the ever-increasing expectations of international legal regimes and what they can actually deliver. Binding sovereign states in this way will make nations more moral without the trouble caused by action, no matter how noble, taken outside the law. But moral suasion without codification has worked when there was political will. As this book demonstrates, NATO allies achieved remarkable consensus during the 1999 NATO bombing to stop ethnic cleansing in Kosovo, despite the Security Council standoff. Only Britain claimed they had an obligation to intervene, and even then it was moral and not legal. Hence the Kosovo war has somewhat awkwardly been deemed "legitimate" by those who called it "illegal." It is an open question whether any new legal regime could close that gap.

International law expert Ann Marie Slaughter believes it can. She argues that states obey international law because of shared values. Eventually, this exercise of shared values will lead to a reconceptualization of sovereignty from national governments that represent a people to branches of global governance that are part of transnational networks. A country's legal system, for example, would be part of a worldwide network of jurists that meet often to find common solutions to problems they face in their respective countries. While she admits that her proposal could lead to the creation of an elite, unelected, unaccountable "global technocracy," she dismisses the threat. She also admits that in order to make her vision of a new world order practicable, government officials (to say nothing about the people) must believe in it. Peter Berkowitz argues that "one should not underestimate the radicalism of Slaughter's proposal, encapsulated in her casual exercise in redefinition [of sovereignty]—as if one could disguise the rejection of a fundamental principle by keeping the name while changing the meaning."[10]

Eric Posner and Jack Goldsmith also counter Slaughter's transnationalist view by arguing that nations obey international law not out of shared values but out of national interests. Just because national leaders increasingly speak in the language of international norms does not mean that the authority of international law has increased, they contend, but only that leaders realize that speaking in this way is more effective for achieving their interests.

Other critics go further and argue that the transnationalist and liberal internationalist desire to redefine sovereignty is dangerous for democracies, because it shifts the authority to interpret law and morality from the people to unelected, unaccountable outsiders who may not have the people's interest in mind: "What is at stake in the doctrine of sovereignty is not whether there are universal principles binding on all states, but who has the authority to interpret them and who has the interest and capacity to protect them."[11]

Because the notion of a responsibility to protect, and of humanitarian intervention more broadly, contradict deeply held attractions to national sovereignty, proponents advanced the idea of a new international norm that would reconcile the problem. Secretaries general of the United Nations and their staff have been outspoken on the need for codification based in law, specifically UN-based law.

Mohamed Sahnoun has lamented the "missed opportunities" of averting the humanitarian catastrophe that took place during his tenure as UN special representative in Somalia. He argues that while the requirement to respect state sovereignty—by nonintervention—was a matter of international law, state sovereignty itself is a matter of political conditions within a state.[12] Sahnoun interprets Article 1 and Article 34 of the UN Charter to back up his argument. Article 1 obliges states to fulfill the purposes of the UN, and Article 34 requires the Security Council to investigate "any situation which...is likely to endanger the maintenance of international peace and security." He maintains that the drafters of the Charter used the word "situation" out of concern that internal conflicts could lead to larger regional conflicts or interstate war.[13]

Former UN Secretary General Javier Perez de Cuellar also pointed toward this "conditional" sovereignty:

One could—and I would even say, should—inquire whether certain other texts that were later adopted by the United Nations, in particular the Universal Declaration of Human Rights, do not implicitly call into question this inviolable notion of sovereignty.[14]

Perez de Cuellar's successor, Boutros Boutros-Ghali, admitted the centrality of sovereignty to the UN system but, like his predecessor, expressed skepticism in his 1992 *Agenda for Peace:*

The foundation stone of the work is and must remain the State. Respect for its fundamental sovereignty and integrity are [sic] crucial to any common international progress; its theory was never matched by reality. It is the task of leaders of states to understand this and to find a balance between the needs of good internal governance and the requirements of an ever more interdependent world.[15]

In 1998, secretary general Kofi Annan said it was the effects of globalization that provided yet another reason for the erosion of state sovereignty:

The understanding of sovereignty is undergoing a significant transformation. Satellite communication, environment degradation, and the globalization of markets are just a few of the contemporary phenomena that are bringing into question the extent of state authority.... The implications of human rights abuses and refugee and other migratory flows for international peace and security are forcing us to take a fresh look at sovereignty from a different perspective: sovereignty as a matter of responsibility, not just power. This idea predates the interdependence among nations that characterizes the current era.[16]

The tension between sovereignty and human rights was debated not only in the case of military intervention. Landmark cases about "universal jurisdiction," such as the extradition of Augusto Pinochet to Chile for prosecution and the work of the International Criminal Tribunals for Rwanda and the former Yugoslavia seemed to provide evidence that nations were willing to put the enforcement of human rights above a strict interpretation of state sovereignty in some cases.

The drafters of the Canadian-sponsored 2001 report on R2P, the International Commission on Intervention and State Sovereignty (ICISS), propose that the traditional right of states to intervene has been "stood on its head" in state practice as a responsibility to protect. The commissioners argue that the Westphalian principle of sovereign equality in the state-centered UN Charter's Article 2(1) and the supporting concept of nonintervention in the affairs of other states codified by Article 2(7) have been eroded by the emerging norm of the equality of all people. The idealist worldview is evident in their assumption that the "community of states has a 'shared ideal' that people are all equal in worth and dignity."[17]

At the heart of the commission's argument is its thinking about the nature of international obligation. The commission asserts that four specific obligations require states to intervene in situations of large-scale loss of life and ethnic cleansing: the obligation "inherent" in state sovereignty, the UN Charter, international legal obligations regarding human rights and common state practice, and UN and regional organization practice in crises such as Kosovo.[18] The bulk of the ICISS document concerns the question of when states should intervene and notably applies just war criteria to answer the question. To garner international political will, it calls for the mobilization of domestic support, using a combination of moral and self-interest appeals, including the prospect of financial gain for states. Their conclusion is that good "international citizenship" is and should be promoted as in the self-interest of states.

The report, released just before the attacks of September 11, 2001, assumed that the nature of sovereignty had changed because state behavior had been significantly influenced by human rights ideals. It assumes people can raise the standard of civilization, and that international politics can be improved by the prudent application of humanitarian intervention. This idealistic optimism was inherent in much of the talk surrounding new definitions of state sovereignty after the Kosovo intervention. In his 1999 report to the General Assembly, just after the Kosovo campaign, Kofi Annan called "unity behind the principle" of protection "the core challenge of the Security Council and to the United Nations as a whole in the next century."[19] Speaking with the confidence typical of the post-Kosovo, pre-Iraq era, he said:

> This developing international norm in favor of intervention to protect civilians from wholesale slaughter will no doubt continue to pose profound challenges to the international community. Any such evolution in our understanding of State sovereignty and individual sovereignty will, in some quarters, be met with distrust, skepticism, even hostility. But it is an evolution that we should welcome. Why? Because, despite its limitations and imperfections, it is testimony to a humanity that cares more, and not less, to end it. It is a hopeful sign at the end of the twentieth century.[20]

After the Iraq war, a disillusioned Annan dropped the campaign to recognize a new norm, but ardent believers soldiered on. For example, an initial report on the Kosovo intervention by the International Commission on Kosovo, chaired by the International Criminal Tribunal for Yugoslavia's first judge, Richard Goldstone, concluded that Kosovo should be seen as an exception to international law and not a precedent. But by 2003, various transnationalist legal experts were arguing the opposite:

> There is nothing in the UN Charter that allows states to take action if another state has killed thousands and thousands of its people. That cannot continue. The moral argument does have a place in law. What is needed is to bring the two strands of international law together: the half that regards relations among states and the half that governs the way states treat their own citizens. It is possible to imagine the UN targeting governments when they repress citizens and further distinguish between that government and the individuals responsible.[21]

Another group of experts let by Robert Keohane and J. L. Holzgrefe asserted that the Kosovo case was precedent-setting and suggested that a coalition of democratic states should draw up a treaty saying so. They argued for an attempt "to create a new norm of customary international law," and that states should act upon it repeatedly in order to establish a new custom or *opinio juris*, that made the act a legal obligation.[22]

While these experts see a solution in codifying moral norms in hard law or custom, others find the appeal to older principles more practicable. The just war scholar J. Bryan Hehir sees the need for a new international norm regarding intervention, but Hehir, even before Iraq, was less adamant about a hard law, proposing that there are other relationships between norms, law, and politics, such as the just war doctrine, that have proved useful:

International law needs to be changed in several ways to accommodate a doctrine of limited humanitarian intervention. While authorization from the Security Council or another regional body is one dimension, the just cause question is another dimension.[23]

Hehir argues that there remains an unresolved tension between the normative reality and the realist debate about intervention. Unlike Slaughter, he finds no answer in legal tradition, nor in the theory of international politics.[24] Instead, he finds an interventionist approach coming from what he calls the "moral tradition," which is in conflict with a noninterventionist "legal tradition." Whereas the ICISS believed the moral, legal, and political ways of thinking could be harmonized in a new norm, Hehir finds a tension among them. He proposes that what he calls the legal noninterventionist school held sway in the twentieth century due to the legacy of Westphalian international relations theory, as well as the institutionalization of what he calls the legal perspective in the UN Charter. This version of the legal tradition, he believes, must be reconciled with the just war doctrine in order to make way for a new custom on humanitarian intervention.

Michael Walzer, in his classic post-Vietnam book on just war published in 1977, did not insist that such reconciliation take place, but rather he suggested that states, either alone or together, must make the moral choice, even if it is not legal:

Any state capable of stopping the slaughter has a right, at least, to do so. The legalist paradigm indeed rules out such efforts, but that only suggests that the paradigm, unrevised, cannot account for the moral realities of military intervention.[25]

Whereas Hehir finds the moral tradition historically leading the cause for intervention and in tension with other ways of thinking, Walzer finds that different ways of thinking have always coexisted in support of the use of force:

Indeed, I have not found any, but only mixed cases where the humanitarian motive is one among several. States don't send their soldiers into other states, it seems, only in order to save lives. The lives of foreigners don't weigh that heavily in the scales of domestic decision-making. So we shall have to consider the moral significance of mixed motives.[26]

Mixed motives have also been used as evidence against the existence of a new custom of humanitarian or rights-based intervention.[27]

The 1985 International Court of Justice declaration in the *Nicaragua* case states that

> While the United States might form its own appraisal of the situation as to respect for human rights in Nicaragua, the use of force could not be the appropriate method to monitor or ensure such respect....The court concludes that the argument derived from the preservation of human rights in Nicaragua cannot afford a legal justification for the conduct of the United States.[28]

In his history of humanitarian intervention in the nineteenth century, Gary Bass argues that the trouble with mixed motives is a long-standing diplomatic conundrum. He finds that the great powers were able to mitigate the accusations of imperialism by recourse to "a combination of multilateralism, self-restraint, and treaties as tools to reassure other states about the good motivations behind a humanitarian mission."[29] As the Nicaragua case and the rhetoric surrounding today's R2P debates show, the challenge of proving good intentions persists. What kind of multilateral regime to apply is a source of conflict among scholars and practitioners of various worldviews, and these perspectives have competed in policy debates. Perspectives of what is the best solution to the legitimacy problem are based upon assumptions about the international order and the way states behave. To understand that, one needs to know what kind of thinking actually informed the decisions.

POWER, PRINCIPLE, AND LAW

The Kosovo and Iraq war decisions demonstrate that the simple dichotomy between the realist and liberal internationalist schools is inadequate to explain the way decision makers actually reconciled the problems of proper authority, justification, and obligation in their decision making about war. More helpful is recognizing the various political, legal, and moral regimes leaders appealed to by tracing three distinct aspects of decision making—power, law, and principle—as they competed and also informed each other throughout the decision-making process. This approach also better explains the role of values. Moral considerations were not separate from concerns about sovereignty and international law in the Kosovo and Iraq cases, but rather moral principle infused thinking about power and law and in some ways made debates highly contentious.

This threefold approach to understanding international behavior, and the same set of three categories, by whatever names, has proven advantageous in the past. Lecturing at the London School of Economics in the 1950s, Martin Wight identified three traditions of international thought evident since the Renaissance: realists, rationalists, and revolutionists.[30] His method placed the ideas and motives of decision makers in the context of specific historical events while relating them to long-standing philosophical and theoretical traditions. Wight proposed that

Statesmen act under various pressures, and appeal with varying degrees of sincerity to various principles. It is for those who study international relations to judge their actions, which means judging the validity of their ethical principles. This is not a process of scientific analysis; it is more akin to literary criticism. It involves developing a sensitive awareness of the intractability of all political situations, and the moral quandary in which all statecraft operates. It requires a sympathetic perception which offers an insight into moral tensions, and it is to be obtained by cultivating the acquaintance of politicians and statesmen.[31]

Others have also found that tracing the debate among the three traditions is essential to understanding the most important questions of international politics. Hedley Bull called their respective advocates Hobbesians, Grotians, and Kantians. Paul Viotti and Mark Kauppi categorized international relations theories into realism, pluralism, and globalism, and more recently Stewart Patrick analyzed the way unilateral and multilateral means are used to achieve nationalist, internationalist, and collective objectives.[32] Janne Haaland Matlary, writing specifically about the legitimacy of military intervention in the cases of Kosovo and Iraq, finds that in addition to realist and positivist approaches to acquiring international legitimacy, a third normative model is necessary to explain contemporary state practice.[33] In the same vein, Euan MacDonald and Philip Alston propose that states seek legitimacy for the use of force on three bases: sovereignty, security, and human rights.[34] In this book, the three traditions are called realist, internationalist, or legalist, and idealist approaches.

In its most basic sense, the realist tradition sees the world as a system of sovereign states organized only by the relative power they can wield. Force is the dominant mode of international interaction, since no authority higher than the state exists to enforce national will, laws, or norms. Its adherents take a positivist approach to international law, emphasizing what *is* rather than what *ought* to be. In theory, the realist approach has both aggressive and defensive forms. On the aggressive side, a realist should be willing to impose interests, or in some cases norms, through the use of force. War, as strategist Carl von Clausewitz put it, is an extension, not a cessation of, politics. Realism's more defensive variant favors the promotion of interest by noncoercive means, such as multilateralism and international law.[35] Again, this is realism in its shorthand version, but it is important to keep in mind that some of the most famous contemporary theorists of realism, such as Hans Morgenthau, George F. Kennan, Herbert Butterfield, and Reinhold Niebuhr wrote about the role of morality in foreign policy, whereas others such as E. H. Carr maintained a strict separation between realism and moral considerations.

Martin Wight observed that Carr viewed the distinction between realism and morality as the difference between reality and utopia. "The implications of his language," Wight said, "are that morality is utopia; a place which *is not*, whereas reality is power. Carr does not keep the balance, the fruitful tension, between morality and power which can be found for instance in Niebuhr's *Moral Man and Immoral Society*."[36] Wight further noted that Carr's view of international law and obligation was typically Hobbesian:

At the core of this [Realist] pattern of thought is the doctrine that power is anterior to society, law, justice, and morality. E. H. Carr in *The Twenty Years' Crisis* restates the Hobbesian position: "Any international moral order must rest on some hegemony of power." Here is Hobbes: "…before the names of Just, and Unjust can have place, there must be some coercive Power."[37]

For his part, Wight found Carr's pragmatic realism and superficial reliance on common material interest a less fruitful social doctrine for British foreign policy than the idea of a common moral obligation.[38]

Henry Kissinger, known for his realist worldview, similarly acknowledged the importance of morality in American foreign policy. Kissinger attributed the failure of nuclear détente between the United States and the Soviet Union to the fact that "in America, a geopolitical interpretation of international affairs had become as necessary as it was, by itself, insufficient."[39] In other words, the policy of détente proved short lived because the American public perceived it as ideologically indifferent to the Soviet Union. Thus, the first tradition may take account of moral considerations even though its primary focus is on power and the anarchial structure of the international system.

The second tradition is an internationalist or legalist perspective that views the world as an international society—more than a system but not quite a state—underpinned by law and institutions, its parts increasingly interdependent. From this perspective, international politics are shaped less by international anarchy than by custom arising from habitual interaction. Sovereignty is central, but cooperation rather than conflict is the dominant mode of international relations in this tradition. This approach recognizes the existence of international anarchy, on the one hand, but appreciates the value of universal norms on the other.[40] It seeks to reconcile the two by finding the "lesser evil" in policy debates; it concerns itself with matters of law and justice, employs the just war doctrine since it alone among the traditions calls for limited war, and sees war as a lamentable but sometimes "necessary evil." It looks for the "law behind the law," often called natural law, and seeks multilateral approaches to diplomacy. In theory, there are both realist and idealist variants of the legalist approach; the realist aspect tends to employ multilateral approaches for coercive purposes, while its idealist counterpart sees multilateralism as a way of fostering shared norms. Liberal internationalists are the most well-known adherents to this tradition today, as well as neoliberal institutionalists who also focus on cooperation but emphasize absolute rather than relative gains. Regime theories also adhere to this tradition, in that they believe that international institutions affect states by creating a confluence of interests.

The third tradition is the one most preoccupied with ideas, norms, values, and morals in foreign policy. This is because it views the world as one of moral solidarity—an international community that should eventually be ruled by a global government or in which sovereign states give way to transnational thinking and the authority of global governance. This third worldview sees the world as made up not so much of sovereign states or institutions as of individuals and ideas in which domestic and international politics merge. A world in moral solidarity is only superficially about relations among states; it focuses more on collective goals, such as human rights, the environment, labor relations, and other matters it considers of importance to humankind and believes that the world can be, and must be, changed. Similarly, this worldview sees the mutual exclusivity of ideals, and adherents may promote their ideal using evolutionary or revolutionary means. The evolutionary form focuses on promoting universal ideals through noncoercive measures, while revolutionary adherents are willing to enforce their ideas, even by violent means. Thus, war for the idealist is total war, war of revolution, "holy war," or "war to end all wars." Marxism is an expression of this tradition, as are proponents of violent religious extremism.[41]

Dedicated to this tradition in its goal of global governance are prominent members of the Obama administration, such as Cass Sunstein, the regulatory czar, Ann Marie Slaughter, the State Department's director of policy planning, and Harold Koh, the State Department's chief counsel, who has argued that the U.S. Constitution should be interpreted in the light of international laws and custom. This brand of transnational progressivism has great appeal to Western intellectuals, as well as global elites such as multinational corporate executives. From a policy perspective, critics find this attraction dangerous for liberal democracies, because they say it downplays the seriousness of transnational threats such as Islamic extremism and erodes the unique cultural and national characteristics of the state, which are fundamental to the working of liberal democratic states.[42]

Another critique of transnationalism is that it is unrealistic because it does not sufficiently account for the role of genuine public opinion and the persistence of differing national interests. Transnationalism assumes that the elites of the world share values and thereby represent common values commonly understood. In this way, this worldview not only circumvents democracy but ignores the persistent role of power. As Martin Wight observed, there is a "contrast between the way powers talk under the pressure of enlightened public opinion and the way they act under the pressure of conflicting national interests."[43] The most extraordinary example of this, he believed, was the signing of the 1928 Kellogg Briand Pact midway between the two World Wars, which was to outlaw the use of aggressive armed force. While idealists hailed a new era of international peace, realists were sadly vindicated with Hitler's march into the Sudetenland. In 1858, Abraham Lincoln argued in his debates against Stephen Douglas that "Public sentiment is everything. With public sentiment, nothing can fail; without it nothing can succeed. Consequently he who molds public sentiment goes deeper than he who enacts statutes or pronounces decisions. He makes statutes and decisions possible to be executed." And in 1830s Europe, the strategist Carl von Clausewitz observed that politics is the embodiment of public opinion:

Policy, of course, is nothing in itself; it is simply the trustee for all these interests against other states. That it can err, subserve the ambitions, private interests, and vanity of those in power, is neither here nor there. In no sense can the art of war ever be regarded as the preceptor of policy, and here we can only treat policy as representative of all interests of the community.[44]

Informing the foreign policy of the George W. Bush administration was a group of foreign policy analysts who were able to appeal to a broad range of public opinions by spanning all three traditions of thought. This group, the neoconservatives, political scientist Francis Fukuyama explained, adhere to four principles:

A belief that the internal character of regimes matters...A belief that American power has been and could be used for moral purposes...A distrust of ambitious social engineering projects...And finally, skepticism about the legitimacy and effectiveness of international law and institutions to achieve either security or justice.[45]

Its distrust of international institutions and emphasis on power make elements of neoconservative foreign policy appealing to realists, while its preference for democratic regimes finds favor with liberal internationalists. To the extent that neoconservative foreign policymakers have advocated war for moral purposes, such as the war to liberate Iraq, their policies appeal to idealists.

The power-based thinking essential to realism is attractive to states, which seek to protect and advance their own interests and security. Humanitarian intervention has challenged but has in turn been informed by this approach, producing such hybrids as the "right to intervene" and the Bush administration's doctrine of limited preemption.[46] Calculations of national interest remain central to the French and German demand for multilateralism, just as they do to the American and British war on terrorism. The persistence of realist approaches to international behavior is also partly explained by the longevity of the "unipolar moment," which brings about attempts to counterweight the power of the United States as the sole remaining superpower.[47]

The liberal international or legalist approach, nonetheless, has become increasingly embedded in international politics since World War II. The number of international institutions has proliferated in recent years, growing by more than two-thirds since 1985. Such regimes aspire to rein in national power and to harness the best of idealist imperatives by codifying their norms in law. The extensive resort to just war doctrine and the continued importance of seeking UN mandates, such as in the Kosovo and Iraq episodes, are evidence of the persuasiveness of the legalist or liberal internationalist tradition.

An upswing of idealist thinking in the form of heightened moralism in talk about war is evident in examining the Kosovo and Iraq crises; the national decisions made in those cases cannot be explained purely in terms of power calculations or the requirements of international law. In the months before the Iraq campaign, the idealist worldview that cast the conflict in terms of a "common humanity" remained even for states that did not focus on the humanitarian aspects of the problem. States sought international legitimacy by casting in moral terms the struggles between freedom and liberation and between multilateralism and unilateralism.

Thus, each of the traditions has a place for the influence of moral norms, such as universal human rights, but they differ on their proper place in policy. The rise of idealism, the institutionalization of liberalism

in legalist thought, and the persistence of realism's power-based decision making promise to make the use of force increasingly contested
in the future. In the Kosovo instance, decision makers satisfied the
demands of all three imperatives; where they do not, consensus will
be unlikely.

CHAPTER 3

The Quest for Legitimacy: Concepts and Context

To understand the unstable and intractable nature of international politics, you need only study the relations between the motives and consequences of a war, or between the purposes and history of an alliance.
—Martin Wight, *Power Politics*, 1946

Today's contentious decisions about the use of force have become quests for legitimacy. National leaders seek to sway constituencies both internal and external about the need for forcible intervention or, conversely, the reasons not to go to war. As the following chapters show, none of the NATO nations in the case of the Iraq war or the Kosovo campaign found satisfaction by relying on the authority of strictly unilateral intervention, that is, intervention without consensus from the UN Security Council, NATO, or a coalition of states. Nor did positive or customary international law or strictly moral arguments provide sufficient justification for war. The contexts for these decisions were shaped by issues introduced here as key concepts and revisited in the chapters that follow.

AUTHORITY IN WORLD ORDER

Fundamental disagreement persists about the legality of the Kosovo intervention. Some argue that interventions other than those undertaken in self defense cannot be called legal if not approved explicitly by the United Nations Security Council.[1] Former UN secretary general

Kofi Annan exemplified this perspective when he claimed that, "Actions without Security Council authorization threaten the very core of the international security system founded on the Charter of the United Nations."[2] Others have argued that NATO has the legal authority to act in circumstances like the Kosovo case and that the intervention as executed was not illegal. Resolving the issue remains illusive because, in addition to questions about the UN Charter, such as what constitutes self-defense and armed attack, the disagreement occurs at different levels of analysis, and from different worldviews.

Reconciling these differences requires examining the main issues in turn. These include the relationship between the UN and NATO and NATO's purpose, specifically whether the alliance has evolved into an instrument of collective security while remaining a collective defense organization. NATO governments agreed in 1999 that the organization's primary mission remained collective defense. Article 5 of the North Atlantic Treaty is the collective defense clause, stating that an attack against one is an attack against all. That said, the alliance's non–Article 5 tasks became increasingly prominent during the 1990s. As NATO's de facto day-to-day missions have moved from a large-scale ground combat readiness to actual collective security operations, UN missions have moved from unarmed peacekeeping to peace enforcement missions increasingly carried out in combat situations. Thus organizations with mandates seemingly on opposite ends of the spectrum of conflict have converged in practice, especially since the humanitarian intervention operations of the 1990s.

Conclusions about who has authority to mandate and who has the competence to conduct such interventions were underpinned by the historical relationship of the two organizations and individual decision makers' attitudes about international politics. Some argued that NATO could not bow to UNSC authority in all non–Article 5 contingencies. This was consistent with the view that idealistic collective security organizations do not work in practice because national self-interest always makes security divisible despite declarations to the contrary. Realists argued that peace and security and the prevention of a wider war in the Balkans had to be achieved with or without a UNSC mandate. Internationalists insisted that the legal order is in itself essential to international peace and security, and that UNSC authority must be respected except in extreme cases of UNSC inaction. Disregarding the UN Charter in practice in this vein is just as likely to weaken the legal order.

The Question of Authority and the Use of Force

At the founding of the UN in San Francisco, the Organization of American States (OAS), the oldest regional organization, lobbied successfully for the inclusion in the Charter of the possibility of regional response to security concerns (Article 52(1)). However, Article 53(1) was supposed to strictly prohibit regional action "without the authorization of the Security Council." Any doubt about the precedence of the UNSC over regional organizations was to be removed by Article 103, which states that, "In the event of a conflict between the obligations of the Members of the United Nations under the present Charter and their obligations under any other international agreement, their obligations under the present Charter shall prevail." Finally, Article 51 was supposed to limit collective or individual self-defense to "an armed attack."

Some, like former UN secretary general Kofi Anan, see NATO as a regional organization under Chapter VIII.[3]

[NATO's intervention] has cast in stark relief the dilemma of so-called "humanitarian intervention." On the one hand, is it legitimate for a regional organization to use force without a UN mandate? On the other, is it permissible to let gross and systematic violations of human rights, with grave humanitarian consequences, continue unchecked? The inability of the international community to reconcile these two compelling interests in the case of Kosovo can be viewed only as a tragedy.[4]

Others argue that this was not the intent of NATO founders.[5] Lawrence Kaplan notes:

There was an inherent conflict between the treaty and the charter that could not be avoided. To announce publicly that NATO would be essentially a regional arrangement like the Rio Pact would have required the acceptance of Article 53, wherein regional associations were obligated to report regularly to the Security Council on which the Soviet Union would sit in judgment of their activities. The only rubric then open to NATO was Article 51 of the charter with its emphasis on the right of individual or collective defense.[6]

Officials of NATO governments traditionally maintained that NATO is not a regional arrangement under article 53.[7] They make a distinction between the purpose of NATO and that of the Organization for Security and Cooperation in Europe (OSCE), which has subordinated itself to Chapter VIII of the UN Charter.[8] Thus, even though the governments of NATO used the organization extensively in the 1990s in support of collective security purposes, they have also maintained its original purpose: collective defense under Article 5 of the Washington Treaty.

NATO: Collective Security vs. Collective Defense Organization

As NATO forces carried out the Kosovo campaign, justified in part by collective security ideals, alliance leaders met in Washington and reaffirmed collective defense as NATO's core mission.[9] The contradiction followed a rise in human rights rhetoric in policy making throughout the 1990s and paralleled a return to Wilsonian arguments about the "indivisibility" of security. In fact, NATO's 1999 Strategic Concept retains four fundamental principles of the military alliance. Two of the four seem contradictory: that "security is indivisible," a collective security principle, and that NATO's security policy is "based on collective defense."[10]

Regarding the "security is indivisible" principle, David Yost points out,

Attempts to build Kantian or Wilsonian "collective security" frameworks have broken down throughout history. In practice, governments reason and act as if security *is* divisible. As Inis Claude has pointed out, the de facto policy of the United States and other powers is one of "selective antiaggression." ... In 1991, then U.S. secretary of defense Dick Cheney commented ... "We have to remember that we don't have a dog in every fight, that we don't want to get involved in every single conflict...."[11]

Inis Claude captured the complexity of the collective security idea, finding that its two essential characteristics—upholding universal values and acting multilaterally—may contradict one another in practice. The requirement to slog through the political process of seeking authorization in an international or regional organization may very often preclude taking action to stop human rights abuses and deal with humanitarian emergencies. Defending their position in Security Council proceedings on March 24, 1999, the allies maintained that taking decisive action even without a UNSC mandate upheld international law and international organizations. David Yost notes that, "Threats do not always fall into tidy compartments ... sometimes the only way to honor and uphold collective security principles might be outside an inclusive international organization, global or regional, ostensibly devoted to such principles."[12] Like many analysts of the war, Peter Anderson argues that the allies' chosen path in 1999 upheld the spirit of international legality—the ethical choice—even if it did not adhere to the letter of the law with a legalist approach.[13]

The Iraq war was also waged without a UNSC resolution, but the verdict in many academic and political circles is far more severe. NATO allies were in a standoff in 2002–03 over justification for the Iraq war. As chapter 7 shows, initially a compromise was possible in crafting UNSC resolution 1441, but diplomacy broke down in talks about a resolution specifically authorizing the use of force. The final showdown was between the Americans and British, who sought a second UNSC resolution authorizing the use of force but were willing to proceed without it; the French, who threatened a veto; and the Germans, who argued that war was not justified even with a UNSC resolution. Thus, none of the four countries demonstrated that there is an absolute requirement for UN approval for the use of force.

The UN–NATO Relationship

One of the key legal arguments against the need for UNSC authorization of NATO's action in Serbia was that NATO is a collective defense organization under article 51 of the charter.[14] The Americans were unwavering in this position. Throughout the summer of 1998 and into 1999, Secretary William Cohen, Sandy Berger, and General Hugh Shelton stated publicly that NATO did not require UNSC authorization for collective defense operations. Europeans, particularly the Germans and the French, insisted that the operation was not in support of collective defense.

The ambiguity and skepticism about NATO's relationship with the UN goes back to the founding of the alliance. When written in 1949, the treaty had to overcome stiff opposition in the United States from three camps: isolationists who were opposed to any permanent entanglement in Europe; the Joint Chiefs, who were dubious of Europe's clamoring for aid; and, most importantly, internationalists, who saw the treaty as undermining the UN and as a return to the anarchical balance of power approach that had brought on two World Wars:

The treaty was made to appear as if NATO was to be just another regional organization that would fit under Article 53 in Chapter VIII of the charter. But that article is not mentioned in the text of the treaty—for good reason. Regional organizations were supposed to report their activities to the Security Council where the Soviet Union sat as a permanent member.[15]

After the Soviet threat collapsed, two phenomena put the question of the UN authority back on the front burner. First was the opportunity for consensus on the Security Council—a chance that it would now work as it was conceived to function. Second was the changing nature of the threat: from plugging the Fulda Gap to containing the leaking sieve of Yugoslavia. Weapons proliferation, state collapse, and international terrorism also became pressing security challenges in the following decade. Already in November 1991, NATO's newly approved Strategic Concept foreshadowed "out of area" missions when it stated that

Risks to Allied security are less likely to result from calculated aggression against the territory of the Allies, but rather from the adverse consequences of instabilities that may arise from the serious economic, social and political difficulties, including ethnic rivalries and territorial disputes, which are faced by many countries in central and Eastern Europe.[16]

The latter caused the allies to discuss whether NATO should be used to perform non–Article 5 operations in support of collective security, a debate unaided by the wording of Article 5, which was intentionally convoluted when written:

> The Parties agree that an armed attack against one or more of them in Europe or North America shall be considered an attack against them all and consequently they agree that, if such an armed attack occurs, each of them, in exercise of the right of individual or collective self-defense recognised by Article 51 of the Charter of the United Nations, will assist the Party or Parties so attacked by taking forthwith, individually and in concert with the other Parties, such action as it deems necessary, including the use of armed force, to restore and maintain the security of the North Atlantic area.
>
> Any such armed attack and all measures taken as a result thereof shall immediately be reported to the Security Council. Such measures shall be terminated when the Security Council has taken the measures necessary to restore and maintain international peace and security.[17]

By this language, Congress would have the opportunity to decide when U.S. force was necessary. This appeasing of the U.S. Congress was an "unavoidable price Europeans had to pay for American involvement," especially American aid to rebuild their countries and ensure security.[18] But the ambiguity in the language, created by three contending perspectives, ensured that those same perspectives continued to clash 50 years later.

In the Kosovo case, there was extreme sensitivity in Congress and in other Western capitals to the Balkans' potential for exploding into the living rooms of their constituencies via television coverage. The possibility created the imperative to react. While the general rule in politics was that the political price paid for inaction was less than the price for action ending in failure (a widespread interpretation of the Somalia intervention in 1992–94), the Balkan exception seems to prove the rule. In debating what to do about Kosovo in 1998 and 1999, decision makers often referred to the horror of Srebrenica, when Serbs ignored UN peacekeepers and marched the Bosnian Muslims from the so-called safe haven to their deaths. Many blamed the faulty coordination between the UN and NATO and the "dual key" policy of trying to get concurrence for action with both NATO and the UN. General Sir Michael Rose noted that the policy "opened a door into disagreement and frustration."[19] Policy makers referred to its failure when calling for forceful and timely military intervention to stop ongoing atrocities.

The UN drew upon other hard lessons. In particular, the failure of political will to stop the genocide of 800,000 Tutsis in Rwanda in 1994 was fresh in the memory of the secretary general and others concerned with building the credibility of UN peacekeeping. When NATO nations showed resolve for an intervention to stop ethnic cleansing in Kosovo, it was difficult for the secretary general to insist that inaction due to a lack of UN mandate was better than action without it. And so, months after the intervention, he did not condemn it but simply called the conundrum "a tragedy."[20] In the years since the terrorist attacks of September 11, 2001, American and European leaders have debated taking action in other humanitarian and human rights crises, such as the ongoing situation in Darfur, the war in Congo, the devolution of Somalia, and humanitarian emergencies, such as in Burma in 2008. In each of these, the question of authority is raised, and the trend is toward shifting the responsibility to regional organizations. Often the lack of consensus at the Security Council is a primary reason for inaction.

The Changing Nature of Peace Operations

The post–cold war 1990s, with their opportunity for consensus on the UNSC and the rise of ethnic conflict, witnessed an almost light-headed approval of peacekeeping missions. The number of operations and personnel under UN command soared to an all-time high. But the new missions did not look like classic peacekeeping—monitoring a stable cease-fire—and many wondered what to call these emerging tasks. *Peacekeeping* seemed a misnomer since there was often no peace to keep. Rather than verifying compliance with a negotiated peace settlement between two parties, UN forces in the 1990s increasingly found themselves in the midst of ongoing ethnic violence or in the chaos of disintegrating states. Sometimes the peacekeepers became the targets and even the hostages. With each conflict coming on the heels of the last, there was little time for the Security Council to find consensus on principles, but ample opportunity for disagreements about practice.

The hand wringing in the UN about what to call the new types of operations—peacekeeping, peacemaking, peace enforcement, complex humanitarian emergencies—shaped the Kosovo authorization debate, and in turn subsequent debates such as the 2002–03 dispute over the Iraq war, which was not principally humanitarian in purpose. Political sensitivities prevented agreement on official definitions. NATO designated them "non–Article 5" missions, since they fell outside the defensive mandate in Article 5 of the North Atlantic Treaty. States have not traditionally sought external authority to carry out humanitarian relief, noncombatant evacuation, search and rescue, or other "non–Article 5" missions. David Yost has noted that it is unclear why the allies acting collectively to perform such mission would need such authorization.[21]

General Wesley Clark remarked that when he was in command of the Kosovo intervention he was "never allowed to call it a war" even though it bore the characteristics of one.[22] Like many of the interventions of the 1990s, it had traits of peace making, peace enforcement, and peacekeeping all at once. As a peacemaking enterprise, it fit more clearly into the collective defense category. With its aim of protecting human rights and averting a humanitarian catastrophe, it fit more neatly under collective security. The overarching term *humanitarian intervention* seemed to lend more irony than clarity and did little to settle the dispute about whether Article 51 should be invoked.

The 1990s witnessed a rise in the enthusiasm among humanitarians for the use of force.[23] Conor Foley has demonstrated the way in which humanitarian nongovernmental organizations (NGOs) gradually embraced the use of force. The transformation of their erstwhile pacifism began ironically with the rise of human rights in its standard setting role. The enforcement of ever-increasing human rights norms lagged behind, and the gaping disparity left many frustrated. Additionally, human rights activists came to staff UN and other official bodies and vice versa. These organizations essentially ended up convincing people like themselves,[24] Foley notes, and it is no wonder that new human rights norms were increasingly promoted as universally accepted and asserted with growing confidence, even at the point of a gun.[25] NGOs actively lobbied for the use of force in Somalia and Biafra and, in return, received accusations they were feeding the killers by delivering aid. By the time activists campaigned for intervention in East Timor in 1999 and for the bringing to justice of Balkan war criminals, these campaigns depended upon the threat of force, a fact, Foley laments, that damaged the advocates' credibility.[26] By the time of the Afghanistan intervention in 2002, the debate had come full circle, from aid as an excuse for intervention to aid being used to support military operations, Foley concludes.[27] This gives new urgency to the old question of whether humanitarianism should ever compromise its neutrality, impartiality, and independence.

Even as the use of force gained credibility among humanitarians, humanitarian missions gained credibility among military planners. Leadership in the Pentagon remained skeptical about adding additional duties onto an already overburdened defense system, and one that had not yet made the transition from its cold war posture to a more agile force structure required for small wars. Yet, as chapter 6 addresses at more length, many in the U.S. Marine Corps, if not in the U.S. Army, already prepared for future humanitarian wars. NATO updated its Strategic Concept in 1999 to account for increased attention to peace operations, a mission NATO leaders pledged would remain in their "networked" approach to security when they launched the process of writing a new Strategic Concept in July 2009.[28]

JUSTIFICATION FOR THE USE OF FORCE

The search for a justification that met the demands of international and national constituencies is essentially a quest for legitimacy. Realist prerogatives of power did not stand alone as sufficient justification for the use of force in either the Iraq or Kosovo cases; there was an effort to fulfill the letter and spirit of international law, even though the extent of those requirements were perceived differently among the four nations. Despite a general perception in some circles that power and legitimacy are antithetical in international politics,[29] state behavior indicates that the two are complimentary. NATO nations in these cases found that their actions would be constrained if not justified in what was seen as legitimate reasons.

This heightens the contrast between the two concepts of international law and international legitimacy. The allies strove for the latter but could not achieve it without taking account of the law. Sometimes leaders disagreed sharply on what constituted legitimacy, such as in the dispute about whether a separate UNSC resolution was necessary in the Iraq war. In less obvious ways, there was consensus about legitimacy. The combination of human rights and humanitarianism is one of the commonalities, and the use of the just war doctrine is another.

Human Rights, International Law, and National Interests

During the presidential campaign in 2008, U.S. President Barack Obama's critics made much of the idea that he saw himself as a "citizen of the world," who would take into account the views of the international community in his decision making and therefore neglect American interests.[30] Historians would perhaps be far less alarmed. Martin Wight asserted that common interests never overcome national interests:

Every power is confident that its interests are compatible in a general way with the interests of the community of powers, but its own interests are its first concern. A Foreign Minister is chosen and paid to look after the interests of his country, and not to be a delegate for the human race.[31]

Michael Walzer has noted that "States don't lose their particularist character merely by acting together. If governments have mixed motives, so do coalitions of governments."[32] Walzer further maintains that such a combination of arguments does not dilute the claim on moral quality of an intervention. He noted that the Indian invasion of East Pakistan (Bangladesh) in 1971 could be seen as a response to operations in which a Punjabi army was inflicting grievous and massive harm on the Bengali people:

No doubt the massacres were of universal interest, but only India interested itself in them. The case was formally carried to the United Nations, but no action followed. Nor is it clear to me that action undertaken by the UN, or by a coalition of powers, would necessarily have had a moral quality superior to that of the Indian attack.[33]

Even though none of the allies believed that a purely humanitarian justification would be acceptable for the use of force, none believed they could justify the use of force absent a moral basis.

The UN Charter prohibits the aggressive use of force in Article 2, paragraph 4:

All Members shall refrain in their international relations from the threat or use of force against the territorial integrity or political independence of any state, or in any other manner inconsistent with the Purposes of the United Nations.[34]

The Charter allows two exceptions to the nonuse of force rule: a state's right to self- defense (Article 51), and the threat or use of force with the explicit approval of the Security Council (Article 53). In 1999, the NATO allies did not justify their action explicitly on either of these exceptions, but in their public statements alluded to both. Chapter VII of the Charter, which deals with threats to and breaches of peace as well as acts of aggression, allows the UNSC to decide which actions, including the use of force, members may take to restore international peace and security. What constitutes a "breach of peace" was central to justification for the Iraq intervention the allies debated in 2002–03. Since the UNSC had invoked Chapter VII in framing its resolutions in the Kosovo situation, individual NATO members pointed to these resolutions when justifying their use of force. While the Charter was written with the idea of stemming the use of force for political purposes—such as advancing the national interest or maintaining the balance of power—or for moral or ethical pursuits—each of the allies in the Kosovo case used both political and moral arguments for the use of force in 1999.

This contradiction has become typical of the humanitarian intervention debates and the justification for the use of force. On one hand, the Charter does not explicitly allow intervention for the purpose of stopping human rights violations or humanitarian emergencies. On the other hand, humanitarian intervention "belongs in the realm not of law but of moral choice, which nations, like individuals must sometimes make."[35] Not finding moral justifications in the strictly legal interpretation of the UN Charter to help the suffering Kosovar Albanians, the allies appealed to higher principles that preceded the Charter.

Writing in 1921 long before the framing of the UN Charter in 1945, Ellery Stowell argued that striving to find political and legal justification for morally based interventions weakens rather than strengthens a state's case. Referring to concurrent protests by Austria, Britain, and France in 1863 regarding Russia's oppressive behavior toward its Polish subjects, he remarks,

Unfortunately the cooperating powers did not understand the perfect justification with humanitarian considerations could give to their concurrent intervention. The inevitable consequence of this misunderstanding was that they weakened the force of their action and wasted their strength in futile efforts to discover some other common ground upon which to base their demands. But despite all their efforts Great Britain and France did not, as will be seen, succeed in discovering any ground other than that by which they set so little store—humanity.[36]

Stowell's observation illustrates that even before the UN Charter, nations grappled with finding common moral ground through legal or political instruments, despite the drawbacks of such an approach. In 1999, the allies did not believe that a strictly moral argument would have sufficed, since it would not have garnered the international support required to achieve success. Instead, each strove to justify the intervention in terms of the common interests acceptable to international constituencies—international law—and in terms of the national interests persuasive to internal constituencies. The French maintained that "To serve the law, recourse to force has become inevitable"[37] but also that "these are universal values of our republican tradition that we are defending."[38] The Americans pointed to the UN Charter and previous UNSC resolutions but also believed that they had "a fundamental interest"[39] in resolving the Kosovo crisis.

Throughout 1998 and 1999 the allies, particularly the Americans, believed that NATO credibility was in the balance. Some U.S. leaders argued that the intervention was necessary to maintain NATO and U.S. credibility, even stating that "America's survival depends on presenting a strong, united front to the world," and, "It is in our national interest to avoid even the perception of a vacuum in our leadership capabilities."[40] The link between national interest, national power, and prestige has a long history:

"Vital interests" is a phrase that did not become usual until the latter part of the nineteenth century. The older expression used to be "the dignity, honor, and interests of such-and-such a crown."... Closely bound up with the idea of "honor" is the idea of "prestige". Honor is the halo round interests; prestige is the halo round power. "Prestige", says E. H. Carr, "means the recognition by other people of your strength. Prestige (which some people scoff at) is enormously important; for if your strength is recognized, you can generally achieve your aims without having to use it."[41]

Within each nation there was a growing attachment in public opinion to human rights norms that had been enshrined in law since after World War II. Thus, in addition to national interests, there were common interests in upholding these values, which were seen as superseding the national sovereignty of Serbia. Some have argued that the interventions of the 1990s may be evidence of a period of idealist thinking in which common interests stratified international society across borders and undermined strictly political or legal concepts of the national interest. The question of whether the allies believed there was an obligation to intervene to deal with human rights violations and humanitarian emergencies is addressed in the chapter regarding international obligation. It is noteworthy that, to varying extents, human rights and humanitarian purposes were part of each nation's justification for intervention into the sovereign territory of Serbia. As the chapter on the Iraq debate shows, the moral imperative to stop Saddam Hussein's tyrannical rule was part of the American and British arguments for war.

The Just War Tradition

Was the waging of the Iraq war justified? Was it justified on humanitarian grounds? Scholars still debate these questions and that fact shows that nations find international law, especially positive law, insufficient. It also shows how strikingly relevant the ancient just war doctrine remains as a tool of international law and politics. In both the Iraq and Kosovo debates, the tenets of proper authority and the use of force as a last resort were central. Britain adhered with the least strictness to international law in 1999, claiming "humanitarian exception" to it. Prime Minister Blair declared, "This is a just war, based not on any territorial ambitions but on values."[42] The French, while not making an explicit case for a just war in 1999, nonetheless couched their justification in terms of the principles of the just war tradition. The same is true of the United States and Germany. In 2002–03 the just war principle of last resort was at the center of the standoff over war. The Americans and British believed that all reasonable peaceful mechanisms for stopping Iraq's illegal weapons programs had been exhausted, and the French and Germans believed that weapons inspections should continue.

As the discussion of the Iraq war in chapter 7 demonstrates, many scholars, religious leaders, and human rights advocates promote the just war ethic as having a presumption against the use of force. This is not the classical understanding of the doctrine, however. It is notable that government leaders in the Kosovo and Iraq debates adhered to the classical approach. Political and ethical reasons for the use of force in both cases were similar to those articulated by St. Augustine in the fifth century, and refined by St. Thomas Aquinas in the thirteenth century, and by Francisco Suarez, Francisco de Vitoria, and Hugo Grotius in the sixteenth and seventeenth centuries. These principles were adapted in the mid-twentieth century to cope with the advent of nuclear weapons and, as these cases show, policy makers struggled to refine them for the resurgence of humanitarian intervention and then the doctrine of limited preemption articulated by the United States under the Bush administration.

Attempts to make the doctrine a legal framework have proven difficult. The reason is that the just war doctrine is not a legal code, nor is it purely a moral code. Stanley Hoffmann and J. Bryan Hehir demark four bases of ethics in international politics: religious and theological, ethical and moral, political and strategic, and international law bases. They include the just war doctrine in the second category, ethical and moral, even though it has its roots in the theological and moral and influences the political, strategic, and international law bases. Within the moral and ethical realm, Hoffman and Hehir see the just war doctrine as the middle way between realism and pacifism. Paul Ramsey noted that "in the nuclear age the nations of the world seem to have an overriding interest in identifying every actionable justice with legal justice, and the principle of all order with the legal order."[43] This observation supports the idea that the twentieth century saw a resurgence of legalistic thinking, even though it witnessed powerful idealist movements, above all communism. That the allies were compelled to make their moral arguments in legal terms in the Kosovo and Iraq cases shows the influence of both traditions at the end of the century. The fact that in neither case did legal justifications suffice is also significant. Nations appealed to just war principles, particularly the need for proper authority, just cause, and right intention.

These three principles were those Thomas Aquinas offered as the original three fundamental requirements for a just use of force.

Referring to proper authority, Aquinas tied national self-defense to the responsibility of a leader to defend his nation. The second, just cause, required that the other side must have done some wrong. The third, right intention, required the state undertaking war to have as its aim the doing of some good or avoiding of some evil:

First, the authority of the ruler within whose competence it lies to declare war ... since responsibility for public affairs is entrusted to the rulers, it is they who are charged with the defense of the city, realm, or province, subject to them. And just as in the punishment of criminals they rightly defend the state against all internal disturbance with the civil arm. ... So also they have the duty of defending the state, with the weapons of war, against external enemies. ... And St. Augustine says in his book, *Contra Faustum* (XXIII, 73): "The natural order of men, to be peacefully disposed, requires that the power and decision to declare war should lie with the rulers."

Secondly, there is required a just cause: that is that those who are attacked for some offence merit such treatment. St. Augustine says (Book LXXXIII q.; *Super Josue*, qu. X): "Those wars are generally defined as just which avenge some wrong, when a nation or a state is to be punished for having failed to make amends for the wrong done, or to restore what has been taken unjustly."

Thirdly, there is required a right intention on the part of the belligerents: either of achieving some good object or of avoiding some evil. So St. Augustine says in the book *De Verbis Domini:* "For the true followers of God even wars are peaceful, not being made for greed or out of cruelty, but from desire of peace, to restrain the evil and assist the good." So it can happen that even when war is declared by legitimate authority and there is just cause, it is, nevertheless, made unjust through evil intention. St. Augustine says in *Contra Faustum* (LXXIV): "The desire to hurt, the cruelty of vendetta, the stern and implacable spirit, arrogance in victory, the thirst for power, and all that is similar, all these are justly condemned in war."[44]

In their justification of the use of force in the Kosovo and Iraq crises, NATO allies considered at length the meaning of proper authority, settling the question to varying degrees of satisfaction by all allies before NATO's decision to threaten the use of force in October 1998, only to find themselves in a bitter dispute in March 2003. The fallout in 2003 centered primarily on just cause or justification for war, and so the four nations did not agree to a specific UNSC resolution authorizing force. In the case of Kosovo, all four nations sought but did not ultimately find necessary a UN mandate. They found acceptable the authority that rested in NATO and, in the case of Iraq, a coalition of sovereign states willing to undertake the mission. In the Iraq case, German and French leaders at various points argued that force was not justified even with a UN mandate.

The second requirement that the opponent must have engaged in some wrongdoing was central to each ally's justification in 1999 and caused a split in 2002–03. Serbian leader Slobodan Milosevic's repeated flouting of UNSC and NATO warnings, his refusal to pull back troops, and his directing them to engage in ethnic cleansing and killings were recounted in detail by policy makers advocating the use of force. Similarly, governments rested their cases for force on the desire to avert an even more severe humanitarian catastrophe such as the ones witnessed in Bosnia and Rwanda. They further stated that they wanted to avoid regional instability, particularly affecting Greece and Turkey. These goals fulfilled the third of Aquinas's conditions for the just use of force, right intention: "either of achieving some good object or of avoiding some evil." Furthermore, NATO decision makers undercut any claim Milosevic had on waging a just war against the Kosovo Liberation Army (KLA). Whereas in March 1998 the allies condemned both Serb aggression and KLA "terrorism," by October 1998 reference to terrorism was generally restricted to Serb behavior.

In 2002–03, the allies did not come to agreement on whether the threat of weapons of mass destruction was imminent, but all four of the nations condemned the Iraqi leader as a "tyrant" who was a threat to his own people as well as to regional stability. Because the humanitarian and human rights abuses were not ongoing at the time of the Iraq debate, including the use of chemical weapons on his own people, French and German leaders did not invoke humanitarian arguments for war, although U.S. and British leaders did. The Americans and British rested their case on the 17 previous resolutions that Iraq had ignored.

In 1998, at the same time the allies watched the rising violence in Kosovo, leaders of these countries including members of Congress and parliamentarians condemned Saddam Hussein as a "tyrant" due to the way he abused his own people and defied UN weapons inspections regimes. At the same time, NATO decision makers referred to Milosevic as a "thug" and "war criminal" and called the killings of Kosovar Albanians "genocide" and a "holocaust," thus attributing to the Serbs qualities that would undermine any claim Milosevic had on a just war argument for his behavior regarding Kosovo. Milosevic, like Saddam, claimed that he had a just cause in putting down internal rebellion. Milosevic, like the Americans and French before changing their minds in 1998, called the rebels in Kosovo terrorists, and he claimed that sovereignty gave him proper authority to act. By labeling him a criminal, while not advocating independence for Kosovo, alliance leaders further diminished the Serb leader's claims of a just war against Kosovars. The just war scholar Michael Walzer supports such a removal of legitimacy and further notes that interventions that aid weak and oppressed people but that do not necessarily take up their political objectives (for independence, for example) are rightly called humanitarian interventions. In Walzer's words,

People who initiate massacres lose their right to participate in the normal (even in the normally violent) processes of domestic self-determination. Their military defeat is morally necessary.

   Governments and armies engaged in massacres are readily identified as criminal governments and armies (they are guilty, under the Nuremberg code of "crimes against humanity"). Hence humanitarian intervention comes much closer than any other kind of intervention to what we commonly regard, in domestic society, as law enforcement and police work.[45]

   A common understanding of the just war ethic today expands upon Aquinas's three requirements and includes criteria for launching the war (*jus ad bellum*) comprising just cause, competent authority, comparative justice, right intention, last resort, probability of success, and proportionality between the wrong done and the action taken. Requirements for just prosecution of the war (*jus in bello*) include restraint, proportionality, the avoidance of unnecessary suffering, and discrimination between civilians and combatants.[46]

   The subject of this book is limited to *jus ad bellum* since it involves the decision to go to war. The standard just war model, from Augustine to Grotius, reserved to sovereign states the authority to launch war. The model favored international institutions but did not posit that they were adequate. Above all, the ethic emphasized that war may be waged only if it is limited. Just war concepts featured prominently in the debates regarding the use of force for humanitarian and human rights purposes during the 1990s and were front and center in the Iraq war debates of 2002–03. Scholars and practitioners still debate the justness of the Kosovo intervention, focusing not only on the dynamics of state disintegration and ethnic conflict, but on the moral aspects of the resulting humanitarian and human rights emergencies. Even before Augustine founded the ethic, his mentor St. Ambrose taught that if one knows that evil is being done and does nothing to stop it, he is equally guilty with the evildoer. The most persuasive arguments in 1999 and to a lesser degree in 2003 were strikingly similar to Ambrose's doctrine.

THE NATURE OF INTERNATIONAL OBLIGATION

   The enduring appeal of the just war doctrine shows how closely moral and ethical considerations are intertwined with matters of law and politics. As one senior Clinton administration official told the

author, values and national interests were like a "wool blend," insepa-
rable, during the heated debates about the Kosovo intervention. The
third, principle of *jus ad bellum*, right intention, is closely connected to
the question of whether or not a humanitarian imperative is present
in any given crisis, and if so whether it presents an obligation—moral
or legal—on the part of states to intervene. National leaders debated
this point throughout the 1990s. In the wake of the Iraq war, scholars
also debate whether there is a right of democratic governance that also
imposes duties on states to intervene.[47] These ethical questions create
tensions with the requirements of international law, such as the principle of nonintervention present in the UN Charter, and compete with
the national interests of states.

Morality and Foreign Policy

International relations scholars have long debated the role of ethics
in foreign policy. The work of E. H. Carr, Reinhold Neibuhr, and Hans
Morgenthau has been invoked to support claims that either all moral
talk is specious, or that moral ideas taken seriously can be detrimen-
tal to a nation's interests.[48] Yet we owe a debt to these thinkers for
probing deeply the double-edged sword of moralization of foreign
policy.

Some argue that policy makers use moral talk without believing in the
norms they promote, and that such talk "heals the moral breach in the
inner life of the statesman."[49] Former national security advisor Anthony
Lake asserted the opposite: that while policy makers hold deeply felt
convictions, they rarely express them in American policy-making circles because they fear others perceiving them as sentimental or weak.[50]
Instead, they offer national interest arguments for moral causes.

Others argue that moral foreign policy comes to ascendancy when
nations' security is sound. Margaret Thatcher once noted that, "No-one
would remember the Good Samaritan if he'd only had good intentions;
he had money as well."[51] Predominant powers are often the promoters
of values because they can afford to take care of needs beyond basic
security:

Morality in international politics is not simply a matter of civilized tradition, but
is equally the result of security.... Once security is destroyed, all the higher objects
of politics are swallowed up in the struggle for self-preservation, a tendency seen
in every war.[52]

Two statesmen with virtuosity in combining moral purpose and
national interest were William Gladstone in nineteenth-century Britain

and Franklin Roosevelt in twentieth-century America. Their influence was linked to the power of their respective nation:

Each of these men in his generation had a moral ascendancy and a power over the public opinion of the world, evoking a trust and loyalty far beyond his own country, which was unapproached by any other contemporary political figure ... [they] made power an instrument and not an end, and subordinated national interest to public justice.... The first thing to remember about the policies of Gladstone and Franklin Roosevelt is that Gladstone's Britain and Roosevelt's America were dominant powers.[53]

The policy maker's difficult choices between public justice and national interest have elicited considerable scholarship on the moral dilemmas of humanitarian intervention.[54] Viewing these choices as dilemmas is itself the exercise of a particular worldview that neither views world order in terms of purely power politics nor in terms of the primacy of one ideology or another. Dilemmas are either a choice between two "goods"[55]—such as justice and security, order and justice, or the like—or a choice of the lesser evil.

While governments have dealt with the role of norms in policy, human rights and humanitarian groups have struggled with the best way to influence states. Some, like the International Committee of the Red Cross (ICRC), have sought the codification of norms in law, while others, such as Medecins sans Frontieres (Doctors without Borders), have used political advocacy. Still others believe that moral outrage, shaming, and other practices advance norms more effectively than law or politics. Policy makers faced all of these practices during the decisions regarding intervention in the 1990s.

Neither the strict realist who would proscribe morality from politics, nor the legalist who would codify it in law, nor the idealist who would see moral solidarity trump interest and law can be completely satisfied with the contemporary practice of humanitarian intervention. Yet, states continue to pursue common policies if not common interests and obligations despite the diverging ways of thinking about the role that values should have in defining policy.

Martin Wight has observed that despite the reality that "the world community is still an anarchy, lacking a common superior, and international politics are still power politics,"[56] values shape attitudes about common interests and obligations:

It is true that there was equally anarchy in the period when men talked in terms of the Law of Nature, so that its influence upon politics was tenuous and remote. Yet in the long run the idea of a common moral obligation is probably a more fruitful social doctrine than the idea of a common material interest. As the French philosopher Julien Benda has said, mankind has always betrayed its obligations, but so long as it continues to acknowledge and believe in them, the crack is kept open through which civilization can creep.[57]

From this viewpoint power, interest, security, and morality are interdependent. Power may be a greater concern to states than any particular interest about welfare, but power is also dependent upon security:

This is the vicious circle of power politics: morality is the fruit of security, but lasting security as between many powers depends on their observing a certain common standard of morality.[58]

Each of the allies found the situation in Kosovo a threat to its national interest to some degree. Each enjoyed a margin of security, however, that allowed it to pursue humanitarian and human rights ideals in the Kosovo case beyond the aim of self-defense.

Humanitarianism

The imperative NATO nations felt to help Kosovar Albanians is exceptional when considered in context. During the wars of religion, enemy wounded were often killed or sold for ransom. Vitoria and Suarez conceded the enemy respect for its cause, but considered even noncombatants enemies. Jean-Jacques Rousseau further argued that war is not a relationship between men but between states. Emerich de Vattel and Rousseau agreed that when enemy combatants lay down their arms after the conflict, those individuals cease to be enemies and the right to kill them is removed. Clausewitz, offering a more realist perspective, maintained that the sole aim of warfare was to overthrow the opponent and that humanely inspired acts, such as allowing neutral areas for hospitals, were dangerous.[59] The fact that NATO nations since the 1990s have been moved to set up rescue missions for suffering populations on the other side both during and after hostilities is an indication of the influence that the humanitarian idea held during this period of international history, at least in Europe.

The humanitarian idea arose from those who emphasize the ideal of a world in moral solidarity. They demand impartial treatment of the wounded on the battlefield and do not take sides in a conflict. Humanitarianism has also been promoted, however, by those who emphasize not just idealism but internationalism through cooperation and custom in international politics.

In its contemporary context, humanitarianism is traced to Henri Dunant, who founded the ICRC after seeing the suffering of the unattended wounded soldiers in the battle of Solferino (1859). The ICRC does not as a rule challenge the legality of war, but it has always challenged the way war is conducted and tried to make it more humane.[60] The ICRC was at the forefront of developing laws of armed conflict, especially the Geneva Conventions and Additional Protocols, which have their roots in the *jus in bello* principle of the just war doctrine. Over time, the focus of humanitarians shifted to other relief work such as famines and natural disasters, and at the same time armies improved medical support for soldiers and, at least in some cases, implemented laws of war. The relationship of humanitarians and war changed dramatically in the 1990s, when relief workers found themselves targets and victims during ethnic conflict and state disintegration.

From its inception, the ICRC has balanced the promotion of fieldwork and the gaining of political influence to help support the work by pressing nations to abide by international humanitarian law. Humanitarianism has not been untouched by those who emphasize the anarchical nature of international politics. These maintain that humanitarian motives may be used to promote national self-interest. Such thinking about the uses of humanitarianism has made application of the idea dubious among smaller states, who suspect that larger states use it as an excuse for intervention. This has also been a constant criticism of the human rights agenda, as the promoters of a "responsibility to protect" are daily reminded.

Human Rights

Closely associated with the rise of humanitarianism after World War II, the rise of human rights has been one of the most important phenomena in the international political and legal arena in the last century. The modern positivist notion of human rights, as differentiated from the more ancient concept based on natural law, transformed the way scholars, policy makers, and even the military talked about war during the 1990s. And as the case of occupied Iraq demonstrates, human rights have had lasting effects on expectations before, during, and after war.

In 1948, a diverse committee with representatives from Asia, Europe, and North and South America drafted the Universal Declaration of Human Rights (UDHR). One of the committee's advisors, Jacques Maritain, expressed the sense of the drafters when he asserted that nations can agree on what constitutes human rights without reaching consensus on where those rights come from.[61] While the committee agreed that human rights were universal, they also agreed that their governments would not necessarily apply them universally. The committee debated whether they should draft a nonbinding declaration or a convention. Eleanor Roosevelt, the leader of the drafting committee, believed with good cause that the U.S. Senate would not ratify a legally binding convention and pressed for a morally binding declaration instead. After the fact she wondered whether naming rights without a legal obligation would move states to observe them.[62] Most large states favored a declaration, while small states pressed for a convention. An exception was Britain, which favored a legally binding document. Mary Ann Glendon surmises this was because it viewed human rights as an instrument to wield against Russian and other states.[63]

The tension between sovereignty and human rights was prominent during the drafting of the UDHR, with France's Rene Cassin claiming that the doctrine of sovereignty had led to the crimes against Germany's own people. His perspective was challenged by Russia's Andrei Vishinsky, who maintained that sovereignty protected weaker states from more powerful ones. France and Russia maintained these same positions in the 1999 discussions during the Kosovo crisis. The declaration's notion of the "human family" was acknowledged at the time of the drafting as challenging the principle of respect for the "domestic jurisdiction" of the members of the United Nations, the principle of nonintervention articulated in Article 2(7) of the UN Charter.[64]

The term "everyone" used in the declaration was borrowed at that time from a UN subcommittee on the prevention of discrimination and protection of minorities. "Everyone" allows for no "other" or barbarian, and thus extends the desired boundaries of international society to its absolute limits.[65]

The question of whether states should be legally or morally bound to protect human rights was also debated from the beginning.[66] At the time, a prominent international legal expert, Hersch Lauterpacht, argued that the UDHR was not a legal achievement of magnitude. Roosevelt countered that neither was the Declaration of Independence, but that rather it set a standard that shaped society. This, she argued, would be the role of the UDHR. The Lebanese drafter, Charles Malik, argued that defining a reference point for morally judging states' behavior would be more efficacious than legally binding them. In 1999, NATO states continued to feel bound by a moral obligation to enforce human rights, even if they continued to disregard legal instruments of obligation.

Thus, the appeal of human rights is also one of the conundrums. Leaders throughout contemporary crises often refer to rights as part of an overall moral justification for the use of force precisely because they are legally imprecise. In other words, the human rights framework is neither purely positive law nor strictly moral in nature, though it has elements of both. Leaders did not point to requirements of positive human rights law, such as the Genocide Convention, because they did not believe that treaty or human rights law more generally were extra-territorial, that is, they did not bind states to apply the law outside their borders. Instead, human rights and humanitarianism were part of broader moral arguments. In particular, they helped policy makers argue that both the Kosovo and Iraq campaigns were part of a broader struggle against barbarism.

Barbarians and Civilization

Samuel P. Huntington's 1996 book *Clash of Civilizations* was at once controversial and enduring in foreign policy circles.[67] A subnarrative in modern war debates, even amidst European self-consciousness about it colonial past, has been the need to defend civilization. In the cases of Kosovo and Iraq, NATO leaders often referred to the "barbarity" of Slobodan Milosevic and Saddam Hussein and to the need for their country to defend "civilization." This language was more than rhetorical. In Western states, the terms carried both historical and moral significance and informed the nature of international obligation to intervene on behalf of suffering populations. The concept of the barbarian in Europe dated to Greek times but was linked specifically to human rights crimes after World War II in both the United Nations Charter and the Universal Declaration on Human Rights.

In the Balkans, Europeans were facing their not-too-distant past of extermination and displacement of peoples. Martin Wight proposed that "The deepest reason why the West was shocked by Hitler was his introducing colonial methods of power politics, their own colonial methods, into international relations."[68] It was one thing to practice these methods on "barbarians" outside international society, but quite anther to use them on Europeans. Barbarians, in the traditional sense, are not considered human because they have no legal rights.[69] Human rights law has sought to increasingly expand the desired boundaries of international society with the intention of making it universal. For one who believes in a universal ideology, all people, even the barbarians civilized through assimilation, are on an equal footing. Believing that human solidarity supersedes both sovereignty and custom in international politics, the idealist will dispense with both when his ideology is breached. Thus, when Slobodan Milosevic continued his campaign of ethnic cleansing, or when Saddam Hussein gassed his own people, the thinking goes, the dictates of humanitarianism and human rights gave civilized states leave to trespass on Serb and Iraqi sovereignty in order to stop them.

During World War II, offices for psychological operations, then called propaganda, were established in Britain, Germany, the Soviet Union, and the United States.[70] While the primary purpose of this use of the airwaves, leaflets, and posters was to bolster the war effort and dishearten enemy troops, one aim was to consolidate support for the war by convincing the home front of the threat of barbarism:

In order to be cohesive, the nation also has, to some extent, to be exclusive; the barriers of language, habits, color, have always tended to divide peoples into "them" and "us".... The outsider may be regarded as being unwelcome or inhuman or both.... The charge of inhumanity was frequently made by the British against the Germans and the other way round.[71]

The fight over who could claim civilization and who was the barbarian was very much at the center of twentieth-century war in Europe.[72] During the crises of the 1990s, media images often reflected images similar to those that artists rendered in the media campaigns during the two World Wars. Juxtaposing the faces of leaders with humanitarian and human rights atrocities implied or led the viewers to infer causality, whether or not newscasters or statesmen made direct connections.

Debating intervention in the case of Kosovo, decision makers on both sides often referred to media images of the suffering Kosovar Albanians. Some offered this as evidence of a moral duty or obligation to intervene, while others warned of a sentimental public that would demand intervention today and cease to support the military in the field when they were no longer confronted with such images. In Britain, some members of Parliament (MPs) argued that government policy should not be determined by editors in Western newsrooms.[73] Still another charge came from those who criticized the content of media coverage.[74] Critics argued that both humanitarian agencies and Western media created condescending, paternalistic images showing Western troops aiding "infantilized" foreigners, especially in Africa, in order to evoke emotional responses from Western audiences who would then be compelled to donate to humanitarian agencies and demand that their governments "do something."[75] Mark Duffield criticizes Western media for ignoring complex political aspects of internal conflicts and reducing them to "ancient ethnic hatred" and "tribal warfare." This, he argues, gave support to those who opposed intervention and even fostered a "new barbarism" that called for isolation from or containment of a "dangerous, unpredictable and unhealthy world."[76]

The way decision makers categorized Serb and Albanian behavior in 1999, and Saddam Hussein's totalitarian behavior between the 1991 Gulf War and the 2003 war that toppled his regime, was in keeping with the way the international human rights movement sought to continue the practice of drawing lines between the civilized and the barbarian. The human rights advocate describes the barbarian as one who does not play by the rules agreed upon by international society and is condemned by "the collective judgment of international society about rightful membership of the family of nations."[77] Samantha Power's Pulitzer Prize–winning book on genocide details the way Saddam Hussein used chemical weapons on the Kurdish population in northern Iraq, and Norman Poderetz has chronicled how leading members of Congress on both sides of the isle condemned his abuses on humanitarian and human rights grounds.[78] Important to overcoming resistance in Congress to the Iraq war was the ability of the Bush administration to link intervention in Iraq to the September 11, 2001 terrorist attacks on the United States and the broader war on terrorism. Like many others, Bush couched that connection in terms of defending civilization from radical extremists who "hate our way of life."

The Bush administration's doctrine of limited preemption, first launched at the president's address to graduating West Point cadets in 2002, then established as policy in the 2002 National Security Strategy, underscored this great struggle. The doctrine says, "In an age where enemies of civilization openly and actively seek the world's most destructive technologies, the United States cannot remain idle while dangers gather."[79]

The human rights movement seeks to make behavior—rather than geography, ethnicity, or culture—the determinant of where the line between "us" and "them" is drawn. Those among the movement with a legalist perspective expect this line to be drawn by international law or custom and by getting states to adopt a strictly multilateral approach to foreign policy. They emphasize participation in international regimes such as the International Criminal Court. Human rights advocates with a more idealist perspective see the limits of cooperation and custom and rely on moral suasion and appeals to common humanity. When advocating the use of force, they dismiss the ability of human law or international organizations to regulate state behavior and extend the realm of civilized society.[80]

The following chapters on the Kosovo and Iraq debates reveal a subnarrative wherein Western leaders, influenced by moral imperatives from the ancient just war doctrine to modern human rights norms, sought to articulate the boundaries of civilization in the contemporary context, and who, by acting outside those boundaries, is the present-day barbarian.

CHAPTER 4

The Boundaries
of Multilateralism:
Who May Authorize War?

The UN is fundamentally a legislature, and a caucus of the free and decent must seize it.
  —Jeane Kirkpatrick, U.S. ambassador to the UN 1981–1985

Debate about the use of force in Kosovo began shortly after the March 5, 1998 Serb massacre of the ethnic Albanian Jeshari family at Donji Prekaz, and it ended with NATO's approval of an activation order on October 12, 1998. That order, authorizing preparations for a limited bombing campaign, was followed the next day by Richard Holbrooke's last-ditch negotiation with Milosevic in Belgrade on October 13, 1998. The talks failed. In seven months, the NATO allies reversed their 10-year policy of treating the Kosovo conflict as an internal matter of Yugoslavia, and within a year, on March 24, 1999, began a bombing campaign to resolve the matter.

Launching the intervention in the Kosovo crisis hinged on resolving the debate among the allies about international authority. The question was whether NATO had authority to act militarily without a UN Security Council resolution specifically authorizing the use of force. In the end, the question was not explicitly resolved, and the strikes were launched without a Security Council mandate. Most governments cautioned that acting without UNSC authority should not be seen as a precedent.[1] The question of unilateral intervention was less contested. While the United States officially maintained the right to act alone, secretary of defense William Cohen said that he was "absolutely convinced that the United States could not afford to act unilaterally from a political point of view...without NATO consensus and support."[2] That consensus depended upon each of the 16 NATO governments answering questions about whether and how to legitimately authorize the use of force. Cohen recalled later: "There was a long debate for months, beginning in 1998, over whether NATO had any legal authority to take action,"[3] and each country had to reach a decision within its own government.

Implicit in the debate about whether the UNSC had to approve NATO action in the Kosovo crisis was the underlying question of where ultimate authority lies in the international order. The question was asked in three ways. First, is UNSC approval ever required before NATO action? Individual governments interpreted the Charter and determined whether they believed NATO was a regional arrangement like the OSCE or rather was entitled to collective self-defense without UNSC permission. While some believe that international law requires UNSC approval for the use of force in cases other than self-defense, NATO governments did not maintain this position. Second, if UNSC approval was required for NATO action, do humanitarian emergencies justify disregarding the Charter? Third, and largely debated after the fact, should such an exception be codified in a new customary law? After the Kosovo intervention, various scholars and some practitioners proposed that consensus already exists that states have an obligation to intervene.[4] Others argue that a "responsibility to protect" has already supplanted the "right to intervene" convention.[5] This question concerns obligation, which is taken up in chapter 6.

On the Security Council, Russia, China, Costa Rica, and Brazil all spoke out in opposition to the intervention and insisted that NATO should not use force without a UNSC mandate. France and Germany initially agreed but reversed their positions. Their initial argument was that if the Security Council did not mandate an intervention, the action would be illegal under international law. In their about-face they continued to use legal arguments—the language of existing resolutions—to support their decisions. France's insistence, however, reflected its national interest. France was intent upon upholding the authority of the Security Council, where it is one of five veto-bearing members. The British and Americans took the opposite position for the most part but did so using legal arguments as well. They asserted that international law provided for taking swift action to stem humanitarian crises, and that NATO action was multilateral. The Chinese explicitly disputed the humanitarian exception, and called NATO action unilateral. Thus, whether a state agreed or disagreed with the need for a UNSC resolution explicitly authorizing intervention, it did so adducing legal arguments in support of national interests. Germany did not share France's motives for bolstering the UN. Instead, German impetus came from a certain conception of international law, born of its postwar commitment to the peaceful settlement of disputes via multilateral institutions. While Germany and France agreed on the principle of UNSC authority, they did so for different reasons. Both the German and French publics were committed to human rights, but polls indicate that the Germans felt this commitment more intensely than the French did. This made Germany's overcoming its initial position regarding UNSC authority even more significant than France's, since it showed that, in the Kosovo case at least, the human rights agenda was more important than the commitment to a UNSC-focused international legal order.[6]

LEGAL BASIS FOR INTERVENTION: UNSC AND NATO

Statements from the North Atlantic Council, NATO's decision making body, show the dramatic shift in alliance policy between May 1998 and April 1999. On May 28, 1998, the North Atlantic Council, meeting at the foreign minister level, set out NATO's two major objectives: to help to achieve a peaceful resolution of the crisis by contributing to the response of the international community, and to promote stability and security in neighboring countries, with particular emphasis on Albania and the former Yugoslav Republic of Macedonia.

The next April, in a statement issued at the Extraordinary Meeting of the North Atlantic Council and reaffirmed by heads of state and government in Washington on April 23, 1999, the NATO objectives developed lacked talk of a "peaceful resolution of the crisis" and outlined instead specific military objectives: a verifiable stop to all military action and the immediate ending of violence and repression; the withdrawal from Kosovo of the military, police, and paramilitary forces; the stationing in Kosovo of an international military presence; the unconditional and safe return of all refugees and displaced persons and unhindered access to them by humanitarian aid organizations; and the establishment of a political framework agreement for Kosovo on the basis of the Rambouillet Accords, in conformity with international law and the Charter of the United Nations.[7]

The Security Council approved three resolutions regarding Kosovo in 1998, all citing Chapter VII of the UN Charter. In these resolutions, too, there is clear indication of shifting blame for the violence from the

KLA to Serbia, and a stiffening resolve that the West would have to intervene militarily. The resolutions were:

- UNSCR 1160 (1998), March 31, 1998, calling upon Belgrade and the Kosovo Albanian leaders to enter into meaningful dialogue, with international involvement, for the return of refugees and a for a solution to the political problems in Kosovo, understanding that the territorial integrity of Yugoslavia should be maintained and the rights of the Kosovo Albanians should be respected.
- UNSCR 1199 (1998), September 23, 1998—calling for a cessation of hostilities, endorsement of international monitoring, and the establishment of the Kosovo Diplomatic Observer Mission (KDOM). The tone of UNSCR 1199 was noticeably sharper than that of UNSCR 1160, and the Serbs were blamed for the violence. The resolution marked the first time since the violence in the Balkans began in 1991 that the UNSC did not regard Kosovo as an internal Serbian matter but as one affecting international peace and security.[8]
- UNSCR 1203 (1998), October 24, 1998—endorsing the agreements between Yugoslavia and the OSCE to insert an observer mission, and between Yugoslavia and NATO that called for the use of force in Serbia in the form of unarmed aerial observer missions to verify compliance with the cease fire and refugee returns. Proceedings surrounding this resolution produced criticism regarding NATO's prospective use of force without explicit Security Council approval from Brazil, China, Costa Rica, and Russia.

Additionally, the UN Security Council issued condemnations of both the Racak massacre (January 19, 1999) and Belgrade's declaring the head of the Kosovo Verification Mission (KVM) persona non grata (January 29, 1999) through presidential statements. It further condemned the barring of the International Criminal Tribunal for the Former Yugoslavia (ICTY) prosecutor from entering Yugoslavia after the Racak massacre, and the shooting of KVM personnel.[9]

Arguably the most contentious UNSC debate regarding the authorization of NATO strikes occurred on March 24, 1999 as the strikes began. In these proceedings Russia and China took the position that only the Security Council may approve air strikes, while Britain, France, the United States, and others claimed the legitimacy of the action on humanitarian grounds. By this time, NATO nations had spent at least nine months wrangling with the issue of legitimate authority to resort to force, both with their own publics and with their counterparts on the Contact Group. The Contact Group was an informal group of nations with particular national security interests in the Balkans and was made up of Britain, France, Germany, Italy, Russia, and the United States. Nonetheless, the UNSC proceedings are helpful in understanding the primary arguments for and against the need for a UN mandate.

Russian and Chinese opposition to NATO action without a UN mandate was based upon the following:[10] Bombing violated the Charter;

NATO members were bound by Article 103 giving precedence to the Charter over other treaties; only the UNSC could decide what measures were needed to restore international peace and security; international law did not recognize the prevention of humanitarian crises as justification for the use of force; unilateral force would lead to grave humanitarian consequences; NATO would set a dangerous precedent by acting as international gendarme; and those who undertook the unilateral approach would bear complete responsibility for the spread of such a method internationally.

The opposing view from the NATO allies comprised the following points: President Milosevic had rejected UNSC demands to end brutality to civilians; Milosevic had refused to withdraw security forces responsible for the oppression; Milosevic refused to cooperate with international organizations engaged in humanitarian relief; Belgrade refused to fulfill its obligations to NATO and the OSCE; Milosevic had failed to pursue a negotiated agreement at Rambouillet; military action was taken with great regret and in order to save lives; the action was legal and justified by international law as an exceptional measure to prevent an overwhelming humanitarian catastrophe; and force would be used only to stop the atrocities and to weaken Belgrade's ability to create humanitarian catastrophe.

It is significant that both sides claimed that their position upheld international law, and both cited humanitarian reasons for bombing or not bombing. While Russia and China claimed that international law did not recognize the prevention of humanitarian crises as a reason to use force, NATO allies cited Milosevic's violations of UN and OSCE-mandated humanitarian cooperation and his refusal to negotiate at Rambouillet as a flouting of international law. China and Russia condemned a "unilateral" approach, but the allies viewed NATO action as multilateral.

NATIONAL PERSPECTIVES

On October 2, 1998, the North Atlantic Assembly, a forum for parliamentarians from NATO member states now called the NATO Parliamentary Assembly, stated:

NATO must preserve its freedom to act: The Allies must always seek to act in unison, preferably with a mandate from the United Nations (UN) or the Organization for Security and Cooperation in Europe (OSCE), the framework for collective security in Europe. Even though all NATO member states undoubtedly would prefer to act with such a mandate, they must not limit themselves to acting only when such a mandate can be agreed.[11]

That NATO leaders were able to make this statement in October 1998, or that NATO nations were able to speak at the Security Council with one voice was not taken for granted. Preserving the trans-Atlantic relationship, much strained by the divergence in post–cold war political priorities, proved to be an imperative in 1999. Given the drastic division during the Iraq debate, the consensus seems even more noteworthy. In their search to justify what they ultimately agreed they had to accomplish, the Allies drew upon their own strategic and political cultures.[12] The fate of NATO's Bosnia mission hung in the balance. For many decision makers, the very existence of NATO and their own government's political positions depended upon resolving the Kosovo situation successfully.

Of the four primary players in NATO's decision—Britain, Germany, France, and the United States—only British prime minister Tony Blair enjoyed a comfortable political position at home. It was he who also struck the most determined and consistent tone throughout 1998 and in early 1999 that the conflict could only be resolved by force, including ground forces. Meanwhile, the American secretary of state, Madeleine Albright, led the cause for military intervention as president Bill Clinton was distracted by an ongoing scandal and the resulting impeachment proceedings in Congress. In Germany, the country faced national elections and would hand over its government to a left-leaning Red-Green coalition. In France, the government was defined by a period of "cohabitation" of the Gaullist president Chirac and the Socialist government led by prime minister Lionel Jospin, and the elites on the left as well as the public were deeply divided over the issue of a Balkan intervention. Russia tried to undermine NATO diplomatically by concluding its own agreement with Milosevic, but the plan was spoiled by Serbia's aggression against the ethnic Albanian Kosovars—the same incidents of Serb atrocities that eventually galvanized the otherwise divided alliance.

The rapidly deteriorating humanitarian and security situation in Kosovo forced NATO allies to make a decision about whether to intervene, and whether a UNSC mandate was required. The decision, however, was more than a knee-jerk reaction to events or the sum of political and strategic calculations. At the Security Council on the eve of the bombings, the allies spoke with one voice regarding action, but they continued to disagree in principle.

THE UNITED STATES

Even though American secretary of defense William Cohen was "absolutely convinced" that the United States could not afford to take unilateral action in the Kosovo crisis, he maintained that the

United States "must reserve the right to act unilaterally whenever it's necessary."[13] In a June 1998 interview, Cohen was told that several NATO partners had said that NATO must wait for UNSC action before going further in the Kosovo case, Cohen replied,

I don't agree with that. We don't agree with that in the administration. NATO, itself, has to make determinations about its security and those actions which are undermining or contributing to destabilizing areas that would also undermine NATO stability as such. And so I don't think that we need any Security Council endorsement or mandate. It would be desirable. We'd prefer to have that, but it's not indispensable. It's not imperative. There are some who disagree with that, who believe that it must go to the Security Council. But that would end up giving other countries veto power over what would be essentially actions that are now contributing to instability in the southern—Southeastern tier of Europe, and we think that would be a mistake.[14]

This same resolve persisted in the administration after the internal and international debates about authorization in the summer of 1998. Whereas Secretary Cohen's remarks indicated a self-defense argument for intervention, the president's national security advisor Sandy Berger made an argument that was based on enforcement action under Chapter VII of the UN Charter using existing UNSC resolutions. In an October 2, 1998 interview, he was asked whether the United States believed NATO would need further authorization from the UNSC. Berger replied,

No. The United Nations last week passed a resolution, 1199 it's called, which both prescribed the steps that Milosevic needed to take—it was a resolution under Chapter VII of the UN Charter, which is the resolution that involves use of force. We feel we have all of the international authority that we need here to act. There may be some further discussion in the UN. The Secretary General on Monday will be reporting back to the Security Council on whether Mr. Milosevic has complied with those conditions. I suspect he will get a highly negative report card, and that I hope will help to galvanize the international community even further.[15]

Concerning the threat of a Russian condemnation of intervention as aggression and their possible veto of any UN resolution, Berger added,

NATO cannot be a hostage to the United Nations or to any other nation not part of NATO, that is, if the North Atlantic Treaty Organization, which has been the most successful military alliance over the last half century, by unanimity if its 16 [nations] believe that something is a threat to the region, and this clearly is, we believe they have the authority to act.[16]

His remarks point to a self-defense argument for intervention, but his reference to "a threat to the region" lacked explanation of what constituted an "armed attack" as required in the Charter. Despite the unapologetic statements that Russian objections did not matter, the administration's behavior toward Russia told a different story. Secretary of state Madeleine Albright worked to get a tacit approval from the Russians in order to minimize the diplomatic costs of intervention without a UN mandate. On the eve of the October 8, 1998 Heathrow airport meeting of Contact Group members, Albright spokesman Jamie Rubin told reporters that the United States still had not broken through French and German concerns about UN authorization nor obtained an agreement from them that force was necessary. He said, "We are continuing to push for early action. NATO is not there yet."[17]

During the Heathrow meeting, the Russians stated that they would veto any attempt to sanction the intervention in the Security Council, but would "make a lot of noise" if action were taken outside the UN.[18] The following January, Secretary Albright received the explicit Russian go-ahead that paved the way to French and German support. While she was visiting Moscow at the end of January 1999, Serb atrocities increased. As part of the diplomatic program, she attended *La Traviata* with Russia's foreign minister, Igor Ivanov. During the intermission, she explained the Contact Group's plan. Ivanov replied that Russia would not publicly disapprove of this up to the point of using force but would not give public approval and would have to veto any move if brought to the UN. He told her that if she could find another way outside the UN, Russia would be onboard. The next day, while visiting the Arabian Gulf, she contacted the Europeans and they agreed to a Contact Group meeting in London on January 29, 1999.[19]

By February 18, Secretary Albright was answering for domestic audiences the same questions about authorization that Secretary Cohen and Sandy Berger had answered in previous months, but she displayed some hesitance regarding the lack of international consensus about authorization.

Well, we have—I've been talking to Foreign Minister Ivanov regularly. I spoke to him twice today. The Russians also do believe that it is time to have a political settlement on Kosovo. And they have been very much a part of the contact group deliberations. And I think that we will keep working with them. And it is my sense that ultimately we will have agreement. Again, what happened at Dayton, as you mentioned Dayton before, the Russians did object to the military annex of Dayton—did not sign on to it. And sometime later they in fact joined the forces in Bosnia. So we're taking this one step at a time. Foreign Minister Ivanov has made quite clear his support for the agreement in terms of the political aspects of what—the negotiations that are being carried on—and the fact that it's time to deal with this, and the Saturday deadline. They have been very much a part of those discussions.[20]

Her tentativeness displayed respect for Russian sensitivities to the back-channel agreement she had made with Foreign Minister Ivanov, and also her comfort in backing off since an agreement with Russia was secure. The secretary and the administration did not have to work hard to convince Congress that NATO could act without the UN but had a difficult time convincing Congress that NATO should act at all. Hence, debates in Congress were not principally about whether NATO needed UN authorization, but rather about whether the United States had any interest in launching another campaign in the Balkans.

One critic described U.S. engagement in the Balkans as "at best half-hearted" and that it "enjoyed only razor-thin political support."[21] While few voices believed that the United States and NATO should be curtailed by a deadlocked UN, centrists from both parties argued that the Kosovo conflict did not involve the nation's vital interests. The right argued that the United States was already overextended and had no vital interests in Kosovo, and the left argued against the need for force and called for diplomatic solutions.

In the end, Congress voted largely along party lines, with 42 Democrats and 16 Republicans voting "yes" in support of airstrikes and 3 Democrats and 38 Republicans voting "no."[22] The debates within the United States revealed a "mismatch between America's external policies and its internal politics"[23] that was not uncommon on the eve of involvement in armed conflict, including both World Wars. Some criticized the Clinton administration for seeking international engagement "on the cheap." When the president announced early that the Kosovo campaign would not involve ground troops—causing consternation in Britain and at home—he was responding to an American mood, an unwillingness to take casualties for what appeared to be second-tier interests.

The president was in a peculiarly bad position to mount the bully pulpit to persuade Congress or the American people, due to a scandal surrounding his relationship with a White House intern, Monica Lewinsky. On September 24, 1998, *The Economist* quoted Lamar Alexander accusing the president of mishandling several major foreign policy issues since the investigation by Kenneth Starr into the Lewinsky affair began eight months earlier: "the nuclear tests by India and Pakistan; Iraq's suspension of UN weapons inspections; the launch by North Korea of a missile or satellite over Japan; and Russia's slide into economic crisis."[24]

On August 5, 1998, Saddam Hussein halted Iraq's cooperation with UN weapons inspectors, violating the terms signed after its defeat in the UN-sanctioned Gulf War. On August 7, terrorists bombed two American embassies. On August 17, 1998, the president admitted to an adulterous affair with Lewinsky. Three days later, the United States

launched cruise missile strikes on Afghanistan and Sudan in response
to the terrorist attacks on U.S. embassies in Africa. In early December
1998, the House of Representatives began impeachment proceedings
and impeached the president on December 19, 1998, two days after the
United States and Britain launched a four-day airstrike on Baghdad.
The Senate began impeachment proceedings on January 14 and acquitted the president on February 12, 1999, while the Serb–Kosovar negotiations sputtered in Rambouillet, France.

As a result of troubles within the administration, the secretary of state
did not achieve the kind of domestic or diplomatic clout of her counterpart in Britain, who was bolstered by the support of his prime minister. The administration, including the Department of Defense, was
dubious about Albright's hawkish approach, and she was unable to
be as effective as she might have been abroad. To some, the president's
distractions prevented his backing several of her important initiatives,
and this undercut her credibility.[25] When she issued an ultimatum to
Israel and the Palestinians to revive the Middle East peace process in
May 1998, Israeli prime minister Binyamin Netanyahu called her bluff,
and President Clinton's lack of support for her was "conspicuous by
its absence."[26] It was the British prime minister who secured implicit
Italian consent to the use of force in June 1998, while Albright had
failed to do so the previous March.[27]

Further weakening the American hand in Europe was a fracture
between the Pentagon and NATO's commanding general, U.S. Army
General Wesley Clark. Clark claims that the Office of the Secretary of
Defense (OSD) and the Joint Chiefs of Staff (JCS) were so focused on
the budget that they would not seriously consider a campaign in the
Balkans. In a pointed anecdote, Clark recounts his conversation with
JCS vice chairman Joseph Ralston when he called to inform the JCS
that war in Kosovo was probable. General Ralston replied that the JCS
simply did not want to fight a war in the Balkans. Clark thus enjoyed
closer ties with the political leadership in Europe than he did with his
own superiors in the Department of Defense, and their support for
him did not enhance his professional standing at OSD or JCS.[28]

The Pentagon's stance was reflective of the immediate post–cold
war period. After the fall of the Berlin Wall in 1989, American perceptions about the U.S. military role in Europe began to change. Congress
and the uniformed military were keenly aware that since the end
of the cold war, most of the European allies had been cutting their
defense budgets, while at the same time lamenting American superpower status, and they looked for military self-sufficiency in the form
of the European Unions (EU)'s European Security and Defense Policy
(ESDP). The United States wanted to maintain its role as a European

power but did not want to bear the entire financial burden of defending the continent. Thus, Washington welcomed ESDP but viewed it with some skepticism and insisted that it not rival NATO. When Europeans rebuffed American insistence that Europe get involved in the Balkans in 1993 and 1994, Congress reacted by pulling American ships out of an arms embargo in the Adriatic in the autumn of 1994.[29] When Americans struck this unilateralist tone, Europeans further pressed for security independence through a separate European Security and Defense Identity (ESDI) but continued to cut their defense spending and perpetuated their reliance on the American military.[30]

And so, in 1998 and 1999, there were voices in Washington insisting that Kosovo was a European problem that Europeans should handle.[31] Even before the votes were tallied on Capitol Hill, however, the administration, Congress, and the public were largely united in the opinion that NATO should take whatever action the United States deemed necessary, and that such action should not be encumbered by other nations, including those on the Security Council.

BRITAIN

Tony Blair came out early with the position that the Kosovo disaster would have to be solved with force, including ground troops. Before the EU summit in Cardiff in early June 1998, he persuaded the Italian premier, Romano Prodi, of the importance of a firm NATO stance toward Milosevic, including the use of force. This marked a shift in the Italian position.[32] One analyst commended Blair's and Britain's leadership role in the crisis:

Far from being a forced alliance, the experience of Britain in the Kosovo conflict indicated that it entered the Alliance willingly and pragmatically. It served the long-standing British interest in having, in Churchill's words, "a place at the top table," or in Blair's rendition, "to punch above our weight."[33]

Blair's view remained consistent throughout the crisis, and he acted as the lead hawk, encouraging the beleaguered American president to take a stronger approach. As opposition leader, he had roundly criticized John Major's tentative handling of the Bosnian crisis, and he seemed determined not to repeat his predecessor's mistakes.[34] During the air campaign, Blair took such a forward-leaning position about the need to resolve the Kosovo conflict with ground forces that President Clinton had to convince him to stop making public statements lest he jeopardize NATO harmony during the 50th anniversary proceedings in Washington in April 1999. While Blair's Labour Party did not use the term "special relationship," he wielded his ties with the White House to suit the British view of the importance of defeating Milosevic.[35]

Unlike American, French, and German leaders, Blair had few political troubles and enjoyed a safe margin in parliament as well as in the polls. Thus, unlike the precarious position he faced during the 2003 Iraq debates, in 1998 he was able to keep dissent relatively calm, especially from within his own Labour Party. The party was traditionally opposed to the use of force, and this may have strengthened Blair's hand. The Conservatives' objections to the government's action were stayed by a fear of being labeled unsupportive of the troops in the field. When the Scottish Nationalist leader compared Operation Allied Force to the German Blitz of London in World War II, Blair accused him of being "shameless," and foreign secretary Robin Cook said the comparison "would be deeply offensive not only to service personnel and their families but also to millions of British citizens."[36] Although British public opinion did not support Blair's advocacy of ground operations—disfavoring them by 62% in March 1998—he remained popular throughout the campaign. One reason Blair enjoyed cross-party support for his anti-Milosevic stance may have been Britain's memory of the high cost of appeasement on the continent.[37]

Britain's national interests in the conflict included maintaining the credibility of NATO and the stability of the Balkans and containing the chance for a wider war. Louise Richardson argues that those interests could have been served by a less aggressive approach to the conflict. She believes that political and strategic concerns do not fully explain Britain's strong support for the use of force in Kosovo, but that only moral considerations can fully explain it—that Blair upheld a tenet of British foreign policy since the end of World War II: that strategic and moral objectives were mutually reinforcing.[38]

In a televised interview shortly after the war, Blair remarked:

I recognized, from the very beginning, that this might be a very long, drawn-out and difficult affair. What's important is to always get back to first principles in situations like this. I always used to go back to question [sic], if we didn't act, then what? Then he ethnic cleanses Kosovo, and the whole region really is then totally destabilized. Europe and NATO are shown to be powerless, and a terrible act of barbarity has taken place with nothing happening from the international community. Those are some pretty major consequences.[39]

Like other NATO governments, Britain did not wish to set a precedent for the use of force without UNSC authorization. However, Britain did not see the lack of a UNSC mandate as a stumbling block to action in the way that France and Germany did. Blair pushed off the legal dispute about authority as separate from international action:

We haven't yet worked out exactly how a doctrine of how the international community should operate, or how the institutions of the international community have to be adjusted. But this is a very, very big part now of a debate that is necessary to have.[40]

Ultimately, Britain rested the case about authority on the existing UNSC resolutions. On March 24, 1999, George Robertson told the House of Commons:

We think that there is a sufficient authority in existing Security Council Resolutions and indeed the use of force in international law can be justified as an exceptional measure to prevent an overwhelming humanitarian catastrophe. Since it is commonly agreed that that is what we are facing there is no doubt about the legality of the operation we are involved in. Speaking as I do on behalf of the United Kingdom and as Chairman of the Defense Council, I have a particular personal responsibility in this regard which would turn into a legal one if it came to it. I am satisfied that the Resolutions lay down very clear demands, especially Resolution 1199, which, as well as the exceptional circumstances, give us an absolute legal base.[41]

That is not to say that the United States and Britain were in harmony throughout the 1998 effort to get NATO nations to endorse the plan to use force in Kosovo. A fissure seemed most detectable among uniformed military. While the Pentagon was trying to minimize American ground presence in Bosnia and stonewalled against the use of force in Kosovo, British General Sir Michael Rose criticized the shortsightedness of the American political process—held hostage to media coverage, he believed—that at once insisted on preserving the "credibility of NATO" with an aerial campaign in Kosovo, and at the same time curtailed their forces on the ground in Bosnia. He attributed this trend among NATO political and military chiefs to American pressure, especially among the military aviation community, saying, that "the words 'maintaining credibility of NATO' is a convenient expression for actually indulging in the use of military force. That is what it actually means, and has usually been driven by the Americans and very often by the air powers."[42]

GERMANY

If the United States was unwavering in its stance that NATO did not need UN authorization for a strike, Germany was just as firm in taking the opposite position. Thus Germany's eventual decision to use force was a watershed event:

Only diehard American neorealists would have dared to predict what happened in the spring of 1999: "For the first time since 1945, German forces are taking offensive military operations against a sovereign state. The historic watershed is all the more remarkable because it is under the control of a 'Red-Green' coalition government, and without a clear U.N. mandate."[43]

Unlike 2003, when Germany would dig in its heels insisting on a UN mandate, political realities, events on the ground, and the inherent contradictions of the use of force for humanitarian purposes combined to reverse Germany's position in 1999. Germany ordered its forces to engage in an intervention in a sovereign state for the first time in its postwar history.

The Kohl government preferred a Dayton-like negotiation and to get Moscow onboard so that a UNSC resolution would be possible. In March 1998, just after the Donji Prkaz massacre of the ethnic Albanian Jeshari family, Secretary Albright made a push among Contact Group leaders for the use of force against Serbia. Meeting with Albright in Bonn, German foreign minister Klaus Kinkel insisted that any action be authorized by the Security Council and put forward a nonviolent alternative that fell well short of Albright's forceful approach.[44]

As the general elections neared, the German political leadership was unable to bring the United States to this position and faced the dilemma of either refusing to participate in strikes in order to uphold the long-held German beliefs about UN authority, or remain a "good ally" by participating and thus betray those beliefs. In the September 27, 1998 elections, the Germans elected a Red-Green coalition of Social Democrats (SPD) and Greens. Both parties historically opposed the use of force. On October 3, Joschka Fischer, then a potential designee for foreign minister, told *Der Spiegel* that international law required NATO to have Security Council authorization and that if the "basis for action" was ignored, "other powerful countries could use this as a precedent."[45] A stalemate occurred as the government-elect prepared to take over. On October 8, incoming chancellor Gerhard Schroeder met with his predecessor Helmut Kohl just before Schroeder's visit to Washington, but no determination on whether the new government would support the NATO action, even to the extent that the previous government had, was forthcoming.

That same day, Klaus Kinkel was at Heathrow airport near London in the fortuitous conclave of Contact Group decision makers. Present were Robin Cook, Hubert Vedrine, Igor Ivanov, Madeleine Albright, and Richard Holbrooke. When the topic of UN authorization for the use of force arose, Kinkel pressed the group for a Security Council mandate. Ivanov was clear that Russia would veto any such attempt, but Kinkel pressed on. Richard Holbrooke recounted it this way:

Ivanov said: "If you take it to the UN, we'll veto it. If you don't we'll just denounce you. Kinkel says he wants to take it to the Security Council as do the British and French. Madeleine and I say: 'That's insane!'" So, Kinkel says: "Let's have another stab at it". But Ivanov says: "Fine, we'll veto it". And Kinkel asks again and Ivanov says: "I just told you Klaus, we'll veto it...." He says: "If you don't we'll just make a lot of noise."[46]

Back in Germany, the Bundestag debated the need for a UNSC mandate in mid-October.[47] The Greens announced they would oppose German participation in NATO military action in Kosovo without a UNSC resolution approving the use of force.[48]

In his Washington meeting with President Clinton, Schroeder—not wanting to take the blame if Holbrooke's negotiation failed and wanting Germany to appear a reliable ally—announced that Germany would support the NATO campaign but would not commit German troops. Just three days later, on October 12, the Clinton administration—perhaps at the recommendation of outgoing German defense minister Volker Ruehe—pressed Schroeder and received just such a commitment.[49]

The circumstances surrounding German support for intervention without a UNSC mandate reveal competing German interests in upholding international law, protecting human rights, and defending legitimate security interests by supporting NATO. German foreign policy was split two ways. Among elites, two groups reached the same conclusion for different reasons. Moralists, mostly Greens and SPD, supported intervention on humanitarian grounds, while others argued that Germany's national security interests required Germany to support NATO and to prove itself a reliable ally.[50] The Greens were split between the "leftists" who opposed military intervention in the Balkans, and the "realists," whose chief spokesman in the Bundestag, Joschka Fischer, supported it.

At the public opinion level, the divide was clearly between former East and West Germans. While two thirds of westerners would have NATO go beyond collective defense to aid a population at risk, easterners, "reflecting a deeply rooted uneasiness with NATO and its missions...wanted to restrict NATO's functions to collective defense."[51]

For most Germans, the prohibition of employing the Bundeswehr (the army) for a purpose other than self-defense was the codification of guilt over Germany's Nazi past. During the cold war, the issue was moot, since the probability of using any NATO troops out of area was slim. In 1983, Manfred Woerner, the West German minister of defense at the time, stated:

For the Federal Republic of Germany, deployment of forces outside the NATO area is out of the question. Moreover, such operations would have no strategic meaning. Any withdrawal of forces earmarked for defense of Europe would increase the present disadvantage of NATO in the East-West force ratio.[52]

Even so, as early as 1994 the way was paved when the Federal Constitutional Court stated that German forces could participate in collective security operations approved by the Bundestag. However, the thinking was that such operations would be for collective security and under the UN umbrella.[53] The ambiguity of whether NATO operations in the Balkans were collective defense or collective security provided ample room for differing viewpoints to press their cases.

As in Britain, the party in office during the Kosovo intervention was one with a strong historical antiwar reputation. The German troika rested on their own antimilitarist legacy to suppress the notion that German military involvement—as monumental as it was in fact—signaled a return to militarism or even patriotism.[54] Schroeder, Rudolf Scharping, and Fischer

[B]elonged to the activist core of a protest generation which had challenged not only the Germany of the 1960s and 1970s, but also the previous generation for its moral and political failures in the 1930s and 1940s. In an interview with *Der Spiegel,* Schroeder related.... "there was a very lively debate regarding Hitler's fascism in which children asked their parents: Why did you not do anything at the time? ....I would like to be able to say in such a situation that I did what was possible and rational."[55]

Not only did Germany not support Britain's forward-leaning policy endorsing ground troops, but Schroeder and Fischer ruled the option out altogether in mid-May 1998. The Red-Green coalition felt its hold on power in peril over the issue. Schroeder went so far as to declare that his country would veto any such move, with or without German troops.[56] The statement reflected the deep division in German public support for the operation, and the diminishing support shown in polling data as the air campaign continued. The country, like the parties that governed it, was conflicted about the Kosovo intervention's inherent contradictions: support the operation and betray their deeply held beliefs favoring the peaceful settlement of disputes, or protest and betray their commitment to humanitarianism and human rights.

FRANCE

Ultimately, France rested its legal basis of the NATO intervention on the authority of the Security Council:

The action of NATO finds its legitimacy in the authority of the Security Council. The Council Resolutions concerning the situation in Kosovo (resolution 1199 of September 23, 1998 and 1203 of 24 October 1998) were taken under the terms of chapter VII of the Charter of the United Nations, which treats coercive actions in the event of rupture of peace.[57]

Yet, France had to claim this legitimacy without the UNSC resolution explicitly authorizing the use of force that it had previously insisted upon throughout the crisis.[58] France's announcement in January 1999 that it would support the strikes on Serbia without a new and explicit mandate contrasted with its refusal in the previous month to join Britain and the United States in Operation Desert Fox, the aerial campaign against Iraq.[59] An examination of France's insistence upon UN authorization reveals competing traditions of thinking among its decision makers, who were faced with the both the urgency of the events of 1998–99 and the inherent contradictions of "humanitarian" intervention in the 1990s.

Throughout the post–cold war period, France maintained that non–Article 5 missions required OSCE or UNSC authorization. Primary arguments included the desire not to alienate China or Russia on the Security Council and not to set a bad precedent of acting unilaterally that Russia, China, India, or other states might follow.[60] Hubert Vedrine met with Richard Holbrooke on July 2, 1998 and then told *The New York Times*, "If we have to use force...without United Nations authority, we would not be in a position to insist that Russia, China, Nigeria or other countries cannot use force without United Nations authorization."[61] But he added that he did not think Russia or China had said their last words yet on Kosovo. A third concern was giving Kosovar Albanians support for independence and a further disintegration of Yugoslavia. *The New York Times* quoted Vedrine: "If the only option was to bomb strategic Serbian military and communications sites throughout the country, the next day the Kosovo Liberation Army could declare Kosovo a sovereign republic, Albania could join...the war could spread to Macedonia and beyond."[62]

France's emphasis on UNSC authorization is linked to its post–cold war identity crisis.[63] Some have argued that while France is often considered the "consummate realist state, with its emphasis on a narrow view of national interest," the Kosovo intervention manifested a change in France's foreign policy, that it had shed its Gaullist independence and autonomous stance and adopted a multilateral approach, spreading influence by working through international institutions.[64] More than a shift from one way of thinking to another, the debates revealed a competition among strongly held traditions within French foreign policy making. Some argue that this crisis of identity was evident in the way the French press covered the Kosovo situation, connecting it to the historical formation of European national and ethnic identities, especially that of France itself. The press further emphasized the incongruence of France's supporting an American-led campaign against France's historical ally, Serbia.[65]

In the case of Kosovo, the institutions through which France sought to exert influence were the UNSC, NATO, the European Union, the Contact Group, and the Group of Eight (G8). France's insistence upon the need for UNSC approval of NATO operations and its wielding of its own status there is thus linked to its expressed national interest. Its promotion of European institutions of which the United States is not a member is equally important for achieving its goal to be a leading European power.[66] While a multilateral approach made France's approach seem less realist, the reasons behind its multilateralism maintained a realist character.

The rising importance of human rights and other value-laden objectives indicates the prominence of idealist thinking in France's foreign policy, at least for purposes of public legitimization. On the other hand, Alex Macleod has noted that the promotion of "a certain conception of Europe and European values, for human rights, even for European civilization" in justifying the Kosovo intervention is part of France's overall objective of achieving a certain rank among world powers.[67] Arguably, achieving and maintaining status as a norm entrepreneur in Europe and across the globe is the way that this middle power—once able to maintain that rank by navigating between two superpowers—is able to hold on to middle-power status in a world with only one remaining superpower.

French insistence upon UNSC authorization for any NATO action also reflected longstanding reservations about American dominance of NATO and European security affairs. France had long been interested in playing a greater leadership role on the continent. Throughout the Kosovo crisis, France was engaged in promoting a separate European Security and Defense Policy (ESDP), the purpose of the December 1998 meeting at St. Malo with British prime minister Tony Blair, French prime minister Lionel Jospin, and French president Jacques Chirac.[68]

All of this took place in a tense climate of trans-Atlantic economic relations. Europeans were preparing to adopt the euro in January 1999 in the hopes that it would soon rival the dollar. American legislation like the Helms-Burton and D'Amato acts, which threatened to impose sanctions on Europeans for doing business with Cuba, Iran, and Libya, were another thorn in Europe's side, even though the Clinton administration worked hard to ensure these sanctions were never imposed.[69] Negotiations for a permanent settlement to this issue were ongoing throughout 1998, but the French particularly resented the "pre-eminence of a single economic, political and cultural 'hyper-power'," as their foreign minister put it."[70]

However, French insistence on UNSC approval and its emphasis on human rights and other norms may not have been entirely inspired by realist considerations. The French held deep-seated beliefs about human rights and humanitarianism, which they debated throughout the crisis. French popular support for intervention was "fragile and confused."[71] The Kosovo crisis divided the left in France in a way that previous conflicts like the Gulf War did not. *Le Monde* noted on April 9, 1999,

Whereas in 1991 a whole section of the left joined up together with pacifist and Christian bodies in opposition to American intervention, the Kosovo crisis is dividing the radical left.[72]

This fact had a more discernible influence on French justification for the intervention than on French decisions about authorization. However, with weak support among the public, and confrontational positions adopted by French intellectuals, it is not difficult to understand why French leaders judged it prudent to seek a UNSC resolution for action and relied on existing UNSC resolutions 1199 and 1203 as their legal justification when it proved impossible to obtain a more explicit UNSC authorization for the use of force.

THE ROLE OF RUSSIA

The issue of whether NATO must seek a UN mandate would not have come to a head in 1998 if not for the threat of a Russian veto on the Security Council. While the United States and Britain campaigned among Contact Group members for an agreement on the need for force in the summer of 1998, Russia pursued a strategy with Milosevic to meet its own ends. Russia saw Serbia as a traditional ally but was also motivated by a U.S. $200 million Serbian debt that it did not want to write off in the event of war. Russian rhetoric against NATO was strong, but there is evidence that this was designed for a domestic audience rather than a foreign one.

Ironically, Milosevic also worked against Russia's achieving a foreign policy coup over the West. When Milosevic traveled to Moscow for talks with President Boris Yeltsin, he agreed to nearly all of the demands of UNSCR 1160 and thus made the argument for the use of force seem hollow. However, the day after the Yeltsin–Milosevic agreement was signed, the Army of Yugoslavia (VJ) reinforced its troops in Kosovo, a move that humiliated Yeltsin and weakened Russian opposition to the strong language of UNSCR 1199 that condemned Serbia for the violence. Alex Bellamy argues that Russia knowingly looked the other way when the North Atlantic Council was preparing to vote on the use of force against Serbia during a meeting in Portugal in September 1998. This helps to explain Russia's acquiescence on September 23, 1998 to UNSCR 1199's invoking of Chapter VII, which paved the way for the Atlantic Council's activation warning the following day, the first step to a bombing campaign. This interpretation is supported by Ivanov's position at the Heathrow Airport meeting of October 8, 1998 among Contact Group leaders.[73]

CONCLUSIONS

Critics argue that American bullying of the allies was pure realpolitik. But the truth is more complex. The American and British insistence that NATO action without a UN mandate upheld international law is a realist approach, because it implied that law is not just what is written in the UN Charter, but is what is posited by sovereign states. When the United States insisted that the UNSC could not dictate American foreign policy, it was making this case. Furthermore, the move to use force without explicit UNSC authorization came from the real need to see success in NATO's Bosnia mission, avert a humanitarian disaster in Kosovo, maintain peace and security, prevent a wider war in the region, and hold the alliance together. That the allies claimed all of these rationales at different times as justifications for making a legitimate exception to international law is itself a realist approach.

The internationalist legal arguments were also front and center. American and British officials made the case that supporting NATO was supporting an international organization and that holding Milosevic to previous resolutions was upholding international law. Thus, the United States and Britain did not argue at the UNSC that cooperation was not possible among nations and that war was inevitable, but that force was necessary to uphold law. They did not eschew multilateralism so much as find an alternative form of it, shifting their focus to NATO.

When the NATO allies tied Milosevic's blatant violation of previous resolutions with continued human rights abuses, they pointed toward what Francisco Suarez[74] called *societas quasi politica et moralis,* an international society that is both political and moral. This social condition is "institutionally deficient" and leads to a limited Lockean contract. The realists' belief, on the other hand, is that a state of unlimited war leads to an unlimited Hobbesian contract.[75] It is the internationalist's viewpoint that was framed in the Covenant of the League of Nations at a time when the great powers saw World War I as an aberration and the capacity for cooperation among nations as the norm. In this context the UN Charter stands in stark contrast. The contracts underpinning both the League and the UN were not archetypically Lockean and Hobbesian, but, as Martin Wight observed, "the difference between the Covenant and the Charter is, in essence, the difference between Locke and Hobbes."[76]

The Europeans were in a considerably stronger position in 1999 than they were in 1945. Britain, France, and Germany had not only been rebuilt after World War II, they were in the midst of putting together economic and military strategies to someday rival American power on the continent. Thus, the idea that American leadership forced the other allies into the operation in a Hobbesian way is not tenable. The international environment in the Euro-Atlantic region had shifted decidedly toward the internationalist paradigm, wherein the terms of law were respected on a declaratory level, even if not necessarily observed by all members of international society. This helps to explain American reliance on legal justification for the use of force.

While the overarching paradigm was internationalist and based in law, nations continued to speak and act in ways consistent with national interests and idealist aims as well. France's insistence on UNSC authority in 1998 was less internationalist than it was realist, because it resulted in large part from a desire to strengthen France's international political clout. In this respect, France's move toward a multilateral foreign policy was also realist, as was its desire to limit U.S. predominance. France's arguments for ESDP and strengthening the EU role in international security affairs appear to have been intended to advance French national interests.

German foreign policy makers, on the other hand, focused more on the desire to strengthen cooperation through international organizations. They insisted on both UNSC approval and the conflicting desire to remain a "good ally" in NATO. Germany was perhaps the NATO ally most genuinely tied to the notion that only a UNSC mandate could fulfill the requirements of international law and cooperation. However, Germany's decision to abandon this position in order to be a faithful ally no doubt had realist underpinnings as well: the Red-Green coalition viewed its response to the Kosovo crisis as a matter of its political survival in an increasingly ambivalent society.

In the same way, the German government's emphasis on defending human rights as a justification for making a legitimate exception to certain international rules stemmed from a need to please domestic constituencies. This was at once a realist choice on the part of the government and idealist on the part of the public. Throughout the post–World War II period, the German people's regard for human rights—in this case moral solidarity with the oppressed Albanian Kosovars—reflected a genuine transformation in German foreign policy. It can be tied to Germany's milestone decision to contribute troops for the Somalia and Bosnia missions, as well as its ordering them to intervene in Serbia, part of the sovereign state then known as the Federal Republic of Yugoslavia. That human rights norms were more important than legal conventions and the sovereignty of Serbia reveals how powerful the idealist strain had become in influencing policy.

German empathy for both sides in the Kosovo conflict revealed the presence of idealist thinking. The sympathy for Serbia's desire not to lose Kosovo to independence reflected convictions about Germany's own reunification 10 years earlier. German backing for the rights of Kosovar Albanians to autonomy sprang from the same source. Thus, there was a conflict between the idealist belief in the enforcement of universal human rights, and the internationalist belief in the peaceful resolution of disputes. For Germany, the idealist argument carried the day, but only just. Public support dipped once the air campaign began, particularly regarding the efficacy of the use of force to protect civilians.[77]

That Germany, the state most committed to the UN paradigm, was also willing to act without an explicit Security Council authorization to use force due to human rights concerns shows the degree to which idealist thinking shaped international politics in the 1990s. This time it was not antimonarchist or communist, but prohuman-rights ideas that trumped attachment to both the sovereign state (for the realist) and the UN (for the internationist).

NATO members were not forced allies, nor did they have a united NATO interest. A striking degree of unity was nonetheless possible, although each nation acted in its national interest and in accordance with its own analysis of legitimate authority to use force. The inherent contradictions in the nature of humanitarian intervention allowed competing and contradictory voices within and among nations to converge on the side of intervention and not abstention, despite the UNSC deadlock.

Tony Blair captured the way in which national interests and multilateralism merged during the debate about the use of force in the

Kosovo crisis when he linked the upholding of international law with national interests and NATO's credibility:

Upholding international law is in our international interests. Our national security depends on NATO. NATO now has a common border with Serbia....Our borders cannot remain stable while such violence is conducted on the other side of the fence. NATO was the guarantor of the October [1998] agreement. What credibility would NATO be left with if we allowed the agreement to be trampled on comprehensively by President Milosevic and did not stir to stop him.[78]

In the Kosovo case, some who argued against the need for a Security Council resolution—a seemingly realist position—did so in order to uphold the international legal order. Real disagreements existed about whether NATO ever needs a UNSC mandate to use force. For example, the commanding general of the Kosovo operation, General Wesley Clark, maintains that "international law was made by nations," and that "the UN Security Council does not have the consent of the governed because that consent ends at the national border. In a democracy, politics gives legitimacy to foreign affairs."[79] At the same time, the leaders of France and Germany insisted that it was law and not politics that lent legitimacy to international action. Even so, they insisted upon UN sanction for partly political purposes. The debate of 1998–1999 brought to light these kinds of paradoxes but did not resolve them before the NATO allies launched their aerial campaign.

CHAPTER 5

Waging War to Save Lives: When Is Intervention Justified?

For the true followers of God even wars are peaceful, not being made for greed or out of cruelty, but from desire of peace, to restrain the evil and assist the good.

–St. Augustine, *De Verbis Domini*

Immediately following the massacre of 50 members of the Jeshari family in March 1998, the UN Security Council agreed to an arms embargo to put pressure on Serbian president Slobodan Milosevic and the KLA to end the violence. American and British leaders concluded that a military intervention had to be considered, and both began constructing a legal case even as they pursued peaceful means of conflict resolution one by one throughout 1998. Three UN Security Council resolutions and active shuttle diplomacy by the Contact Group did not bring the Serbs and Kosovar Albanians to the negotiating table. By October Britain, France, Germany, and the United States agreed that Milosevic "only understood force," and on October 12, 1998, the North Atlantic Council approved an activation order authorizing preparations for a limited bombing campaign. Milosevic then assented to the terms of UNSCR 1199 in the "October Agreement" he made with Richard Holbrooke.

Following the agreement, there were signs that the Serbs would cooperate. It became clear within weeks, however, that Milosevic was not dissuaded from his efforts at ethnic cleansing in Kosovo. The Serb massacre of ethnic Albanians in Racak on January 15, 1999 was a galvanizing event for proponents of the use of force in the West and a slap in the face for those who had insisted peaceful means would resolve the issue, including Russia.

UN Security Council members who were reluctant to use force maintained throughout 1998 that getting the Serbs and Kosovar Albanians to the negotiating table was the object of their decision to threaten force. The Contact Group warned the Serbs that air strikes would ensue if they did not attend negotiations in Rambouillet, France, in February 1999. The allies similarly told the Kosovar Albanians they would be left to their fate without outside assistance if that party failed to participate. Once the two sides agreed to the talks, the Contact Group brandished the same threats in an attempt to force the two parties to sign the agreement. The Kosovar Albanians eventually signed the accord, while the Serbs refused. The failed negotiations left critics pondering whether the talks, as conceived and conducted under the threat of force, fulfilled the legal requirement to exhaust peaceful means of dispute settlement and the just war requirement of last resort. After the talks, the allies agreed to follow through with their October 12, 1998 decision to use force against the Federal Republic of Yugoslavia (FRY), but they were not in concert about the legal grounds for the action. On the eve of the campaign, the allies' justifications varied widely and were not articulated in fine detail.

In each of the UN Security Council discussions regarding Kosovo in 1998 and 1999, human rights and humanitarian organizations as well as private citizens within each country called on leaders to stop the ethnic cleansing in Kosovo, even if it meant using force to do so. This legitimization of the use of force for normative reasons stands in stark contrast to the strict politically realist and legally positivist position, taken by the Chinese, who maintained that Kosovo was an internal matter of a sovereign state, and that humanitarian concerns give states no legal grounds to intervene.

The Chinese position had been the de facto policy of the allies from the beginning of the Balkan crisis in the early 1990s. But by 1998 the situation had changed, leaving the allies deteriorating policy options to maintain the fragile peace in the Balkans. First, it was becoming clear that Kosovo might unravel the nascent UN, OSCE, and NATO peacekeeping and reconstruction efforts that began in 1995 with the Dayton accords. Western leaders translated this into a threat to international peace and security, as well as a challenge to their national and personal reputations. Second, due to Milosevic's recalcitrance, decision makers in the West increasingly saw him, not as an authority with whom to make deals, but as a "thug" and "war criminal" to be distrusted. Finally, the 1994 genocide in Rwanda and the other humanitarian crises of the decade had convinced most Western leaders that the consequences and costs of failing to stop genocide were greater than the consequences and costs of military intervention. Furthermore, the allies hoped that the threat of force alone would suffice, as it did when coercion caused Milosevic to compromise his position against allowing OSCE monitors into Serbia. The allies expected that if the use of force was required, it would be of short duration and limited to no greater force than was required in Operation Deliberate Force in August and September 1995.[1]

Each government rested its case in some measure on humanitarian concerns—France less so than the rest, and Germany and Britain more so than the United States. There was no disagreement among the allies that the ongoing ethnic cleansing and potential for large-scale disaster gave them legitimacy for military intervention. The difficulty was finding the proper calculus of legal, ethical, and political justifications on which to rest their convictions.

NATIONAL PERSPECTIVES

The United States based its justification on four grounds: the humanitarian necessity, the threat to neighboring states and regional stability, Serbia's violation of international humanitarian law and human rights, and the existing UN Security Council resolutions referring to Chapter VII provisions of the UN Charter. Michael Glennon categorized the U.S. legal case as a combination of customary law, treaty law, and the UN Charter.[2] The French rested their case almost entirely on existing resolutions, because the resolutions pointed to international peace and security and Chapter VII of the Charter. Implicitly, however, they expressed their case—including national interests and values—in terms of the just war doctrine. The British rested their case on "overwhelming humanitarian necessity." Their legal argument was based largely on customary law rather than on the provisions of the Charter. The Germans rested their case on the threat to international peace and security and the need to avert a humanitarian and human rights emergency. They did not cite previous UNSC resolutions as a legal basis, because objections by China and Russia left doubt about whether such an appeal was valid under international law. These varying legal, political, and normative justifications for the use of force stemmed from diverse and sometimes conflicting political cultures and national interests. The ultimate agreement to act together despite national differences was a converging of three traditions of thinking about intervention.

THE UNITED STATES

During the UN Security Council proceedings, the United States based its legal justification of the campaign on previous UNSC resolutions, the impending humanitarian emergency, and a threat to peace and security in the region. In the debates within the U.S. government, justification was framed in terms of the national interest. Clinton administration officials relied heavily on national interest arguments because, by the end of the 1990s, the administration felt it "could not go back to the Congress with yet another request for the use of force" if national interests were not at stake.[3] In an October 6, 1998 letter to Senate leaders, President Clinton justified the use of force against Serbia in terms of three U.S. national security interests: first, avoiding regional instability affecting NATO allies Greece and Turkey and the exacerbation of tensions in the Aegean, including radical Islamic fundamentalists establishing a foothold in Southeastern Europe and thereby increasing the threat of terrorism; second, averting a major humanitarian and human rights crisis; and third, upholding NATO's credibility.[4]

President Clinton typified this format at a policy briefing on the eve of the Rambouillet talks:

If [the violence] continues, almost certainly it will draw in the neighboring countries of Albania and Macedonia. Both of their Prime Ministers came here today to meet with me and urge me to have the United States help to stop this war. It could potentially involve our NATO allies, Greece and Turkey. It could spark tensions again in Bosnia and undo what we just spent three years trying to do. Certainly, if this conflict continues we'll see another massive humanitarian crisis; there will be more atrocities, more refugees crossing borders, more people crying out for justice and more people seeking revenge.[5]

Justification in the UN Charter

The UN Charter provided the Americans a legal basis for pursuing their national interest of maintaining regional stability. While humanitarian concerns and matters of U.S. and NATO credibility could not be easily defined in legal terms, the threat to regional security and the possibility of a wider war could be covered by Article 51 of the Charter, which provides for self-defense:

Nothing in the present Charter shall impair the inherent right of individual or collective self-defense if an armed attack occurs against a Member of the United Nations, until the Security Council has taken measures necessary to maintain international peace and security. Measures taken by Members in the exercise of this right of self-defense shall be immediately reported to the Security Council and shall not in any way affect the authority and responsibility of the Security Council under the present Charter to take at any time such action as it deems necessary in order to maintain or restore international peace and security.[6]

Some government officials from NATO countries argued that the repression of Kosovar Albanians by Yugoslav forces could cause the unrest to spread to neighboring countries and eventually draw in Greece and Turkey, thus requiring defensive force to protect NATO allies. In a February 23, 1999 interview, national security advisor Sandy Berger made the case that a threat to international peace and security existed when he stated that the Kosovo crisis could lead to the Balkan war spreading to Greece, but he did not tie this specifically to self-defense under Article 51 of the UN Charter or collective defense under Article 5 of the North Atlantic Treaty. Given the favorable ties between Greece and Serbia—and between Macedonia and Serbia—this case would have been difficult to make unless there was an attempt to create a "Greater Albania" based on ethnic Albanians in Macedonia and northern Epirus in Greece. The United States and other allies never explicitly justified action in self-defense terms.[7]

Also precluding a self-defense argument was the fact that American military officials did not try to argue that Serb aggression could threaten American lives. The Defense Department determined that there was no threat to American forces involved in peacekeeping in Bosnia or Macedonia, and it seems reasonable to conclude that Article 51 was not seriously entertained as a justification involving threats to Americans.[8] In his remarks at the NATO Commemorative Ceremony on April 23, 1999, while the campaign in Serbia unfolded, Clinton stated, "No member of NATO has ever been called upon to fire a shot in anger to defend an ally from attack."[9] By this statement, the president clearly avoided claiming publicly that the NATO action in the Kosovo crisis was a defensive measure to safeguard Greece and Turkey. The American case therefore rested primarily on previous UNSC resolutions.

On the eve of the bombing campaign in 1999, the United States sent classified cables to its NATO ambassador containing the several principles of its legal case. Here, the reference to collective defense was explicit, but the cable was an internal document. Included were the reliance on Chapter VII provisions in UNSC resolutions, collective defense of NATO's southern tier, the growing threat of a humanitarian crisis, collective action with UNSC approval, and an observance of the laws of armed conflict.[10]

Military and Political Goals

There was no doubt that political and military aims also informed the U.S. justification. From his vantage point at Supreme Headquarters Allied Powers Europe (SHAPE), General Clark saw two reasons for forcible NATO intervention in Kosovo. He said, "Success in Bosnia hinged on success in Kosovo; we had to prevent another war. That would have meant the end of the NATO mission in Bosnia and the end of NATO."[11]

Even so, the Clinton administration strove to emphasize the legal justification for the use of force rather than the military-political or humanitarian aims. One National Security Council (NSC) staff member has argued that one will not find a "shred of evidence" that the American case was humanitarian, rather than legal. He argues that the administration believed that stating its justification in humanitarian terms would set an undesirable precedent, and making a general legal argument was thus more desirable.[12]

The United States had reasons not to define its legal case in great detail, however. First, the United States, and the State Department in particular, did not want to set a legal precedent that might bind the United States to intervene in future crises. Second, it wanted to avoid giving a legal pretext for China and Russia to intervene in their "near abroad."[13] Third, the administration did not have to argue its legal or humanitarian case in great detail to internal constituencies, since members of Congress were not pressing it on upholding international law or fulfilling human rights or humanitarian obligations.

Values as Interests

Secretary of state Madeleine Albright stressed that most NATO leaders agreed that the Kosovo crisis could threaten NATO credibility and Western values. Speaking in Brussels on October 8, 1998, the secretary of state linked the alliance to preserving Western values as well as peace and urged NATO nations to approve an activation order, which they would do four days later:

One of the keys to good diplomacy is knowing when diplomacy has reached its limits....I believe that we are at a crossroads in the history of the Balkans as well as NATO. The decisions we take in the days ahead will be crucial for us all. NATO is our institution of choice when it comes to preserving peace and defending Western values on the continent. It must be prepared to act when a threat of this nature exists on Europe's doorstep.[14]

The secretary of state was consistent. On February 4, 1999, after the president had delivered a message to the American people that emphasized regional stability and stemming humanitarian disaster, Albright again stressed the imperative of upholding the credibility of NATO and Western principles of human rights and the rule of law. She did so, however, in the language of the national interest:

America has a fundamental interest in peace and stability in Southern Europe, and in seeing that the institutions which keep the peace across that continent are strengthened. America has a fundamental interest in preserving Bosnia's progress toward peace....America has a fundamental interest in strengthening democratic principles and practices in the Balkans and throughout Europe....And America has a fundamental interest in seeing the rule of law upheld, human rights protected, and justice done.[15]

The idea of preserving Western values was not a primary argument, as it was for France, but it was echoed in some quarters domestically, most notably by Secretary Albright, Senator John McCain, and former Senator Bob Dole. Dole stated, "Freedom and liberty—the principles that America stands for—are at stake. American credibility and European stability are on the line. What is urgently needed now is American leadership."[16]

Congress and the National Interest

A Republican majority that was generally unsympathetic toward the Clinton administration controlled the Congress during the Kosovo crisis. The most influential members of Congress in the Kosovo debates had a shared history of debating intervention and humanitarian aims throughout the 1990s. After the October 1993 incident in Somalia, in which U.S. Army Rangers were killed and Americans watched television images of one soldier dragged through the streets of Mogadishu by an angry crowd of Somalis, Congress withdrew its support for the mission, and U.S. forces left the country in March 1994. However, after the successful resolution of the Bosnian crisis in 1995, and feeling a vested interest in making the Dayton Accords work, members of Congress had gained some confidence in the use of force in operations other than war. One lesson generally taken away from the decisions about interventions in the 1990s was that force should be used only in cases involving important or vital national interests.

In the case of Kosovo, Congress was generally supportive of military intervention, with few exceptions. Those who dissented from the use of force maintained that the national interests at stake were not sufficient to risk American lives. For example, Senator Sam Brownback (R-Kansans) said that

This is not in our strategic and vital interest of what is taking place. Yet we are going to go forward and start a bombing campaign. We need to have a thorough, extensive debate here, involving the American people, as to whether or not this is in our vital and strategic interests. The administration has not brought the Congress along, and this is an inappropriate, ill-timed event and action for us to take and is not being supported by the American people.[17]

Senator Strom Thurmond (R-South Carolina) similarly criticized the use of force as failing to serve vital national interests:

I am unconvinced that trying to resuscitate these failed nation-states is in the U.S. vital interest....The question is simple: is it in the United States' best interests to have our troops in imminent danger, preoccupied with defending themselves against people whom they have come to help, who have shown little inclination for reform at a great cost to America? We are now involved in a steady run of civil wars without clear solutions which involve failed nation-states. We will soon drown in this kind of foolishness. Stemming civil wars should not be the main strategic challenge for the United States.[18]

Senator Kay Bailey Hutchinson (R-Texas) argued that as a last resort, force was not yet required:

Have we done everything we can do first? If we have—and I don't think we have—if the administration makes the case that we have, then, and only then, should we be considering other options.[19]

Senator John Kerry (D-Massachusetts) supported air strikes and opposed the use of ground troops based upon the premise that while only American military power could achieve peace in the Balkans, it had to be preserved for more important security interests such as the Persian Gulf and Southwest Asia:

Congress should not tie the President's hands or give Mr. Milosevic the slightest reason to believe the United States will not join with its allies....When that question [of ground troops] does arise, I will oppose any deployment of U.S. personnel on the ground in Kosovo. The stability of the entire planet depends on the readiness and availability of the U.S. Armed Forces. We should not fritter them away in peacekeeping missions in countries which do not rise to the level of vital American interests. We should keep them ready for the contingencies that are truly in our league: Iraq and the Persian Gulf, the Koreas, Russian nuclear forces. Europe contains wealthy countries with the militaries that could take on local European missions like Kosovo. It is their problem, and they should step up to it.[20]

Kerry's colleagues rebutted him using national interest arguments as well. Senator Robert Byrd (R-West Virginia) argued:

The United States cannot stand idly by and watch the catastrophe unfolding in the Balkans. It is in our national interest to support stability in this volatile region, to prevent the downward spiral into violence and chaos, and to stem the humanitarian disaster spreading out of Kosovo like a contagion. Having raised the stakes so high, a failure to act decisively could have untold consequences.[21]

Notably, there was no significant dissent from the left. Rather than protesting the use of force, some members of Congress who professed to favor "nonviolence" made an exception in the Kosovo crisis for humanitarian reasons, even claiming that the United States had a moral obligation to intervene.[22] It is noteworthy that members of Congress did not declare that human rights or humanitarian concerns were a national interest, but rather linked such abuses to the national interest of preventing regional instability. Congressional attitudes regarding the obligation to intervene solely for humanitarian and human rights reasons are addressed in the following chapter.

Credibility and Regional Stability

The primary justifications members of Congress gave for supporting air strikes were the threat of regional instability, the humanitarian crisis, and the credibility of the United States and NATO. The chairman of the Senate Armed Services Committee, John Warner (R-Virginia), claimed credit for getting the Senate to focus on Kosovo and credited senators Kay Bailey Hutchison (R-Texas), Byrd, and Carl Levin (D-Michigan) for bringing the debate to the floor.[23] Senator Levin argued that "The risks of not acting are greater than the risks of acting," and that "the conflict in Kosovo could spread to the neighboring countries of Macedonia, Albania, and Bosnia and could involve nations such as Greece, Turkey, Bulgaria, and Hungary."[24] In an October 1, 1998 interview, Senator John Warner and Senator Joseph Lieberman (D-Connecticut) also expressed the opinion that the wider war would involve NATO members Greece and Turkey and that the violence would be worse than seen in Bosnia, even if the humanitarian emergency was less severe. Warner stated, "Already you've got Albania in the state of revolution. It could spread into Montenegro and other areas in that area, and you'd have an all out civil war."[25]

Senator Joseph Biden (D-Delaware) argued that the instability could cause Greece and Turkey to go to war. This was due, he said, to the possibility that if Kosovar Albanian refugees ended up in Macedonia, they might contribute to the oppression of Muslims there, drawing Turkey to their defense, and if they entered Albania they might contribute to the abuse of the Greek minority there, drawing in Greece to protect them. He further noted that refugees in Western Europe would cause a financial burden on governments that could negatively affect U.S. trade with the EU, hitting Americans "in their wallets." Biden admitted that none of the scenarios would directly threaten the United States, but he argued rather that "the history of this century has shown that in a relatively short time the kinds of instability I have described could carry a higher cost than the current air strikes."[26]

Senator Frank Lautenberg (D-New Jersey) rested his support on U.S. and NATO credibility, citing President Bush's "Christmas warning" to

Milosevic, given as a message through the U.S. embassy in Belgrade in December 1992, declaring that the United States would use force to stop aggression in Kosovo. President Clinton reissued the warning in March 1993.[27] Lautenberg stated:

The fundamental United States interests which are at stake here: The first is U.S. credibility, going all the way back to the Christmas warning issued by President Bush and reaffirmed by President Clinton. . . . The second is the credibility, cohesion, and future of NATO. . . . Third, we need to prevent this conflict from spreading.[28]

American credibility was important to several members of Congress. Senator John McCain (R-Arizona) criticized the Clinton administration's faith in the efficacy of the U.N. rather than reliance on NATO military power. He believed that "U.S. and allied credibility had descended to new depths" when, after Secretary Albright's warning Serbia that it would "pay a price" for its aggression, the only consequence of further violence was a show of force by NATO fighter jets in June 1998.[29] He likened Clinton foreign policy "to what would happen if Thucydides' Melian Dialogue were reversed, and the weak were dictating to the strong."[30]

Several lawmakers had traveled to Kosovo in the previous 10 years, and some stated that personal experience had confirmed that Milosevic was a "thug" or a "war criminal."[31] The contrast between such a bad character and the might of the American republic was used to argue that Milosevic should not be allowed to defy the Christmas warning and subsequent threats by the United States and NATO. Members of Congress urged their colleagues not to allow the ongoing impeachment proceedings to distract them from foreign policy. Some even argued that because the presidency was handicapped by scandal, Congress had a responsibility to promote American leadership abroad. Senator Biden made it a matter of American survival, a vital national interest:

America's survival depends on presenting a strong, united front to the world. Now, in the middle of a domestic political crisis . . . we must not allow ourselves to be distracted from our task of protecting America's security, leadership and credibility abroad.[32]

*   *   *

The American justification for intervention in the Kosovo crisis was articulated, by both the executive and legislative branch officials, in terms of the national interest. Yet policy makers used the national interest as an umbrella term under which they put humanitarian relief, human rights, regional stability in southeastern Europe, and other goals that had never been officially defined as American interests. That is not to say that humanitarian and human rights goals were not genuinely believed to constitute a valid justification for the use of force by some policy makers. In fact, several made deeply personal and persuasive appeals to such causes, including the terms "genocide" and "holocaust." Even so, few relied solely on these arguments, and they framed them in terms of American interests when they did.

Clinton administration officials used national interest arguments because they believed they would not get Congressional support without them, and members of Congress likewise used national interest arguments to gain support from their constituencies. American political culture fed the desire to ensure that the use of force was believed to be important if not vital to American interests. Few American officials referred to the requirements of international law or to previous UN Security Council resolutions when speaking to internal audiences. Conversely, previous UN Security Council resolutions and the threat to international peace and security were used to justify action to international audiences.

BRITAIN

Rather than relying on specific UNSC resolutions, the British cited the principle of humanitarian emergency as their core justification for the use of force in Kosovo. British secretary of state for defense George Roberston argued:

The principles of international law—indeed, international law itself—did not start with the UN. International law preceded the UN, and these principles are there whatever the UN charter says. They are clear. There are those in the House who doubt that there is a legal base, and have questioned the legality of the action.... We are in no doubt that NATO is acting within international law. Our legal justification rests upon the accepted principle that force may be used in extreme circumstances to avert a humanitarian catastrophe. Those circumstances clearly exist in Kosovo....

The use of force in such circumstances can be justified as an exceptional measure in support of purposes laid down by the UN Security Council, but without the Council's express authorization, when that is the only means to avert an immediate and overwhelming humanitarian catastrophe.... The precedent, the principle and the emergency situation were the same [in the case of the Kurds in Iraq in 1991], and we took action to save the Kurds.[33]

Pointing to UN Security Council acceptance of the use of force in the cases of Bosnia and Somalia as a legal basis, "overwhelming humanitarian necessity" remained London's justification for action without an explicit UNSC mandate. The United Kingdom's UNSC representative used identical phrasing in both the March 24 and 26, 1999 Security

Council proceedings when he said that "The action being taken is legal. It is justified as an exceptional measure to prevent an overwhelming humanitarian necessity."[34]

Even when critics began to point out the increased humanitarian emergency after the beginning of the campaign, George Robertson rested legal justification "upon the accepted principle that force may be used in extreme circumstances to avert a humanitarian catastrophe."[35]

Humanitarianism and International Law: A Just War Argument

The British were comfortable making their case in humanitarian terms without an explicit UNSC mandate only after resolving how this argument could be resolved with international law. A UK Foreign and Commonwealth Office note sent to other allies in October 1998 pointed toward general international law, but also the UN Charter and existing UNSC resolutions. It outlined three criteria for making a case of overwhelming humanitarian necessity: convincing evidence, no practicable alternative, and force that is necessary and proportionate to the overall aim of meeting the humanitarian need.[36] This is essentially a just war argument. Tony Blair made the just war argument explicit in an April 1999 address in Chicago, this time linking political, economic, and strategic interests explicitly to values:

Awful crimes that we never thought we would see again have reappeared—ethnic cleansing, systematic rape, mass murder. I want to speak to you this evening about events in Kosovo. But I want to put these events in a wider context—economic, political and security—because I do not believe Kosovo can be seen in isolation.

 No one in the West who has seen what is happening in Kosovo can doubt that NATO's military action is justified. Bismarck famously said the Balkans were not worth the bones of one Pomeranian Grenadier. Anyone who has seen the tear-stained faces of the hundreds of thousands of refugees streaming across the border, heard their heart-rendering tales of cruelty or contemplated the unknown fates of those left behind, knows that Bismarck was wrong.[37]

Blair's justification of intervention went beyond humanitarianism into a defense of values. While he offered humanitarian concerns as providing grounds for an exception to the rules, he proposed that the values at stake fulfilled the requirements of the just war doctrine:

This is a just war, based not on any territorial ambitions but on values. We cannot let the evil of ethnic cleansing stand. We must not rest until it is reversed. We have learned twice before in this century that appeasement does not work. If we let an evil dictator range unchallenged, we will have to spill infinitely more blood and treasure to stop him later.[38]

Finally, Blair maintained that the allies had fulfilled the last resort requirement of the just war doctrine, stating that "We should always give peace every chance, as we have in the case of Kosovo." [39] Robertson echoed the fulfillment of the last resort requirement:

What alternatives are there? We have tried diplomacy to exhaustion over the past year. Every chance has been given....We could try appeasement. That was the policy before the second world war. There were those who believed in it. Why do not we give them Kosovo?[40]

Strategic Interests: NATO Credibility and Regional Stability

While Britain's UN Security Council representative referred extensively to the humanitarian emergency during the October 24, 1998 deliberations regarding UNSC Resolution 1203, he also stated that "The situation in Kosovo represents a threat to international peace and security."[41] Public statements by Prime Minister Tony Blair clearly pointed to British strategic interest in halting a spillover of the Balkan crisis into the rest of Europe. Blair said, "We cannot contemplate, on the doorstep of the EU, a disintegration into chaos and disorder."[42]

In the House of Commons on March 25, 1999, foreign secretary Robin Cook defended the action on several grounds, including the humanitarian necessity, the prospect of a wider war, the exhaustion of peaceful means, and NATO credibility.[43] Cook stated,

The first reason why we took action was that we were aware of the atrocities that had been carried out and we had the capacity to intervene, but that is not the only reason. Our confidence in our peace and security depends on the credibility of NATO. Last October, NATO guaranteed the cease-fire that President Milosevic signed. He has comprehensively shattered that cease-fire. What possible credibility would NATO have next time that our security was challenged if we did not honor that guarantee? The consequences of NATO inaction would be far worse than the result of NATO action.[44]

On February 3, 1999, General Sir Michael Rose had told the House of Commons that concern for NATO credibility was essentially an American issue:

The words "maintaining credibility of NATO" is a convenient expression for actually indulging in the use of military force. That is what it actually means, and has usually been driven by the Americans and very often by the air powers.[45]

Rose maintained that NATO governments that used the credibility argument did so with an American "hand on their back" to justify the use of force by "people out there who think you solve these problems by the use of force"[46] and pointed the finger at "inconsistent and short-term" U.S. foreign policy making held hostage by the American policy-making process and the media.[47]

Strategic Interests II: Balancing the Atlantic and European Agendas

If some British officials thought Tony Blair had an American hand on his back, some Europeans believed he had his eyes on the continent. The day Operation Allied Force began, German newspapers hailed Blair as "the first British head of government since Edward Heath to want to make the partnership with Europe a success."[48] They welcomed his efforts to subdue the substantial "anti-Euro forces" in Britain, especially among the Conservatives, and were particularly hopeful at the prospect of the rescinding of the British rebate—a reduction of the British contribution to the EU budget by 2 billion pounds per year—at the EU summit in Berlin, lamenting that "the German side is really tired of the role of the EU's main financier."[49]

A second pro-European Union stance credited to Blair in 1998 and 1999 was the dramatic change he enabled in defense and security arrangements. Under Blair, Britain reversed its decades-long objections to an "autonomous" EU defense capacity.[50] The prime minister confirmed the about face at the Franco-British summit meeting at St. Malo on December 3 and 4, 1998, but he had alluded to the change at an informal meeting of the EU heads of state and government in Pörtschach, Austria, on October 24 and 25, 1998. At a press conference following the Pörtschach meeting, Blair pointed to the way in which the Kosovo crisis strengthened the new resolve. He recognized the serious shortcomings in the European Union's ability to handle a Balkan crisis, for a second time, without American leadership and forces. He therefore balanced his pro-European Union actions with words that recognized the material need to keep America in Europe, and the political need to allay U.S. concerns about EU defense and security capabilities:

The only thing that was ever going to work in Kosovo was diplomacy backed up by the credible threat of force, and that is all that has brought Milosevic to the position he is in, and we need to keep him in that position now. But I think Kosovo simply underlines the need for Europe to take a very hard-headed review of this and to make sure that it can fulfil its obligations and responsibilities properly.... The European security and defence identity is very much within NATO. Now as I say, let us discuss the best way forward, though I repeat to you, nothing must happen which in any way impinges on the effectiveness of NATO, anything that suggests it should be complementary to that, because NATO for us is the absolute correct forum.[51]

Blair's anticipation of U.S. concerns was well founded. Madeleine Albright followed on the heels of the December 4, 1998 St. Malo agreement with a guarded American acceptance of the plan that also gave a nod of support for Tony Blair. Washington insisted on no decoupling of the transatlantic link, no wasteful or divisive duplication of alliance capabilities and decision-making structures, and no discrimination against non-EU NATO members. In the December 7, 1998 *Financial Times*, Albright wrote,

Kosovo carries another lesson: political will is more important than additional institutional structures. The problem in Kosovo before we acted together was not the lack of appropriate institutions; it was the lack of agreement to use the institutions we have. As Europeans look at the best way to organize their foreign and security policy cooperation, the key is to make sure that any institutional change is consistent with basic principles that have served the Atlantic partnership well for 50 years. This means avoiding what I would call the Three Ds: decoupling, duplication, and discrimination.[52]

*   *   *

Even though Britain's justification was the most overtly humanitarian and idealist, its approach was informed by realist interests in regional stability, NATO credibility, and balancing the European and Atlantic agendas abroad and at home. British justifications for the use of force in Kosovo were formulated during a critical period of trans-Atlantic relations in which Britain saw itself as the linchpin. Its strongly humanitarian case reflected more the sentiment among the German population than that among pragmatic British decision makers, but this may not be surprising considering Blair's pro-European agenda at the time. Likewise, his constant accommodation of American concerns about his initiatives in European Union defense activities reflected Blair's desire to sustain the special relationship with the United States. The unblinking insistence that the Kosovo conflict was a threat to international peace and security was identical to the American position. Thus Britain's appeals to humanitarian concerns and the European Union's security responsibilities served its European interests, and its consonance with the American position served its Atlantic agenda: taken together, a realist position. Yet few doubted the sincerity of Robin Cook's principled foreign policy, or Tony Blair's belief in the universality of human rights. The fact that the British claimed humanitarian exception to international law indicates that they were willing to eschew a legalist approach in favor of upholding their values. Since they chose not to argue their humanitarian justification in legal or political terms, it stands as an idealist position, one that puts moral solidarity among individual human beings above the strictures of law and the national interest.

GERMANY

The Kosovo intervention highlighted the marked change in German policy toward military operations in the decade following reunification in 1990, but a change in German attitudes about the use of force is less clear. The German debate about justification revealed two strong trends: pacifism and antimilitarism on one hand, and the responsibility to be a reliable international partner on the other. Humanitarian and human rights concerns, stemming from the same post-1995 guilt as antimilitarism, ironically tipped the scales in favor of intervention. Together, the arguments were enough to convince Germans to order their military to participate in offensive military operations for the first time in 50 years.[53] While the government's internal justifications relied heavily on human rights and humanitarian arguments, external justification was couched in the language of maintaining international peace and security.

German Foreign Policy

During the cold war, peacekeeping fell within the domain of the UN. NATO did not undertake non–Article 5 operations until the 1990s, so Germany did not debate the issue extensively. During the 1980s, even though legal experts differed on the airtight nature of the Basic Law (the constitution of the Federal Republic of Germany)'s restrictions, officials left the subject alone for political reasons. When the United States asked allies for assistance in escorting Kuwaiti oil tankers in 1987, the first signs of disagreement appeared among German foreign policy makers. Even so, when Iraq invaded and occupied Kuwait in August 1990, thereby initiating the 1990–91 Gulf War, Germany was preoccupied with the final stages of negotiating the Treaty on the Final Settlement with Respect to Germany (sometimes called the Two-plus-Four treaty, concluded in Moscow September 12, 1990). As long as this treaty and other agreements had not been ratified, the government remained cautious about addressing the subject. While the allies understood Germany's reluctance to send troops to Iraq, they were alarmed by the government's initial lack of open support for the operation—launched with a UNSC mandate by a broad coalition—while a vocal German minority dissented loudly.[54] Some later criticized Germany's "checkbook diplomacy." SPD leaders stated that Germany would not be obliged to defend Turkey under Article 5 if it was attacked by Iraq, on the grounds that Turkey would have provoked Iraq by allowing U.S. aircraft to operate from its soil.[55] It was the burgeoning of peacekeeping and humanitarian operations in

the early 1990s, particularly requests for German military participation in Somalia and the Balkans, that pressed decision makers for a
clear policy regarding operations in support of collective security.[56]
Politicians sought a ruling from the nation's Constitutional Court,
which affirmed in 1994 that the Bundeswehr could be employed in
operations in support of collective security that have been endorsed
by the Bundestag.[57]

The Reliable Partner

Throughout the Kosovo debate, German officials often referred to
Germany's "responsibility" in the crisis. This term had evolved significantly since the Bonn Republic. The "policy of responsibility"
(*Verantwortungspolitik*) or "policy of good example" (*Politik des guten
Beispiels*) meant antimilitarism and a "culture of restraint" as opposed
to "power politics" (*Machtpolitik*) during the initial period of unification.[58] By the late 1990s, officials of the German government were
applying the term *Verantwortungspolitik* to refer to shouldering international burdens as opposed to standing by and allowing the other
allies to perform military operations missions. The nature of the missions of the 1990s, with their humanitarian and human rights purposes, allowed German officials to bring about radical change while
using familiar language. Indeed, the nature of the new missions was
consistent with the concept of German responsibility in helping to
achieve world peace, contained in the preamble to the 1949 Basic Law,
the constitution of the Federal Republic of Germany:

Conscious of their responsibility before God and Men, Animated by the resolve to
serve world peace as an equal partner in a united Europe, the German people have
adopted, by virtue of their constituent power, this Basic Law.[59]

Human Rights Arguments

Postwar German attitudes, and those of the governing coalition in
particular, emphasized a deep commitment to human rights, and the
government used this issue to justify military action against the Serbs.
During the crisis, foreign minister Joschka Fischer emphasized the
humanitarian and human rights abuses against Kosovar Albanians,
whereas after the intervention he emphasized the need to maintain
regional stability as the core justification.

Throughout the debate, German officials were sensitive to the fra-
gility of public support for the use of force. The defense minister,
Rudolf Scharping, said that he had "great problems with the term war"

when referring to the operation.[60] Like Scharping, chancellor Gerhard Schroeder avoided using the word *war*, instead calling the campaign part of a peaceful solution to a humanitarian crisis. On March 24, 1999, the chancellor emphasized the preventive aspects of the intervention and claimed public support for breaking the half-century-long practice of keeping the Bundeswehr out of combat operations:

Dear citizens, this evening NATO began the air strikes against military targets in Yugoslavia. With this, the coalition wants to avert further terrible and systematic violations of human rights and prevent a humanitarian catastrophe in Kosovo. We are not leading a war, but we are leading a peaceful solution in Kosovo including military means. German soldiers are also participating in the NATO mission. And thus the federal government and the German Bundestag have decided this—in agreement with the will of the vast majority of the German people.[61]

Balancing Domestic Politics and International Standing

The governing coalition was keenly aware of the power of public protest in German politics. Public demonstrations in the early 1980s were massive and sometimes violent; security policy was often the focus. The American war in Vietnam had also sparked such public outcry, and during the Bundestag debate over Kosovo, at least one dissenter from Fischer's own party made the connection between the two conflicts explicit.[62] Critics advanced various arguments. Some members of the Bundestag complained that the Rambouillet talks did not exhaust diplomatic means. Greens countered by claiming credit that the talks were held at all.[63] A group from the Party of Democratic Socialism (PDS) went so far as to challenge German participation in the campaign through legal channels, but the Federal Constitutional Court dismissed the challenge as inadmissible, further noting that it did not address the legality of German participation.[64] The majority of Bundestag members did not dissent, however, and instead used parliamentary debate to emphasize political unity and resolve to respond to the humanitarian emergency.

Contrasting with the extreme sensitivity inside Germany about the use of force was the pressure German leaders felt from the allies for Germany to bear its share of international obligations. On August 4, 1998 Gerhard Schroeder, the SPD candidate for chancellor, met with President Clinton in Washington and assured him that Germany would remain a "reliable partner."[65] He used the same phrase as chancellor in his February 6, 1999 speech at a conference in Munich: "Germany remains a reliable partner in Europe and in the Atlantic Alliance. A partner which is fully aware of its national and global responsibility in the politics of peace and security."[66]

   This was a marked shift from previous policy. Whereas German politicians hesitated before sending Luftwaffe AlphaJets and Hawk and
Roland surface-to-air missile units to Turkey for that ally's defense in
the event of an Iraqi attack in conjunction with the UNSC-mandated
liberation of Kuwait in 1991, they sent 15 German Tornado aircraft into
the 1999 campaign without a UNSC resolution explicitly authorizing the use of force. By their incremental decisions during the 1990s,
German decision makers led the public to accept a change in foreign policy. In an interview, Defense Minister Scharping declared the
Kosovo operation, "very clearly...a turning point in German foreign
policy...in my view, this is a turning point in a certainly positive way."
Like Schroeder, he referred to German responsibility among nations,
stating: "for the first time we accept responsibility in such a fundamental matter, and Germany is part of Europe, of the western democracies,
and not opposed to them as it was until the end of World War II."[67]

National Interest and International Law

   Cold war West German foreign policy, shaped by postwar guilt about
Nazi aggression and militarism, comprised "multilateralism (never
again going it alone), European integration (with an emphasis on
regaining recognition, trust and economic wealth) and anti-militarism
('culture of restraint'; 'civilian power')."[68] That officials felt constrained
by public opinion is evident in their asking the Constitutional Court to
clarify the circumstances under which Germany could legitimately use
force, in addition to national and collective self-defense.
   External justification, expressed in the UN Security Council, was based
primarily on the threat to international peace and security. Officials
noted the 1.3 million refugees from the former Yugoslavia living in
Germany, including 300,000 ethnic Albanians, most of them from
Kosovo.[69] The reference to a threat to international peace and security
was an appeal to Chapter VII of the UN Charter. At the UNSC, the
German representative emphasized this legal grounding:

The explosive situation in the Kosovo region constitutes a clear threat to international peace and security. The genesis of the war in Bosnia and Herzegovina,
which in the beginning was considered by some to be an internal matter, is still
very much alive in our memories. The outside world cannot simply stand by and
watch a new, potentially even more devastating conflict develop in the region.[70]

Unlike the French, the Americans, and the British, the Germans did
not appeal to previous UN Security Council resolutions as justification
for the use of force in Kosovo. The stated reason was that the Chinese
and the Russians had accompanied their votes with legally valid

statements against the use of force. The German commitment to upholding international law is enshrined in the Basic Law, which refers to
international law as "part" of the Federal law. Article 25 subordinates
federal law to international law, but it also obliges Germans to fulfill
the duties prescribed by international law:

> The general rules of public international law form part of the Federal law. They
> take precedence over the laws and directly create rights and duties for the inhabi-
> tants of the Federal territory.[71]

The German branch of the International Association of Lawyers
Against Nuclear Arms (Ialana) declared the Kosovo operation a violation of international law under the UN Charter and the Treaty on the
Final Settlement with respect to Germany, pointing to this passage in
the Basic Law, and claiming that a violation of international law therefore violates national law.[72] Even among the largely unified Greens,
some members of the party, including Angelika Beer and Ludger
Volmer, admitted that the basis for intervention in international law
was less than solid.[73]

*   *   *

The nature of the interventions of the early 1990s—operations with
humanitarian and human rights elements—allowed diverging interests in Germany to merge and paved the way to a change in German
foreign policy. German decision makers combined appeals to human
rights and humanitarianism that resonated with the German public,
with legal statements regarding international peace and security in
the UN Security Council that satisfied allies and fulfilled the letter of
federal law. While political and security considerations such as the
concern about additional refugees were also used to justify action,
these arguments were secondary. Using different arguments to satisfy
diverse audiences, German officials displayed a realist approach to a
difficult foreign policy decision. But it is clear from German hesitance
to rely on previous UN Security Council resolutions that there was a
genuine desire to adhere to the letter of international law.

The strenuous appeals to human rights and humanitarianism rather
than to the domestic problem of refugees reveal German idealism,
since they elevated those universal moral principles to the level of
political and even strategic interests. In the words of Defense Minister
Scharping, "human rights are valid all over the world."[74] Ludger Volmer,
the Greens' parliamentary state secretary, said that he had evidence
that Milosevic had counted on the Greens' pacifism to split NATO and
stop an intervention. That the Greens compromised their position he
attributed to the difference between holding to pacifism in theory as an

opposition party and having to put it into practice "in the complicated web of international relations" in government.[75]

FRANCE

In October 1998, President Chirac emphasized both the vital nature of a Security Council resolution authorizing force and the exceptional nature of the humanitarian situation that could occur when he said that:

Any military action must be requested and decided by the Security Council. In this particular case, we have a resolution, which does open the way to the possibility of military action. I would add, and repeat, that the humanitarian situation constitutes a ground that can justify an exception to a rule, however strong and firm it is.[76]

Despite Chirac's statement and French experience with humanitarian emergencies such as Rwanda in 1994, French statements in the UN Security Council lacked appeal to the human tragedy of Kosovo. Instead, the French rested their legal case on Chapter VII provisions of existing resolutions. In his brief statement during the deliberations about UNSCR 1203 on March 24, 1998, the French representative mentioned the FRY's threat to international peace and security four times.[77]

This was a shift from France's previous assessment of the Kosovo situation. Whereas the United States, Britain, and Germany unhesitatingly argued that a threat to international peace and security existed during the March 31, 1998 Security Council proceedings regarding UNSCR 1160, France was more reserved in its approach, calling the resolution "balanced," criticizing both Serbs and ethnic Albanian Kosovars, and avoiding the term that would give Chapter VII sanction.[78]

It was in the March 31, 1998 deliberations that terrorism was most condemned. The FRY defended its massacre of the Jeshari family as antiterror police work, and only a week before U.S. diplomat Robert Gelbard had called the KLA "without question a terrorist group."[79] Both China and Russia adamantly opposed reference to international peace and security, a stance they maintained throughout the crisis. France eventually gave way on this point and adopted language closer to that of the other allies, but never with the same commitment to the humanitarian justifications for the use of force.

French Foreign Policy

French foreign policy since Charles de Gaulle had among its aims independence, an autonomous Europe, and global ambitions.[80] France's

policy in the Kosovo conflict reflected these goals and revealed its struggle to maintain them in the new security environment dominated by
American power. French justification for the use of force followed just
war doctrine, particularly Aquinas's three primary requirements for
proper authority (defined by France as the UNSC), right intention (to
promote peace and human rights) and injury by the enemy (Milosevic's
barbarity and broken agreements). The French argument highlights
the uneasy fit between moral and legal justifications with which all
the allies struggled and also reveals an admixture of the three different worldviews in their arguments. While the primary case the French
made was based upon just war principles, a legalist approach, French
realism was obvious in its officials' arguments of national power (the
need to avoid *impuissance,* or lack of power), and the balance of power
(the need to contain U.S. *hyperpuissance,* or hyperpower). French idealism showed itself in assertions that French values had to be defended
from "barbarity." French values, according to president Jacque Chirac
and prime minister Lionel Jospin, were also European and universal.
Together, these three ways of thinking converged to constitute French
justification for the use of force in Kosovo.

President Chirac's policy in the Kosovo conflict went contrary to the
Balkan policy his predecessor, Francois Mitterrand, had articulated.
That policy included the need for explicit UNSC consent for action and
the desire not to allow NATO to overshadow EU decision making on
the continent.[81] Chirac did not even mention UNSC authority when he
addressed his constituencies on the day the campaign began.[82] While
France agreed to act without an explicit UNSC mandate, French officials
strove to claim UN authority, resting their case in the Security Council
on previous UNSC resolutions and Chapter VII of the UN Charter.
French leaders twice referred to the UN secretary general's reports on
Belgrade's failure to comply with UNSC resolutions as lending further credibility to the intervention argument. Speaking to the National
Assembly, prime minister Lionel Jospin quoted Kofi Annan as saying
that "the recourse to force can be legitimate."[83]

The French aim to promote more autonomous European security
arrangements included strong Franco–German relations. France was
determined to integrate Germany into as many European institutions
as possible during the cold war in order to ensure that Germany would
never again become a great power that would threaten peace on the continent. This was the idea behind the forging of the European Coal and
Steel Community of 1951, and the European Atomic (Euratom) and
Economic Communities of 1957.[84] At the center of Franco–German
relations were the 1963 Elysee Treaty between Konrad Adenauer and
Charles de Gaulle,[85] the 1986 French declaration in which France's

president promised to consult with the German chancellor before using nuclear weapons on German soil if time permitted,[86] and the plan for ESDI outside NATO.

France's relations with the United States have been influenced by the desire for greater European autonomy. Successive presidents have desired to maintain the transatlantic link while strengthening France's role on the continent. In 1983, President Mitterrand made a landmark speech in the Bundestag arguing against West German resistance to the prospective deployment of U.S. Pershing II ballistic missiles and cruise missiles on the continent to counter Soviet SS-20s: the Alliance's "dual track" decision. In the mid-1990s, when the Balkan wars were raging, the predominant French concern was more about U.S. disengagement than dominance, but this was clearly changing by 1999.

French Politics

French domestic politics in 1997–2002 were marked by a period of cohabitation in the government, a reality that forced politicians to share power with political opponents. This was the third period of cohabitation in French politics since the adoption of the constitution of the Fifth Republic in 1958, and the first time a Gaullist president served with a Socialist prime minister. Cohabitation was first experienced by the Socialist Mitterrand, who accepted the Gaullist Chirac as his prime minister. Traditionally, the president took the lead in foreign policy, leaving domestic policy and administration of government to the prime minister. While prime ministers appointed government posts, the defense and foreign ministers needed the president's approval. Even so, the powerful office of the presidency designed by de Gaulle in 1958 had been decidedly weakened by 1998. Both President Chirac and Prime Minister Jospin attended international summits, for example, and this uniquely French practice was sometimes awkward.

The kind of dissent evident in Washington and Bonn was not usually prominent in Paris.[87] Lionel Jospin had lost the presidential election to Chirac in 1995, but Chirac felt obliged to select him as prime minister in 1997 when "la gauche plurielle," or plural left—a coalition of Socialists, Communists, and environmental parties—won a majority of seats in the National Assembly in the legislative elections. While Jospin and the president would diverge dramatically on foreign policy in later years—such as policy regarding the Arab–Israeli conflict— such a cleavage was not evident in 1998. Even though foreign minister Hubert Vedrine insisted upon the continuing differences between the right and left in French politics, many found them hard to discern in 1998.[88] The nature of French foreign policy decision making fostered this perception. France was the most centralized government in Europe, with a weak legislature, and foreign policy making was consolidated among a few officials at the top. In fact, the debate over intervention in the National Assembly did not take place until after the campaign began; and when he finally appeared there to answer questions for the government, Prime Minister Jospin explained that his participation in the Berlin summit was more pressing than the National Assembly debate.[89]

Weakening Chirac's hand in 1998 was the fact that he had dissolved the National Assembly in 1997 and called for legislative elections. The move was a miscalculation that forced him to work with a majority of NATO-skeptical Socialists after the vote and left him without the option of dissolving the National Assembly again until mid-1998. This may have been a factor in France's hesitance to support the American and British stance in early 1998. In the March 1998 meeting of the UN Security Council, France criticized both KLA terrorism and Serb aggression equally. By October 1998, France condemned Milosevic outright, and its final justification for the use of force was grounded in Milosevic's recalcitrance and his human rights violations against Kosovar Albanians.[90]

Just War Arguments for Intervention

French officials chose justifications that were largely based on just war principles. In his brief address on March 24, 1999, Chirac justified France's participation in Operation Allied Force in terms of preserving peace and defending human rights. His statement highlighted the three original just war principles: last resort, just cause, and right intention.

French public statements in March 1999 were meant to establish that the use of force in the Kosovo conflict was a last resort. Chirac claimed credit for initiating, hosting, and cochairing the Rambouillet talks, thus fulfilling the requirement to exhaust peaceful means. He blamed Milosevic's "unjustifiable and incomprehensible obstinacy" in rejecting the proposed terms of political settlement "without reason." At the same time, he made clear that the peaceful option remained open and put the responsibility on Milosevic to choose it, saying that the FRY president could "at any moment return to the negotiating table to sign the peace accord." Barring this, Chirac concluded that "there were no longer any other options than to intervene militarily" in the Kosovo conflict.[91]

Lionel Jospin gave a lengthy and dramatic description of the 10 previous years of Serb obstreperousness in his March 26, 1999 speech in the National Assembly, and again in his March 30, 1999 appearance there. Like Chirac, he assigned Milosevic full "responsibility" for the political deadlock, concluding that the lengths to which the allies went to resolve the crisis peacefully were "in vain" since Milosevic "obstinately refused" to cooperate. He declared that "the military intervention was absolutely necessary. Because the irrationality of the Yugoslav regime left no other choice; because we could not reconcile ourselves to impotence."[92] Six days into the campaign, when public criticism of the military solution began to rise, Jospin retorted,

Yes, we prefer to use dialogue, we prefer peace, a political solution, how can we engage in dialogue, how can we effectively practice the diplomacy which has been at the heart of French policy for several months, particularly with the Rambouillet process, if the Serb leaders and Mr. Milosevic reject it?[93]

While there was little outright dissent before the military action, it is clear that disputes arose in the National Assembly only a few days into the operation. In his March 31, 1999 appearance there, Jospin acknowledged that there was agreement between the Assembly and the government on only two points: Milosevic's guilt and the proper intention of the military action, that is, that the goal was a political settlement.[94]

Responding to objections that the campaign lacked proper authority, Jospin admitted that the government "would have preferred a mandate from the UN," and he was silent on the issue of whether diplomatic channels were exhausted before NATO's use of force. Extolling France's right intention, Chirac insisted that "everything has been done to achieve a rational solution, one of peace. One complying with human rights." He insisted that "what was at stake today is peace on our soil, peace in Europe—which we are part of too—and human rights."

French officials' insistence that the intervention into a sovereign state was not violating territorial integrity but instead supporting a political agreement that respected both the independence of the FRY and the autonomy of Kosovo within Serbia was to lend more credibility to the argument that the allies had right intention. On March 30, 1999, Lionel Jospin told the National Assembly that "the sole objective of the air operations over the Federal Republic of Yugoslavia...is to destroy the Serb repressive military machine."[95]

Discrimination between civilian and military personnel during war is also a requirement of just war, and Chirac emphasized that the bombing was only directed at "clearly targeted Serb objectives in order to contain a tragedy."[96] In a March 29, 1999 interview, Hubert Vedrine made a limited war case, contrasting the Kosovo operation with World War II.

NATO's objective was simply to "destroy the ability of the army to carry out the repression" against Kosovar Albanians. He first insisted, as the Germans did, that the word *war* did not apply to the Kosovo case but then reversed his position: "It's a war against a repressive machine." Contrasting it with total war, he added, "It's not a matter of crushing Serbia." He offered as evidence of the campaign's limited war nature the fact that "the possibility of a ground war has been clearly ruled out by all the Western leaders."[97]

Whereas Chirac remained silent on the issue of authority during his March 24, 1999 address, referring only to the unanimity of the allies, Jospin was careful to describe to the National Assembly the legal basis of the government's position. He relied on the previous UNSC resolutions, Chapter VII of the Charter, Milosevic's flouting of international law, and, finally, the UN Secretary General's tacit approval of the use of force when he stated that "the recourse to force can be legitimate."[98] Vedrine pointed to both legal and political legitimacy. In an interview on March 25, 1999, he rested the legal case on the strong wording and reliance on Chapter VII of UNSC demands, on UNSCR 1199 and 1203, and on the fact that "the United Nations Secretary General has deemed it legitimate."[99] Apart from the legal case, Vedrine stated that legitimacy was granted by all the political leaders who tried to resolve the case peacefully, including the Contact Group and Serbia's neighbors, "which had been asking for an intervention for an extremely long time."[100]

The case France made in Security Council deliberations was based predominantly on the UN Charter, especially previous UNSC resolutions, but also on agreements Milosevic had made and broken with the OSCE and NATO. It is in these deliberations that the attempt to cast just war doctrine into the mold of international law is most evident. The October 24, 1998 argument was brief and based entirely on the threat to international peace and security. In just war terms, this was a reference to Serbia's "aggression" and the harmful effects it would have on neighboring states. The requirement that the "enemy" has done "harm" was laid out in the March 23, 1999 proceedings in which the French blamed Milosevic for not respecting international obligations and agreements, and for causing an "impending humanitarian catastrophe" by the actions of his security forces against the civilian population. This also reinforced the right intention of France, since it made clear that the purpose of its using force was to avert new massacres, restore peace, and preserve human rights. Here, the language was almost identical to Chirac's in addressing the French people on March 24, 1999: "what is at stake today is peace, peace in Europe—but human rights are also at stake."[101]

On March 26, 1999, France's rebuttal to Russia's claim that the action represented a new "lawlessness" was short and posed in legal terms. France again relied on existing UNSC resolutions, the threat to international peace and security, and Milosevic's violations of international agreements.[102]

All of these arguments sprang from an internationalist or legalist way of thinking. They were attempts to fit the moral and political case into international law and relied on the framework of the just war doctrine to do so. Yet France could not contain all of its argument in legal terms. The term "regional stability" was often used, but this could mean either destabilization because of a humanitarian emergency such as refugee flows, or a spread of fighting among ethnic groups that could lead to an "attack" on a NATO ally. The latter offered a sounder case for self-defense, but the former was the more likely scenario. There were two more compelling arguments that did not fit into a legal framework: defending French values and maintaining the balance of power.

Civilization vs. Barbarity

French officials argued that they wanted the Balkans, "in which democracy is growing stronger," to become "a full part of modern Europe."[103] The Serbs could not do this, however, unless they shared civilized European values, the values upheld by France. It is telling that when he wanted to justify military action to the French people, Chirac did not rely heavily on legal arguments, but rather on appeals to promote their values, among them peace and human rights. Chirac told the French people:

Because it is a matter of peace on our continent, because it is a matter of human rights on our continent, I know that the French people will understand that we had to act.[104]

Chirac described the action as at once a show of French independence and its solidarity.

He sensed that the French people believed that republican values were universal:

Finally, you will be able to invoke the duty of solidarity. At the moment when French pilots are carrying out an action which France has decided on in full sovereignty, with every one of its allies, to further the cause of its ideals of peace, I would like the whole nation to demonstrate its solidarity. These are universal values of our republican tradition that we are defending.[105]

Chirac emphasized that the NATO allies were not imposing these values on others, but rather defending them. Referring to the Rambouillet agreement, drafted by the Contact Group and given to both the Kosovar Albanians and the Serbs to sign under threat of force, Chirac insisted that

This agreement, as you know, isn't one imposed by the West, but one which has the support of the whole international community and particularly that of all the Europeans, Russia and the United States.[106]

Thus he described "republican" values, and in particular human rights, as French, European, and universal. Lionel Jospin echoed Chirac's words and the interchangeability of French and European values when he addressed the National Assembly on March 26, 1999. He did so after a detailed description of the "barbarity" of the Serbs:

Ladies and Gentlemen, France's involvement in this operation is consistent with our values. It is prompted by what makes the very spirit of the Europe we are building: the desire to place respect for individuals at the heart of what our States do, to put an end to the settlement of differences by violence and hatred.[107]

Jospin pointed to France's role in rebuilding Western Europe after World War II in its own image, and the peril in which the barbarity of conflicts in the former Yugoslavia put that project:

For decades Europe, at any rate our Europe, has been being rebuilt on new foundations of peace, respect for human rights. To accept the flouting of these values on the European Union's doorstep would have meant betraying ourselves. What is at stake in today's conflict is a certain conception of Europe. Do we accept the return of barbarism on our continent or do we rise up against it? For us, the choice is clear.[108]

On March 31, 1999, Jospin told the National Assembly that France was faced with the issue of "civilization or barbarity."[109]

Humanitarian Considerations

The French did not give humanitarian concerns the same treatment as human rights. They were instead used either as part of the legal argument regarding regional stability, or as part of the argument to prove Milosevic's barbarity, or simply as a problem that "we have to do something about."[110] Neither Chirac nor Jospin used the suffering of the Albanian Kosovars as a primary reason to launch air strikes, nor did they ask the French people to understand that force must be used in the name of humanitarianism. They may have implied this by referring to barbarity as opposing French values of human rights and respect for the individual, but the French, like the Americans, did not claim humanitarian exception as the British did. Jospin suggested that humanitarian values had to be weighed in the balance with other values of a civilized nation, including justice, order, and democracy:

> I should like to tell you that we appreciate the scale of this humanitarian catastrophe, but have to make it plain to European opinion and to the French listening to us, that this humanitarian catastrophe is reversible on only one condition: that the current conflict does not end on Mr. Milosevic's terms, but on the conditions set by the civilized nations in Europe of the end of the twentieth century...so that he emerges from this conflict the loser and that we can then bring about the conditions for a prosperous, democratic Europe and not a Europe tempted by a return to barbarity.[111]

Hubert Vedrine made the distinction when criticizing earlier French proponents of intervention in Bosnia: "In such cases the dividing line is not between compassion and indifference, but between responsibility and irresponsibility."[112]

The Balance of Power

The final part of France's justification for the use of force in Kosovo was strategic. French officials appealed to the necessity of avoiding France's "impotence," a matter of national survival and sovereignty, and to the need to maintain the balance of power by containing U.S. power in Europe. From December 1998 to February 1999, Chirac, Jospin, and Vedrine made statements expressing concern about "a new American unilateralism."[113] In January 1999, Prime Minister Jospin announced,

> We're confronted with a new problem on the international scene. The United States often behaves in a unilateral manner and has difficulty in assuming the role it aspires to as organizer in the international community.[114]

In February 1999, Foreign Minister Vedrine described the United States as a "hyperpower" that had to be counterbalanced.[115] In an interview with *Liberation*, a French newspaper, Hubert Vedrine suggested five steps to counter American power:

> 1) Have solid nerves; 2) Perseverance; 3) Methodically widen the bases of agreement among Europeans; 4) Cooperate at each stage with the United States, combining friendship and the will to be respected, while defending in all circumstances

organized multilateralism and the prerogatives of the Security Council; 5) Prepare politically, institutionally and mentally the moment when Europe will have the courage to go further.[116]

Chirac offered a plan to counter U.S. "unilateralism"—a proposal to the French diplomatic corps that the UN General Assembly consider reshaping the international order based upon "collective sovereignty." He listed seven principles and aimed the first at the unnamed Americans, advocating "collective responsibility" in international action and "excluding unilateral temptations and leading to shared management of the global risks and threats that weigh on our peoples."[117]

* * *

To their domestic audience, French officials justified the use of force in Kosovo in terms of France's responsibility for building a civilized Europe based upon French values of democracy and human rights: an idealist approach. To their external audience, French decision makers' justifications were indicative of an legalist approach based upon just war principles, international law (previous UN Security Council resolutions), Milosevic's breach of international agreements, and the threat to international peace and security caused by ongoing violence and repression in Kosovo. They did not claim that the relief of human suffering in itself was a justification for intervention, nor that it placed a duty on France to intervene independent of other circumstances. The French reliance on the UN was part of a multilateral approach that fulfilled France's larger aims of maintaining its influence in Europe and the world while containing the influence of the United States, a realist position.

CONCLUSION

Each nation's particular combination of political, moral, and legal arguments depended upon both long-standing and immediate political realities. Governments found that legal arguments alone were not sufficient, nor were purely moral arguments about ending human suffering. Likewise, no nation chose to justify its action solely in terms of strategy or the national interest without appealing also to a moral cause and a legal basis for the use of force.

Russia and China asserted that Western claims of a humanitarian exception were no more than a patina over prerogatives of power. This analysis does not support that claim. Rather, this analysis reveals an admixture of thinking among and within states that have been a part of Western thinking about international politics for centuries.

The limits of international law precluded states from making a purely legal case for stopping the ethnic cleansing in Kosovo. That said, no state was willing to dismiss the law, and all chose to refer to the UN Charter and previous UNSC resolutions in their justification for intervention. No ally was entirely comfortable in justifying the use of force entirely on moral grounds either. Both France and the United States regarded national interest arguments for the use of force as acceptable and desirable. Neither Britain nor Germany made strong national interest arguments, but rather, in keeping with their legalist thinking, found the use of moral arguments benign and even central. Their participation, however, required strong evidence of international cooperation in the form of customary law for Britain, and in upholding the letter of international law for Germany.

Thus, while all three of the traditions of thinking were evident in each of the NATO nations in 1998–99, there were differences in emphasis among the allies. While France and the United States preferred policy based upon the primacy of the state in international politics, Britain and Germany were more influenced by the efficacy of multilateralism. Even so, both London and Berlin needed to interpret the humanitarian situation as severe in order to proceed with the intervention. The lesson of the debate of justification for the Kosovo war was that British policy making in the future would be based upon a strong moral purpose, with a preference for international cooperation, but not hindered by the lack of it. Germans could be expected to continue their preference for international approbation for intervention. Finally, one could expect American and French policy regarding intervention to be guided by strong national purpose, and to refer to international cooperation and custom to the extent that they further national aims. These lessons were indeed borne out in their attitudes about justification for the Iraq war three years later.

CHAPTER 6

My Brother's Keeper: Are Nations Obligated to Intervene?

> The idea of common interest can never have much vitality if it is separated
> from the idea of common obligation.
> —*Martin Wight,* Power Politics, 1946

As NATO aircraft struck targets in Serbia in April 1999, prime minister Tony Blair declared before an American audience in Chicago that "In the field of politics...ideas are becoming globalized. As problems become global...so the search for solutions becomes global too. What amazes me, talking to other countries' leaders, is not the differences but the points in common."[1] As they faced the common problem of whether to intervene in the case of massive human rights violations or humanitarian emergencies, did the four leading NATO nations of Britain, France, Germany, and the United States share the same idea toward an obligation, responsibility, or duty to assist the Kosovar Albanians with military force? The notion of obligation in this case is used to mean that nations believed they were bound to intervene either by a treaty or established custom that included a responsibility or duty to protect civilian populations other than a nation's own citizens. This is in contrast to a perceived moral duty that persuaded governments to intervene when self-interests alone would not have led them to do so.

During the 1990s, NATO nations were compelled to air their attitudes about international obligation in a public way due to the numerous humanitarian emergencies that confronted them in Somalia, Sierra

Leone, Haiti, Rwanda, the Balkans, East Timor, and elsewhere. Because of the complexity of each nation's policy-making situation, it is not enough to say that because nations chose to intervene in such emergencies, there is evidence of a shared acceptance of responsibility to protect the suffering populations. This chapter examines whether the Kosovo case provides evidence of a common recognition of obligation and, if so, the nature of that obligation.

Among the key issues two stand out: the tension between the concepts of sovereignty and human rights and the issue of humanitarianism and war. Each NATO nation made policy from its unique background and existing political realities.

The debate about intervention in the United States was shaped largely by the question of whether humanitarian operations were a suitable role for the world's only superpower, whose military had to maintain readiness to fight two conventional wars nearly simultaneously. The American human rights tradition in foreign policy was influenced by a cold war utilitarianism used in the rivalry with the Soviet Union. A second influence came from the growing alliance between human rights and humanitarian groups who held sway with members of Congress beginning in the 1970s. The effect of this latter influence increased sharply after the end of the cold war.

Britain's military had extensive experience in operations analogous in some ways to humanitarian interventions during the small wars of its colonial period and did not shy away from the unconventional military role of humanitarian operations. Britain's approach to human rights in foreign policy, like that of the United States, had a pragmatic quality that was in part a legacy of its colonial period. However, Britain was led during the Kosovo crisis by a prime minister who declared that he was seeking both a more principled foreign policy and a more continental one.

France's military, like Britain's, had experience in peacekeeping and humanitarian operations due to a special role in its former colonies, notably in Francophone Africa. In particular, France's interventions in Rwanda in 1994 and the Central African Republic in 1996 shaped its policy debates regarding the obligation to help the Kosovar Albanians. As the preceding chapter demonstrates, human rights were considered essential to French values, those values were thought to be universal, and France believed it bore a special responsibility for extending and safeguarding a culture of civilization against the culture of barbarity, especially on the European continent.

For Germany, the interventions of the 1990s brought a sea change in military and foreign policy that had been marked by antimilitarism after World War II. Britain and the United States shared strong martial traditions, and the pacifist movement in France had been discredited after 1945, but German reticence to employ troops in combat was in direct conflict with the strong popular support for upholding human rights standards. Therefore, the 1994 Constitutional Court decision clarifying the conditions under which the Bundeswehr could be employed for purposes other than national and collective defense was ironically made possible because of a strong humanitarian and human rights consciousness among the population, closely linked with antimilitarism.

The various ways NATO nations perceived an obligation to intervene on behalf of human rights and humanitarian crises was influenced by several key factors. These included each nation's attitude about the role of norms in foreign policy, especially the tradition of defending civilization against barbarity that was a part of Western traditions of foreign policy; each country's military tradition, including the use of force for humanitarian purposes; each nation's human rights tradition, in particular its attitudes about the idea of a responsibility to protect individuals against human rights abuses and to take action in humanitarian emergencies; and the influence of the media regarding these factors. Each NATO ally had a different history and outlook on these issues, which resulted in an emphasis on different traditions of thinking. Likewise, the emphasis on a particular tradition of thinking informed the approach each nation took to the key issues during the intervention debate.

THE UNITED STATES

The day after the Rambouillet talks failed, President Clinton prepared the American people for intervention. While recounting horrific humanitarian scenes of the last decade, he did not claim that they were obligated to stop the current disaster, but he did insist that it was in American interests, even vital interests, to intervene:

As we prepare to act we need to remember the lessons we have learned in the Balkans. We should remember the horror of the war in Bosnia, the sounds of sniper fire aimed at children, the faces of young men behind barbed wire, the despairing voices of those who thought nothing could be done. . . .

This is a humanitarian crisis, but it is much more. This is a conflict with no natural boundaries. It threatens our national interests. If it continues, it will push refugees across borders, and draw in neighboring countries. It will undermine the credibility of NATO, on which stability in Europe and our own credibility depend. It will likely reignite the historical animosities, including those that can embrace Albania, Macedonia, Greece, even Turkey. These divisions still have the potential to make the next century a truly violent one for that part of the world that straddles Europe, Asia and the Middle East. . . .

But we must weigh those risks against the risks of inaction. If we don't act, the war will spread. If it spreads, we will not be able to contain it without far greater risk and cost. I believe the real challenge of our foreign policy today is to deal with problems before they do permanent harm to our vital interests. That is what we must do in Kosovo.[2]

The president did express a sense of responsibility as he ended his remarks, but it was not to the suffering Kosovar population, but rather to leave his successors a Europe "stable, humane and secure."[3]

Clinton also addressed the nation once the aerial campaign was underway on March 24, 1999. This time he was more insistent on American moral responsibility to act, but again he combined it with national interests: "Ending this tragedy is a moral imperative. It is also important to America's national interests."[4] To understand the meaning of the U.S. president's remarks regarding "humanitarian" intervention, it is essential to understand them in the broader context of American war fighting.

The American Way of War

In his 1973 book, *The American Way of War: A History of United States Military Strategy and Policy,* Russell Frank Weigley catalogued the war of attrition that American military commanders had pursued from the Civil War through Vietnam.[5] Max Boot has argued that the United States also has a long history of "small wars" similar to the interventions it faced in the 1990s, but that in the 1990s it did not embrace these missions nor maintain proficiency at them.[6] The predominant strategy of overwhelming force, on the other hand, maintained support as late as the 1984 Weinberger doctrine and 1992 Powell doctrine.[7] The crises of the 1990s challenged the predominant thinking regarding the American way of war and caused a mismatch between military strategy and political objectives in facing the "new wars" of the 1990s. According to Mary Kaldor, the new wars represented

A new type of violence...blurring the distinctions between war (usually defined as violence between states or organized political groups for political motives), organized crime (violence undertaken by privately organized groups for private purposes, usually financial gain) and large-scale violations of human rights (violence undertaken by states or politically organized groups against individuals.)[8]

Richard Haass points to the way these new wars brought change in American uses of force.[9] American thinking regarding the justification for the use of force, Haass argues, is traditionally based upon Thomist and Augustinian notions of the just war, built on Grotian notions of the right of self-defense, developed in line with classical strategists.[10] He notes that after the cold war, the sole superpower was no longer restricted to the aims of self-defense nor inhibited by superpower rivalry. Yet, even during the cold war, the United States used force to effect regime change, to aid populations within sovereign states, and for purposes other than self-defense.[11] Post-Vietnam thinking emphasized the Weinberger and Powell doctrines. The doctrines required that national interests be at stake before committing forces, that political and popular support be present, that political objectives were tied to military means, and that force would be used only as a last resort. [12] Former chairman of the Joint Chiefs, General Colin Powell described the beginning of the doctrines as a response by secretary of defense Caspar Weinberger to the bombing of the Marine Corps barracks in Beirut, Lebanon, on October 23, 1983, and in opposition to secretary of state George Shultz's readiness to "commit America's military might...in a no-man's land like Lebanon."[13]

The Somalia Effect

Ten years after the October 1983 Beirut bombing, the tension between the traditional doctrine of attrition and the realities of the new wars was brought starkly to light in the Somalia intervention. The lessons that American decision makers drew from the episode were the backdrop against which subsequent decisions about intervention were made. On October 3, 1993, 18 U.S. Army Rangers were killed, and Americans watched television images of a fallen soldier treated with the utmost disrespect by an angry crowd in Mogadishu. The United States pulled its troops out shortly afterward. One lesson president Bill Clinton drew from the political costs associated with the debacle was the need for the United States to maintain operational control of future operations:

My experiences in Somalia would make me more cautious about having any Americans in a peacekeeping role where there was any ambiguity at all about what the range of decisions were which could be made by a command other than an American command with direct accountability to the United States here.[14]

The United States had already applied this lesson to the Haiti operation in 1994. In this case, a US-led multinational force (MNF) was used and an American commander chosen for the follow-on UN mission, rather than putting U.S. troops under foreign control. The UN, for its part, learned a different lesson with the same result: the communications failures between the U.S. military and the UN during the second

UN-led mission in Somalia (UNOSOM II) made the UN leery of putting a contingent under an entirely U.S.-planned operation in Haiti.[15] Madeleine Albright expressed American domestic skepticism about UN competence in leading peace operations early in her tenure as the U.S. ambassador to the UN: "If I had to choose a single word to evoke the problems of UN peace-keeping, it would be 'improvisation.' ... A kind of programmed amateurism shows up across the board."[16]

The Clinton Administration: Pragmatic Wilsonianism

American convictions about human rights are reflected in the Declaration of Independence and the Bill of Rights, conceived to prevent the state from infringing on individual rights. According to Mary Ann Glendon, the American rights tradition, like the British, is individualistic in nature, placing its emphasis on claiming rights. The European or "dignitarian" tradition holds the rights of the community above those of the individual.[17] Consecutive American administrations in the second half of the twentieth century took a pragmatic approach to human rights, placing more importance on traditional notions of the national interest and responding to concerns that the United States should not forfeit its national sovereignty by allowing international institutions to impose a foreign version of rights on U.S. citizens. This helps explain why the United States has been one of the founders of major human rights instruments but has sometimes had difficulty gaining the advice and consent of the Senate for their ratification.[18]

Likewise, the Clinton administration claimed that attention to human rights issues played a major role in shaping its foreign policy, but the administration compromised on human rights positions, even on policies previous administrations had maintained, such as its delinking of Chinese human rights policy from normalized trade status. On the other hand, the administration tried to use sanctions to influence human rights abroad. At the time of the Kosovo crisis, almost half of the 125 unilateral sanctions imposed by the United States since World War I took effect between 1993 and 1998, and most of the sanctions imposed by the Clinton administration were based on human rights violations, rather than security concerns.[19]

When it took office in 1993, the Clinton administration claimed it would break from the its predecessors and follow a deliberately international and Wilsonian path in its foreign policy.[20] The multilateral aspect of its Wilsonianism was eventually overshadowed by the exceptional nature of the American mission. In the case of the Bosnia conflict in the beginning years of the decade, the United States allowed the Europeans to take the lead. When its allies were unable to stop the

Bosnian war without American involvement, it consolidated the opinion among decision makers, which was often articulated by Secretary of State Albright, that the United States was the "indispensable nation."

The Somalia and Haiti crises were ongoing when the Clinton administration took office. Learning quickly by inundation in these emergencies, the administration attempted to organize what it learned into Presidential Decision Directive 25 (PDD-25). Bureaucratic politics as well as disagreement on the underlying issues undercut the document's effectiveness. From PDD-25's publishing in May 1994, bureaucrats, especially those involved in negotiating its language, used it as cover to meet agency objectives. Since the PDD bears the ambiguous language typical of a document requiring interagency agreement, officials could claim that since they were part of its drafting, they could correctly interpret the document's meaning to suit their agency's interest.[21] Thus, the directive provided little help in codifying the lessons learned from Somalia, or curbing interagency wrangling in successive crises.

Despite personal convictions among some Clinton administration officials, they quickly learned from the Somalia case that in order to secure domestic support for a military operation, they had to articulate a credible national interest. The Powell doctrine that had emerged from the first Bush administration therefore gained strength under Clinton, making its way into PDD-25:

Peace operations should not be open-ended commitments but instead linked to concrete political solutions; otherwise, they normally should not be undertaken. To the greatest extent possible, each UN peace operation should have a specified timeframe tied to intermediate or final objectives, and integrated political/ military strategy well-coordinated with humanitarian assistance efforts, specified troop levels, and a firm budget estimate.[22]

The doctrine's insistence that military means be tied to specific political objectives and the support of Congress, to include a firm budget, reflected the influence of the lessons of the Vietnam War among senior military officers, and the deference that decision makers gave the military in matters involving the use of force. In particular, it reflected the military's resistance to the use of the armed services for peacekeeping or other uses they called "military operations other than war" (MOOTW).

Conversely, the military learned from the Somalia operation that politicians could and would withdraw support from an intervention with soldiers still in the field. Concerns about the erosion of war-fighting capability, lack of experience in MOOTW, and thinning budgets were also at the heart of the military's reticence about pursuing peace operations. But perhaps the most notable lesson policy makers chose to take from the Somalia experience, and one that would have direct consequences on the way they approached the Kosovo campaign, was the seeming intolerance for American loss of life in operations other than war. Some believe this was a phenomenon of the post-Vietnam all-volunteer force:

> The unlimited liability clause and the voluntary consent to kill and destroy make the soldier's contract a morally weighty one...Only if the soldier, sailor, or airman trusts that political authority will only call on military services for morally legitimate and weighty causes can the contract be entered into with confidence and moral security.[23]

The human rights idea that each life is of equal value is in keeping with this idea of a servicemen's compact, but the two principles seemed to collide in practice. Harkening back to historical questions about dealing with "the barbarians," policy makers in the 1990s had to decide how many of their nation's sons and daughters should be lost to save the lives of foreigners with whom their own people felt little or no connection. The lack of connection felt by the general public challenged human rights advocates who maintained the self-evidence of the equality of all individuals and the responsibility to protect each individual regardless of nationality.[24]

The choice of an aerial campaign in Kosovo conducted at 15,000 feet instead of a ground invasion was evidence that such an equation was not widely held among the allies. The way the Kosovo campaign was conducted, both as an aerial campaign and as a US-led NATO operation rather than a UN multilateral arrangement, reflected some of the conditions encountered in previous decisions about intervention. As early as the 1992–94 Haiti operation, UN secretary general Boutros Boutros-Ghali seemed to take a step back from the ambitious call for intervention he had put forward in *An Agenda for Peace*. By the time the UN Security Council was faced with the 1994 Rwanda genocide, American confidence in UN responsiveness was already low. Facing a similar situation, Slobodan Milosevic's ethnic cleansing campaign in 1998, U.S. decision makers believed they had little reason to hope the Security Council could overcome its inherent weakness—the need for consensus among its permanent five members—in time to avert another genocide. Hence the allies' bold justifications before the NATO operation, analyzed in chapter 5, not only showed the need to achieve and maintain domestic support, but also to maintain tight control of the operation.

The Argument That Wasn't: Treaty Obligation

The United States ratified the Genocide Convention in 1988, 40 years after signing it. The treaty had faced strong resistance in Congress and so the Americans ratified it with reservations that would allow it to opt out if action was deemed unconstitutional or was taken without specific consent of the United States in each case.[25] While some advocates believed what was occurring in Kosovo qualified as genocide, American officials steered clear of calling by that name in 1999.[26] From 1988 through the administration of George W. Bush, Americans maintained that the Genocide Convention is not extraterritorial. That is, it does not apply outside its own borders, nor obligate states party to it to take action in another country. This has also been the position of the Europeans. Even so, the Clinton administration went to great lengths to make sure it did not call the Rwanda genocide by that name. Likewise, the Senate resolution authorizing air strikes stated that an "Assault on the civilian population has been reported to include atrocities which could be considered war crimes, crimes against humanity and genocide."[27] Thus the Senate further avoided the claim that the United States was bound by a legal obligation to act under the Genocide Convention.[28]

Public Attitudes and Public Pronouncements

American public officials relied on national interest arguments to gain public support for sending in troops,[29] but voters supported the idea that NATO was responsible for stopping Serb atrocities against Kosovar Albanians. Polls revealed 60–67 percent support for the notion of a "responsibility" to do something to halt ethnic cleansing. Responding to polls taken early in the bombing campaign, Americans answered the question, "Do you think NATO (North Atlantic Treaty Organization), including the United States, has a responsibility to do something about the fighting between ethnic groups in Kosovo, a province of Serbia, or doesn't NATO have this responsibility?" Sixty-one percent expressed a sense of responsibility, 22 percent disagreed, and 13 percent did not know. Of those who did not believe the United States had a responsibility, 63 percent believed Europeans did, 25 percent believed they did not, and 13 percent did not know. After the president's March 24, 1999 speech justifying intervention, a poll revealed that 66 percent found his argument that the United States and NATO had a responsibility to stop systematic killing and ethnic cleansing "excellent/good," while 29 percent found it "not so good/poor" and 5 percent did not know. Overall, about 45 percent of those polled did not believe the president had done a good job of explaining why they were involved in the air campaign. While around 60 percent polled favored air strikes (a similar proportion of those expressing responsibility), 64 percent opposed the use of ground troops if air strikes failed, and only 29 percent favored the idea. This may indicate an aversion to American casualties or a prolonged engagement in Kosovo. In any case, it indicates that the sense of responsibility had its limits.

Ian Johnstone has noted that public justifications, especially in the UN Security Council, were based upon legal and not self-interested arguments in order to be persuasive to other governments.[30] As discussed in the previous chapter regarding the case of Germany, however, the fact that humanitarian and human rights arguments were not at the forefront of decision makers' public pronouncements does not mean that these ideals were not deeply held. To the contrary, those closest to American decision makers in the Kosovo case believe that the humanitarian idea and human rights played a "huge role" in the coalescence of the Western position:

If you want to see the effect [human rights concerns] have, take a look at the solutions proposed. Look at the war crimes tribunals, access to humanitarian services, etc. The definition of a "durable solution" is humanitarian. This is a big change from previous times. This may sound Reaganesque, but most leaders measure success by how they affect the lives of individuals. We asked, will this solution improve the life of a Kosovo farmer? General Shalikashvili was very open about asking things like, "Will bombing and killing people do more harm than good to the average citizen?[31]

Individual decision makers were deeply moved by the human tragedy in the Balkans. One Clinton administration official tells a story of Vice President Al Gore:

He saw a picture of a girl who hung herself after being raped in a refugee camp following the Srebrenica massacre. He kept saying, "She looks just like my daughter."[32]

A member of the U.S. administration's Principals and Deputies Committees maintains that the massacre in the Kosovo town of Racak in January 1999 had a major influence on the committee in favor of intervention. The massacre was reported immediately before the convening of a deputies meeting at the White House:

I remember everyone arriving to that meeting fuming and we got up from that meeting determined to push the government to use force. The principals meeting followed shortly after that.[33]

For many policy makers, there was a strong personal conviction and sense of responsibility not to make the mistakes of their predecessors regarding human rights atrocities:

> Every member of [the principals and deputies committees] had been through the Holocaust Museum. Policy makers [during World War II] knew what was going on and did not stop it. All of us had a strong feeling we didn't want to leave behind a similar scar, yet we knew to get political action we needed substantial national interests at stake.[34]

The administration was cautious about using humanitarian and human rights justifications with Congress by the mid-1990s. One administration official said that part of the reason the Clinton administration did not seek authorization to intervene during the Rwandan genocide in 1994 was its belief that Congress would not allow another humanitarian operation:

> We had to pass an emergency supplemental every time we used force so we had to go to Congress. Moral arguments did [very little] with Congress, and with the American people for that matter. The people of the US were not moved by humanitarian arguments where these were likely to require the use of military force.... How many times could we go back to Congress? We knew it was violent [in Rwanda] but we did not know that it would be a chain reaction. We were straining the limits of our carrying capacity [to ask Congress to support the use of force].[35]

By this account, it was conservatives in Congress, the Pentagon, and the general population that were the most resistant to intervention based on human rights and humanitarian ideals. Meanwhile, it was the liberals in the administration and among human rights and humanitarian groups that were most convinced of the obligation to intervene on moral grounds.

This is not to say that members of Congress, the military, or the general population did not hold humanitarian and human rights as deep convictions, only that they weighed those convictions with other factors in decisions about whether to use force. Domestic politics, party politics, interagency competition, as well as competing national interests were all taken into account by various policy makers in the decision to apply force in Kosovo.[36] One Clinton administration official responsible for planning humanitarian operations in the Department of Defense contends that human rights organizations "boxed the US in" at the UN and made it harder for the administration to fight the sectors of the American population that were most reluctant to use force for humanitarian reasons.[37]

Scoundrels, Victims, and Civilization

Madeleine Albright asked Serbians at Rambouillet the same question written on the flyers dropped from allied planes during the aerial campaign: Did they want to be part of Europe? It was neither a geographical question nor a strictly political and economic question, but a question of shared values. Implied in it was the West's own indecision, after witnessing nearly a decade of Serb aggression in the Balkan wars, about whether Serbians were Europeans or barbarians, deserving or undeserving of the rights and privileges of international society, including the right of nonintervention. When George H. W. Bush's secretary of state, James Baker, met with Milosevic in 1991 he used a similar standard:

I raised human rights—of Albanians in Kosovo, of Hungarians in Vojvodina, of Serbs in Croatia....I went on to note that while we sought to isolate no one in Yugoslavia, those who trampled on minority rights would isolate themselves from the international community."[38]

In Richard Holbrooke's opinion, Milosevic was a "scoundrel," an opportunist concerned with power rather than a nationalist dedicated to his country.[39] His comment was indicative of the shift in Western sympathies by October 1998 to the Kosovar Albanian side. Holbrooke publicly described the Serb practice of intimidating Kosovar Albanians who came to receive international humanitarian assistance administered by Serbs.[40] He also emphasized the ongoing cooperation of the Kosovar Albanians with U.S. State Department representative Chris Hill. During the summer of 1998, the State Department was involved with various Kosovar Albanian leaders, trying to put together coherent representation that could eventually agree to the settlement the Contact Group was crafting. In an October 23, 1998 interview, Sandy Berger commended the diverse Kosovar Albanian side, ranging from moderate Ibrahim Rugova to the extremist KLA, for coming together: "In two weeks, as I say, this Kosovar delegation, never in the room together before, representing various factions of Kosovo, have come together around a blueprint for Kosovo."[41]

*   *   *

There is no indication that U.S. policy makers' attitudes about sovereignty and human rights changed during the 1990s. Previous administrations, particularly at the beginning of the twentieth century, had exercised the right of intervention in Latin America based upon a combination of humanitarian and national interest arguments. Similarly, the complexity of the policy-making environment in 1999 resulted in the Clinton administration's multifaceted justification for the use of force in Kosovo to its domestic audience, including a heavy reliance on national interest arguments. Such a complexity does not support the idea that there is a consensus among Americans about an emerging norm of humanitarian intervention. This does not mean that Americans did not feel a moral responsibility to help Kosovar Albanians.

Even though there was a sense of responsibility to help the Kosovar Albanians among the public, and individual policy makers in many quarters felt responsibility as well, the administration did not express this responsibility publicly. First, it believed that this argument would draw the ire of some members of Congress where there was opposition to the intervention due to a lack of vital national interests. Second, the administration was concerned about setting a precedent, political and legal, which would make opting out of future interventions more problematic.

BRITAIN

The British found a moral obligation to intervene, even while they found no legal obligation to do so. Before the Kosovo crisis, a UK Foreign Office memorandum made explicit the difficulty with using international law as a basis for the right or obligation to intervene:

The overwhelming majority of contemporary legal opinion comes down against the existence of a right of humanitarian intervention, for three reasons: first, the UN Charter and the corpus of modern international law do not seem to specifically incorporate such a right; secondly, State practice in the past two centuries, and especially since 1945, at best provides only a handful of genuine cases of humanitarian intervention, and, on most assessments, none at all; and finally, on prudential grounds, that the scope for abusing such a right argues strongly against its creation. . . . In essence, therefore, the case against making humanitarian intervention an exception to the principle of non-intervention is that its doubtful benefits would be heavily outweighed by its costs in terms of respect for international law.[42]

As the following analysis shows, this legalist line was outweighed in parliamentary debates and official statements by talk of a "humanitarian exception" to law that imposed a moral if not a legal obligation to intervene.

War and Humanitarianism

Unlike the U.S. military, the British army did not have the responsibilities of a global power projection role and had ample experience with peacekeeping in the "small wars" of the British colonial and postcolonial period. While a legacy of peacekeeping did not preclude some parliamentarians from criticizing an intervention in Kosovo as a potential quagmire, it meant that the Blair government did not have to contend with a military resistant to engaging in conflicts other than major war. Instead, debate over intervention in Kosovo, like that regarding Bosnia during the Major government in 1992–95, was split between Conservatives who emphasized the lack of national interests involved, and the hypocrisy of pursing a moral foreign policy in Europe while neglecting comparable moral issues in other parts of the world.

During a lecture on British foreign policy in 2003, British foreign minister Jack Straw endorsed the assertion that "Britain had lost an empire but had failed to find a role," made by U.S. secretary of state Dean Acheson in 1962.[43] Britain's national identity had gone through an upheaval following the loss of its position as a hegemonic power after World War II, and especially after the run on the pound following the Suez crisis of 1956, the process of decolonization in the 1960s and 1970s, belated entry into the European Economic Community in 1973, and receipt of an International Monetary Fund loan in 1976.[44] By the end of the 1990s, however, Britain had become the world's fourth-largest economy and was second only to the United States in foreign investment.

Britain's special relationship with the United States continued during the 1990s. At the same time, Britain leaned closer to Europe. After 18 years of Conservative-led government under Margaret Thatcher (1979–90) and then John Major (1990–97), Britons elected Tony Blair's Labour party in May 1997. Blair came from the right wing of the party and was hailed as the most Europeanist prime minister in 30 years. Championing interdependence in his "doctrine of the international community," Blair placed himself opposite the Whig tradition that promoted British identity as Anglo-Saxon and Atlantic, the superiority of British parliamentary tradition over the European Parliament, and the goodness of national sovereignty against integration as a hedge against the evils of European conflicts.[45] The Anglo-Saxon belief in a moral British foreign policy gained strength after the cold war, even among Europeanists like Tony Blair. This tradition maintained that Britain, alongside the United States, had vanquished the evils of Nazism in World War II and had likewise conquered communism in 1989.

Despite continued political party debate on the subject, British social and economic behavior showed a preference for the Europeanist school, especially since the 1980s.[46] One historian argues that the study of British history had been "more fundamentally reconstructed" in the 1980s and 1990s "than at any time in the last hundred and fifty years,"

away from a promotion of British individualism and British excep-
tionalism and toward interdependence and integration.[47] The result
of social and economic interdependence was a more fertile ground for
political integration and favorable attitudes towards the enforcement
of universal human rights.

The Rise of Human Rights and Legal vs. Moral Obligation

The British date their rights tradition to the Magna Carta (1215–95)
and Bill of Rights of 1689. Official documents extol the broad political
agreement concerning Britain's major role in drafting the European
Convention for the Protection of Human Rights and Fundamental
Freedoms, begun in 1948 and finalized in 1951 by the Council of
Europe.[48] Even so, the British, like the other strong democracies emerging from World War II, did not favor a binding convention of rights
either at the UN or in the Council of Europe except as a way to bind
smaller states.[49] The British resisted incorporating European human
rights laws into British common law until the mid-1990s and then
explained its incorporation as a pragmatic measure taken in order to
process European law in British courts due to the rising costs of taking
them to the court in Strasbourg for trial.[50]

The Labour party's Election Manifesto of 1997 made adoption of
European rights law a priority. The paper followed a party consulta-
tion paper, "Bringing Rights Home," published in 1996, and was followed by a government White Paper, "Rights Brought Home," and the
Human Rights Bill in 1997–98, published after the Labour government
took office.[51] British public opinion favored Blair's move to incorporate European rights law, of making minority rights a priority and of
putting "the promotion of human rights at the forefront of our foreign
policy."[52] For example, in 1996 one scholar found that the public was
more willing to ban attacks on minority religions than on Christianity,
and more supportive of the rights of Nigerian and Indian citizens to
vote in the UK than of the rights of Australians and Canadians to do so;
and that, if "someone in Britain objects to a law passed by Parliament
and takes the case to the European Court of Human Rights," the public
would back the court against the parliament.[53] Thus, at the same time
the British public elected a liberal internationalist prime minister, they
also became more willing to accept a liberal internationalist approach
to human rights.

Tony Blair maintained that NATO nations, especially the United
States, had a moral obligation to intervene in Kosovo, stating that
"just as with the parable of the individuals and the talents, so those
nations which have the power, have the responsibility."[54] British public

opinion backed his position. Support for the NATO campaign in Kosovo increased between March 28 and May 2, 1999, from 55 to 70 percent believing it was "right" for the UK to have joined NATO in conducting the operation. Those believing that no British life should be lost to help the Kosovar Albanians dropped by more than half between March 28 and April 2, 1999 from 56 to 25 percent, with an overall settling at 45 percent by May 2, 1999. Meanwhile, support for the Labour party increased from 27 to 30 percent during the campaign, and support for the Blair government rose from 49 to 60 percent during the same period.[55]

Perhaps most striking was the public sense of obligation to intervene. On the fourth day of the NATO operation in Kosovo, 87 percent of the public polled believed that Britain had a moral duty to stop human rights abuses in Kosovo.[56] It was this sense of obligation promoted by the Labour government, with strong support from the Liberal party, for which the Conservatives took them to task. The Tory shadow foreign secretary, Michael Howard, condemned it, saying that "if that is the Government's view, then I can only say that the obligation has been honored more in the breach than in the observance."[57] He tried to pin down the government, stating that the minister of state had made statements during a television interview that had proposed a legal obligation to intervene. The minister, Tony Lloyd, insisted it was a moral obligation to intervene.[58]

Conservative criticism generally followed three points: the hypocrisy of defending human rights in one arena while failing to so in other places like Africa and the ensuing lack of credibility in such a foreign policy; the lack of national interests in the Kosovo case; and the danger of intervening in a civil war and the possibility of a military quagmire in the Balkans. The government dismissed the first argument by insisting that there was a humanitarian exception and a moral obligation to intervene. Regarding the second argument, there were a few members of parliament (MPs) who supported the prime minister by referencing concern among Balkan refugees in constituencies.[59] The government's case regarding interests, however, rested primarily on the need to preserve the credibility of NATO and to prevent the destabilization of the region, including the drawing in of NATO members Greece, Turkey, and Hungary.[60] On the third point the government maintained that its military aims were limited. George Robertson insisted that Britain had "not set ourselves the task of defeating the Yugoslav army. We are engaged in an effort to reduce Milosevic's repressive capacity."[61] At the same time, however, it announced publicly the need for ground troops to protect against further human rights abuses. The Tory front bench never mounted a successful campaign against the government's moral premise.

Meanwhile, Tony Blair declared that values and interests had merged in British foreign policy, and that promoting human rights was a matter of national security:

Now our actions are guided by a more subtle blend of mutual self interest and moral purpose in defending the values we cherish. In the end values and interests merge. If we can establish and spread the values of liberty, the rule of law, human rights and an open society then that is in our national interests too. The spread of our values makes us safer.[62]

The strongest opposition to Blair's moral aims, and to the closely related aims expressed by Robin Cook, came from the veteran MP Tony Benn, who insisted that all moral justification for military action in the name of humanitarian action was specious and sought to dispel romantic versions of World War II as a fight between good and evil:

In all fairness—this is an important point—we did not fight Hitler because of his persecution of the Jews; we fought because he challenged the power of the west. When Hitler died in 1945, the obituary in *The Times* did not mention the holocaust. I contributed in a minor way to the war, but that war was not about human rights—it was a bit more than that.[63]

Sovereignty and Nonintervention

Some in parliament attempted to steer the debate away from human rights and on to the matter of violating Serbian sovereignty:

We are not debating history or Srebrenica ... we are debating whether we are within our rights and whether it is proper for us to bomb a sovereign country, effectively an act of war, without the authority of the United Nations or of this House of Commons, in pursuit of the interests of one side in a civil war.[64]

Such arguments were generally countered by detailed descriptions of Serb atrocities and a challenge for the dissenting member to offer an alternative solution for stopping them. Alternatives were not forthcoming. Meanwhile, Tony Blair came out unambiguously on the subject of sovereignty and nonintervention, siding with those in the human rights movements who would label as barbarians those who committed human rights violations and proscribe them from the rights granted civilized society:

Non-interference has long been considered an important principle of international order. ... But the principle of non-interference must be qualified in important respects. Acts of genocide can never be a purely internal matter. When oppression produces massive flows of refugees which unsettle neighboring countries, then

they can properly be described as "threats to international peace and security"...
there are many regimes that are undemocratic and engaged in barbarous acts.[65]

Countering this, Tory parliamentarians reminded the House of
Commons of the danger of violating sovereignty. Bowen Wells pointed
out that the conflagration in the Balkans began when German foreign
minister Hans Dietrich Genscher opposed their own British position and
granted recognition to the breakaway states of Slovenia and Croatia:

That was an illegal action. It was outside the United Nations—it was outside all
commonly perceived ideas of the UN and, indeed, of the international rule of
law. That is what started it. At that point, the Serbs, or all those who wanted to
keep Yugoslavia together, were perfectly justified in taking up arms against the
decision.[66]

*   *   *

There was thus a mixture of motives, realist, legalist, and idealist
in British thinking about obligation. The Kosovo crisis came to a head
fewer than two years after Britain had elected a center-left Labour party
that was determined to put human rights at the forefront of its foreign
policy. While British national identity tended to favor strong national
sovereignty as opposed to political integration, the Blair government
was equally assertive in its Atlantic and European agendas, including
the "bringing home" of European Union human rights law into British
common law in 1997. Together with the foreign secretary Robin Cook,
Tony Blair insisted on a moral foreign policy that linked the protection of human rights abroad with security at home. They were supported by the majority of British public opinion when they announced
that Britain had a moral duty to intervene to protect ethnic Albanian
Kosovars and eschewed warnings from those who equated their violation of Serb sovereignty to Germany's "illegal" and ill-fated recognition of Slovenia and Croatia, which some observers argued helped
instigate the Balkan wars.

Britain enjoyed a favorable disposition toward military operations,
and the British military's experience in peacekeeping operations gave
it further confidence in pursuing a limited campaign in Kosovo. There
was no pacifist or antimilitarist counterweight to the human rights
movement splitting the left as it did in Germany. British military
experience with small wars also meant the government did not face
the resistance that the U.S. military services mounted in Washington
against participation in the operation.

The Blair policy and the public opinion that supported it tended
toward internationalizing obligations such as human rights norms,

sacrificing a degree of British sovereignty for European integration, and leaning toward a moral obligation to stop human rights abuses that overrode the principle of sovereignty. This last tendency was linked to a categorization of the Serbs as "barbarians" and therefore outside international society and undeserving of full sovereignty. That said, there remained resistance to these trends. Adoption of the Bill of Rights was slow in 1997–98, opposition remained to the adoption of the euro and other measures of full integration with the European Union, and a legal obligation to intervene was never claimed by the Blair government. London insisted after the intervention, along with some other allies, that the Kosovo case should not be seen as a precedent for humanitarian intervention in the future.

Thus, on the matter of the obligation to intervene in Kosovo, the British approach combined the idealist belief in the primacy of moral solidarity that made intervention a moral obligation, and the liberal internationalist tendency toward interdependence in its integration of European rights law into British law. The realist position was muted but was acknowledged by Blair when he claimed that the promotion of human rights abroad was a national interest. Even so, the more traditional realist arguments regarding sovereignty, national interest, and military concerns were generally ineffectual in the case of Britain, and this explains why Tony Blair was able to become the most outspoken of the NATO leaders in favor of intervention on moral grounds.

GERMANY

While Germany's geopolitical division between East and West was one of several factors that fostered its antimilitarism and multilateralism, the continuation of these policies after reunification was not was not predicted by many students of international politics.[67] Harmut Mayer has observed:

With German unification and recovery of sovereignty, many analysts questioned whether Germany would continue its multilateral foreign policy or whether it would opt for more unilateral or nationalistic paths. Most remarkably, throughout the period 1989–97 the German government continued to be the most enthusiastic proponent of binding the country into an ever closer European Union, thereby even surrendering some of the sovereignty just regained. Germany remained committed to cooperative self-binding (*Einbindungspolitik*).[68]

Mayer's analysis finds that the result of a debate among German policy makers about the future of the international system led to an agreement in favor of "cooperative self-binding." German debates about the nation's future after the fall of the Berlin Wall were informed by American academic debates at the time. Some supported Germany's antimilitarist stance, while others looked to the rise of multinational firms, financial institutions, and interest groups as a harbinger of the erosion of state sovereignty and an impetus for Germany to continue a multilateral and economics-focused foreign policy.[69]

Sovereignty, Identity, and Security Policy after Reunification

Those like Helmut Kohl who were moved by the realist predictions of continued inter-state conflicts emphasized the imperative of European integration as the only hedge against repeating the wars of the first half of the twentieth century. Still others were impressed with the idea of a cultural dispute between Western and non-Western peoples replacing the East–West ideological feud of the cold war. Wolfgang Schauble, leader of the Christian Democratic Union (CDU) in the Bundestag, argued:

> Huntington's thesis of a war between cultures might be, in its consequences, exaggerated, but there is no doubt that these global cultural conflicts and challenges exist, and that we Europeans have to give an answer to them. For me it is unquestionable that the answer can only be a common European answer...however, we can only become a real community if we manage to discover our common roots. One of the most decisive foundations is doubtlessly our common historical and cultural heritage...the peoples and nations of Europe are united in a common identity, in a community of common values with roots reaching back to the Christian medieval and to the archaic ages.[70]

The result of these seemingly diverging concepts about Europe's future led to a consensus about the need for a united Europe or a Europe of common destiny (*Europa als Schicksalsgemeinschaft*), whether as a hedge against war within Europe and the conflicts of a new cultural and ideological divide, or to capitalize on a more pacific world order marked by international cooperation.

Policy regarding Germany's role within a united Europe raised further debate. Least influential were those on the right of the Christian Democratic Union (CDU), the Christian Social Union (CSU), and the Free Democratic Party (FDP), who emphasized the rebuilding of Germany on nationalistic lines. The left wings of the Social Democratic Party (SPD), the Greens, and the Party of Democratic Socialism (PDS), focused on German leadership in global issues and global governance.[71] The majority of German policy makers—in the center of the CDU, the CSU, the FDP, and the SPD—were Europeanists who accepted an increased level of integration as healthy. Counterbalancing them were the more conservative members of their parties, who were skeptical of pooling sovereignty and who emphasized a strong Deutschmark, the preservation of NATO and trans-Atlantic ties, and increased German international responsibility.[72]

There emerged a split in the left wings of the parties between absolute pacifists who opposed all uses of force, and pragmatic pacifists who allowed limited military operations. Tamar Hermann describes those decision makers with a desire for political power as attached to a pragmatic pacifism that allows the use of force, and those embracing absolute pacifism as more focused on personal conviction.[73] The Greens were divided over this issue in the 1990s, with the *Realos* (realists), led by Joschka Fischer, advocating limited uses of force, and the *Fundis* (fundamentalists) holding fast to the party's traditional line.[74]

During the Kosovo campaign, Fischer met strong opposition from the left wing of his party, who called for a halt to the bombing. At a meeting of 800 delegates of the Greens in Bielefeld in May 1999, he was denounced as a "warmonger" and "murderer" as he pushed through a violent crowd of pacifists throwing rotten eggs and stink bombs and was hit by a paint bomb that burst his eardrum. After his plea beseeching his colleagues not to "cut him off at the knees," the delegates voted 444 to 318 in favor of a resolution implicitly accepting participation in NATO strikes but urging a temporary cease-fire and continued negotiation.[75]

The Pacifist Movement in Germany

The New York Times noted the irony of Germany's position:

Gerhard Schroeder, now often called the Kriegskanzler, or War Chancellor, has found himself steering a coalition made up largely of former pacifists toward involvement in a war that has ended with the planned deployment of 8,000 German troops.[76]

The evolution of the pacifists in Germany from the well-educated youth who violently protested American policies in Vietnam and NATO during the 1970s and 1980s to the ruling party officials who sent German troops into the NATO-led campaign in Kosovo is an excellent example of the way that conflict caused diverging traditions of thinking to converge in a policy of intervention.

The Greens' pacifist platform was connected to a peace movement among the population that also had an element of anti-American sentiment.[77] Some anti-American feelings resulted from Allied bombing during World War II, fostered by the Nazi anti-American propaganda campaign. During the rebuilding of West Germany under the U.S.-led

Marshall plan, this sentiment was driven underground as pro-American sentiment became a vehicle for distancing oneself publicly from Germany's Nazi past. Harald Mueller and Thomas Risse-Kappen argue that pro-American sentiment also sprang from personal desires to find some moral good in world politics after the horrors of World War II. This caused many, they argue, to put the United States on an exaggerated moral high ground, so that U.S. policies during the Vietnam War brought disproportionate disillusionment and caused many to equate American behavior in Southeast Asia with that of the Nazis.[78]

NATO's decision to deploy 572 intermediate-range nuclear missiles to Germany (the "dual-track decision" of 1979) fueled the West German peace movement between 1979 and 1983.[79] Some Germans even proposed that they were victims of the American global strategy.[80] Attitudes toward the United States, like attitudes regarding German foreign and security policy in general, were a function of generation, diverging among three postwar groups (those born before 1940, between 1941 and 1960, and after 1960).[81] Joyce Marie Mushaben contends that those who were involved in the peace movement set the "critical foundation for the national security orientations of the Western Germans throughout the 1990s," and that generational ramifications will continue to affect German policy towards NATO.[82]

Since formal ties between Americans and West Germans were exceptionally strong throughout the cold war period, some explain the emergence of tensions as a function of personal experiences: there were changes in perceptions about the United States, from enemy in the 1940s, to an idealized country in the 1950s, to an imperial state during the Vietnam War in the 1960s, to a dangerous state under President Reagan in the 1980s. The Green party platform included German withdrawal from NATO in favor of a collective security arrangement. This anti-American and anti-NATO sentiment was present in the Kosovo debates in the Bundestag. Hans Christian Stroebele, adhering to the more strict interpretation of the Greens pacifist policies, argued against intervention for this reason:

Years ago I sat before the television and saw how the war in Vietnam was conducted.... Hundreds of thousands of humans lives the cost, while we sat here in Europe and could do nothing to change it.... [M]y whole political commitment begins with the fact that German soldiers take part in no more war.[83]

Human Rights, Sovereignty, and Security

In a speech at the 54th session of the UN General Assembly in September 1999, Joschka Fischer noted that the Kosovo conflict had marked a turning point in international affairs, and that "the role of the nation state has been considerably relativized by the increased importance of human rights and the globalization of the economy and society."[84] In a seeming contradiction, he insisted that NATO's intervention should not be seen as a precedent "for weakening the UN Security Council's monopoly on authorizing the use of legal international force," and that humanitarianism should not become a "pretext" for the use of force as it was in the nineteenth century, but he nonetheless asserted that there was an obligation for the "international community" to intervene in the "internal affairs" of states who "use the cover of the principle of state sovereignty to violate human rights."[85] Germany's official statement on the principles and objectives of its human rights policy further links human rights and security, defining the "protection and promotion of human rights" as "in the political interest of states," serving "stability, peace and development."[86]

Fischer's commitment to intervention on behalf of human rights violations reflected both his party's and the German population's favorable dispositions toward policies promoting universal human rights. German attitudes toward human rights, like those regarding antimilitarism, were shaped by the country's Nazi past and search for a new national identity after World War II. This was the same period in which the international human rights regime was shaped by such instruments as the European Convention for the Protection of Human Rights and Fundamental Freedoms and UDHR. Andrew Moravcsik argues that European perspectives on human rights are a reflection of internal policies, noting that the European Convention on Human Rights was supported by weak democracies such as Germany, which ratified it in 1952, wanting to stem the negative influence of future governments.[87] This is consistent with Mary Ann Glendon's analysis of various degrees of support among Western powers for the founding of the UDHR.[88]

Germany's perspective on international human rights is also informed by its experience at the end of the cold war. The Alliance 90 party from the German Democratic Republic (GDR, East Germany) that joined with the Greens (Die Grunen) from the Federal Republic of Germany (FRG, West Germany) had grown out of the major human rights groups that protested communism and "effectively brought down the Berlin Wall in 1989."[89] Alliance 90 was composed largely of former dissidents and focused heavily on civil rights in its first national platform. While the Greens received only 4.8 percent of the vote and no Bundestag seats in 1990, Alliance 90 gained 6 percent of the East German vote and therefore eight seats in the Bundestag that year. Like the Greens, Alliance 90 drew support from young, urban, middle-class voters with an interest in the environment and the promotion of human rights. The two parties merged in January 1993 in anticipation of the federal and *land* elections. It was the combination of the two parties, together called the Greens, that came to power in coalition with the SPD in September 1998, as the Kosovo crisis came to a head.

By the time this coalition government had to make arguments in favor of intervention in Kosovo on behalf of human rights, members had already chosen sides on the issue of the use of force during the fractious debate between the *Realos* and *Fundis*. Thus while some remained firmly pacifist, others leaned heavily on human rights and humanitarian justifications for intervention, even to the point of insisting on an obligation to intervene. Wolfgang Thierse (SPD) argued:

[I]n all clarity the result of the brutal procedure of the Yugoslav army against the population in Kosovo is over 250,000 refugees, many villages burning, and even more refugees crossing the border. This brutality must be terminated. It is an obligation due to the experiences from the first half of this century and it is an obligation due to our own ideals to not permit that in Europe the fractious wars of the first half of this century, and the past determines the future. It is thus our goal of terminating a humanitarian disaster by adhering to the agreements already made.[90]

Geopolitics and Self-Determination

Relations with Central European neighbors, a concern for regional stability, and the influx of refugees were also cogent arguments for Germans to participate in the Kosovo intervention. During Bundestag debates, Gernot Erler (SPD) recognized this reality:

We have large respect for the Serbian contribution to the European culture. We live together well with 500,000 Serbs, in the Federal Republic. From this debate a message must also go out: we want that the Serbs blend as fast as possible again into the European integration. We want to have it here in Europe.[91]

The German government was keenly aware of the influence of minorities on foreign policy. When Yugoslavia began to unravel in 1991, Germany was the first external power to recognize the states of Croatia and Slovenia, while other governments remained undecided on the best course of action. Their early recognition caused some political difficulty for the other member states of the European Community and, arguably, might have contributed to the ensuing humanitarian emergency in the region. Critics of Germany's early recognition admit that the government was under pressure by a sizeable Croatian minority as well as the influence of the newly recognized right to self-determination of the people of the GDR.[92] The Kosovo case presented the Schroeder government a similar conundrum, with the question of the future of Kosovar Albanians who openly advocated independence from Serbia.

A counterweight to German sympathy for the right of ethnic Albanian Kosovars to self-determination was the country's sensitivity toward Russian interests. More than any other bilateral relationship, Germany's ties with Russia influenced the post–cold war European order. The relationship was rooted in their historical competition for influence in East and Central Europe, Russia's policies during Germany's cold war division, and Germany's dependence upon Russian compliance to make reunification successful.[93] Germany, more than the other allies, was outspoken about the need for the Contact Group and NATO to take into account Russia's objections to the campaign and its potential negative reactions to the bombing of its historical ally, Serbia.

Human Rights as Self-Interest and Ideology

The German decision to intervene in the Kosovo crisis was, as one analyst put it, "the culmination of a period of great change and partisan contestation" in Germany's foreign policy.[94] As discussed in the preceding chapter, the CDU/CSU-FDP government used German participation in Somalia and Bosnia as a way of regaining political latitude by leading the German public to accept increased German responsibility in international security operations. The right and center of the SPD and the Greens, once in power and faced with the difficulty of putting the idealistic antimilitarist platform of these parties into practice, supported participation in the Kosovo campaign for the same reason.[95] However, the shift was not simply a matter of abandoning idealism, since they faced increasing criticism that pacifism meant the inability to respond to massive human rights violations and humanitarian emergencies.[96] The failure to provide safe havens for refugees during the Bosnia crisis, and the Srebrenica massacre in particular, stood as testimonial for many of the decision makers. When the SPD found itself in danger of losing support in the Bundestag for the NATO campaign, it stepped up the use of human rights and humanitarian justifications to regain support from its leftist members.

Defense minister Rudolf Scharping used images and stories of the atrocities in public speeches and private meetings. He was severely criticized for his mentioning of a Serb plan called "Operation Horseshoe" for ethnic cleansing of the ethnic Albanian Kosovars, since the plan was never officially discovered.[97] Despite this, such emotional appeals to human rights abuses were effective in keeping the SPD support in the Bundestag intact and free of the violent divisions apparent among

the Greens. Meanwhile, the CDU and the CSU, the parties most ame-
nable to the use of force in exceptional cases, did not have to rally their
members around human rights arguments but instead could appeal to
the potential threat to the national interest posed by waves of refugees
about to flow from Kosovo toward German borders.

* * *

The use of human rights and humanitarian justifications for intervention, even to the point of claiming an obligation to intervene, was
both opportunist and deeply felt by policy makers. Those who claim
that German behavior in the Kosovo case derived from a consensus
on an obligation to intervene must account for two aspects of the
German position. First, the government has publicly insisted that the
case should not be used as a precedent.[98] Second, the use of humanitarian and human rights justifications, while they may have been deeply
believed by some policy makers, were nonetheless intended in part to
secure domestic political cohesion. While Joschka Fischer later called
the Kosovo crisis a turning point for international attitudes about the
compromising of the principle of sovereignty in favor of upholding
individual human rights, Germany's behavior during the crisis showed
extreme sensitivity to supporting Serbian sovereignty over Kosovo
due to Germany's special relationship with Serbia's ally, Russia. Even
though German Greens and Social Democrats may have strong personal beliefs in favor of a new norm of sovereignty and intervention,
their behavior in the Kosovo case gives cause for tempered expectations about their acting on this in the future.

FRANCE

French officials did not categorize their nation's participation as
a "humanitarian exception" as British officials did, nor did they use
value-laden justifications to overcome a strong antimilitarist movement as German officials had to do. As in the American case, human
rights were knit together with the idea of the national interest. Unlike
the Americans, however, the French saw these values as central to
their national identity and foreign policy. Thus, French leaders did
not have to contend with strong opposition based on national sovereignty arguments in parliament as the Americans did with Congress.
Instead, opposition within political and intellectual circles was weak
and unable to mount a significant case. French officials were able to
use rights and humanitarian language liberally to sway the public into
supporting participation in the NATO campaign, and there are indica-
tions that this strategy was successful.

French Foreign Policy: Identity, Security, and Values

In 2000, Hubert Vedrine, then France's foreign minister, looked back at the 1990s and asked, "Is moral outrage a sufficient basis for cogent State policy?"[99] His question indicated how far French foreign policy had come from the Gaullist state-centered approach that drew its status as a great nation from its nuclear weapons and its ability to successfully wend its way between the superpowers.[100] Like Britain, France faced its reality as a middle-rank power after the Suez Crisis of 1956.[101] While Gaullism still informed French policy into the 1970s and 1980s, the fall of the Berlin Wall in 1989 and European integration after 1992 posed new challenges to the Fifth Republic's foreign policy in several ways. First, reliance on possession of nuclear weapons for its international status was undermined when the United States and the Soviet Union agreed to nuclear arms reductions. Second, a united Germany constituted an economic and military rival reemerging on the continent.[102] Third, the economic and security requirements of Eastern and Central Europe were a source of competition for military aid and humanitarian support directed to the south, especially toward France's former colonies in Francophone Africa.[103]

Post–cold war challenges to French foreign policy emerged at the same time NATO leaders were dealing with the humanitarian and human rights crises of the 1990s. For France, it meant that the realist tradition that emphasized French security in a statist way encountered the strong internationalist trend emerging from European integration. This latter phenomenon brought a perception that threats would no longer come from outside the country, but rather from within France, due to the side effects of economic and cultural globalization. France's foreign policy stressed the spreading of French values as a priority, and chief among them was human rights.[104] The emergence of the United States as an empire—an idea already pondered in the post-war era by the preeminent French scholar of international politics, Raymond Aron—became an increasing concern in French political and intellectual circles.[105] These intellectuals were willing to forgo French sovereigntist policy in favor of multilateralism, seeing it as part of the French mission to spread French culture and the values of civilization throughout international society.[106]

Cultural Global Reach: The Francophonie and Souverainete

The strengthening of ties with the Francophonie and Souverainete, states associated with France due to common language and former or current politic ties, was linked to France's renewed emphasis on

spreading its language, culture, and values as part of its security policy. In November 1997, France adopted a charter for the Organisation
Internationale de la Francophonie (OIF) and appointed a secretary
general, the Egyptian diplomat and former UN secretary general
Boutros Boutros-Ghali, to coordinate political, cultural, and economic
cooperation among members of the Francophone community (some
51 states, 131 million people comprising two and a half percent of the
world's population). Thus began a renewed emphasis on spreading
French values, beginning particularly among those states France help
to found. The formalization of the Francophonie, a step analogous to
what the British had done in 1965 with the Commonwealth, was tied
to French identity as well as security.[107]

France also extended its global reach through its overseas possessions, the Departements d'Outre-Mer and Territoires d'Outre-Mer
(DOMs and TOMs), mostly seized by France in the 1630s and 1840s.
The possessions give France Exclusive Economic Zones in the Indian,
Pacific, and Atlantic Oceans, which comprise 11 million square kilo-
meters of water and the world's third-largest area of maritime control.[108] What France spent to support the welfare of these possessions
(as much as 2.3% gross domestic product—GDP—per year), it gained
in maintaining vestiges of its great power status. Jacques Chirac stated
that, "Without the DOM and TOMs France would only be a little
country."[109]

Sovereignty, Revolution, and Politics

Unlike the leaders of Germany, the French government did not have
to contend with a strong pacifist movement protesting French participation in the Kosovo campaign. The French were less influenced by
peace movements than other Europeans in the twentieth century. Before
the World Wars, however, French and German roles were reversed,
with France leading the pacifist movement on the continent. World
War II "tainted pacifism in France and reinvented it in Germany."[110]
The nature of French politics in the last two decades of the century had
a chilling effect on several social movements, including antimilitarism.
While these sprang up in the 1970s, the Socialist victory in 1981 quashed
them, since social movements in France relied heavily on party support. The Socialists did not actively court new members by supporting
movements that were not concerned with their traditional issues, such
as class and labor.[111] The French communist party and the intellectuals
committed to the revolution similarly split in the late 1970s for political
reasons.[112] French security policy under the Socialists in the 1970s and
1980s was based upon the Gaullist model and marked a turnaround in

President Mitterrand's attitude after his election in 1981,[113] reflecting little influence from the intellectuals of the left.

The sovereigntist vs. the integrationist foreign policy perspectives became a central issue after the signing of the Maastricht Treaty in 1992. While communists struggled to articulate how the revolution would take place within European integration, the left could not entirely oppose economic integration and market liberalization since it was tied to many issues important to its constituencies such as immigration, the environment, and democratization. Similarly, prime minister Lionel Jospin's *gauche plurielle* or "plural left," which governed from 1997–2002, had deep divisions within it. He set himself apart from the center-left leaders Blair and Schroeder, who formally established a "Third Way" in 1997.[114] Thus, a complex set of attitudes regarding French statist vs. internationalist policies emerged during the 1990s. In France as in most European countries, the extremes of the parties still opposed the trend toward multilateralism and globalization, while the center supported it.[115] The center, however, remained somewhat conflicted regarding sovereignty issues. In 1999, there were few politicians willing to upset the unity of the *gauche plurielle,* so the government had significant latitude on foreign policy choices, especially when prime minister Lionel Jospin (a Socialist) and president Jacques Chirac (a Gaullist) could agree.

French Culture: Civilization vs. Barbarity

The government chose to use strongly worded human rights language in advocating French participation in the NATO action in Kosovo.[116] This combined an appeal to the public's deeply held convictions regarding human rights and a statist view that by promoting these rights, France was taking a lead in spreading French culture and ensuring peace and stability.

The French people accepted their country taking a leading role. Concern in the early 1990s about potential American isolationism had been replaced by a concern about American unilateralism and a loss of French influence on the continent. Just as the government was working with Britain on pursuing the European Union's European Security and Defense Policy during this period, it was also intent upon taking a leading role in resolving the Kosovo crisis. France insisted on hosting the formal negotiations between the Serbs and the ethnic Albanian Kosovars on French soil, and French press reports in the first week of the Rambouillet talks were filled with expectations that Europe would avenge its circumscribed role at Dayton. The French seemed eager to correct the perception that they had been "asleep" in Bosnia.[117]

Other parts of Europe echoed French sentiment. From Brussels, one reporter noted:

Contrary to the Bosnian experience, this time it is Europe that is coming to the United States' rescue, the peace accord brokered by Richard Holbrooke in Belgrade being doomed to failure. Besides, Europe hints that it is ready to go it alone in Kosovo if Washington does not follow. Germany offers its unconditional contribution. This is a nice revenge on Dayton, where Europeans were considered totally insignificant.[118]

As noted in the previous chapter, French leaders carefully and continually made the case in their public pronouncements that Milosevic was a barbarian. They insisted that the French had no quarrel with their former allies, the people of Serbia, and that while they did not support terrorism on the part of Kosovar Albanians, they saw the ethnic Albanian Kosovars as the victims in a battle against the values of civilization.[119]

The government believed that this case would resonate with the French people, and polls taken during the conflict seem to bear out their assumptions. In a BVA poll, belief that France was right to join the NATO action was 58 percent on March 27, 1999. Nor did overall support flag during intense criticism of civilian casualties incurred in the first weeks of the campaign. To the contrary, public support rose to 66 percent between April 15 and 17, 1999, and returned to 57 percent from May 17 to 18, 1999.[120] Some speculate that public support may have been weaker than suggested by these poll findings, and that public support was emotional and a reflection of the reaction to television images and media reports sympathetic toward Kosovar Albanian refugees.[121] This impression strengthens the perception that the French were genuinely moved by humanitarian and human rights arguments.

Human rights arguments for intervention resonated among the French public because of the experience of the public, media, and French leadership during the previous human rights and humanitarian disasters of the decade.[122] The media investigated and sometimes strongly criticized French officials for hypocrisy and even alleged complicity in previous cases, including the Rwanda crisis of 1994. Meanwhile, French intellectual leaders like Bernard Kouchner, who helped found Medecins sans Frontieres (MSF) as a breakaway group from the International Committee of the Red Cross when that agency would not intervene in the Biafran civil war, had promoted the idea of the right of intervention during the 1990s. MSF did not support every call for intervention of the decade, but the concept that human rights was a justification for intervention beyond the sovereignty of borders and dictates of the law had already been accepted among sectors of the French public before Chirac used it in the Kosovo crisis.

*   *   *

The tension between France's embracing of universal human rights and its Gaullist foreign policy dates back to the beginning of both regimes in the late 1940s. For France's patron of universal human rights, Rene Cassin, the French Republic was a revolution and a vanguard for spreading international obligation for the rights regime. For France's leader, President de Gaulle, France was a fortress, and human rights were not central to France's foreign and security policy.[123] Since their inception, then, France has struggled between its role as patron of international obligation regarding rights and its own strongly nationalist foreign policy.

France intervened in the Kosovo conflict due to a perceived obligation to uphold humanitarian or human rights ideals, not only because they were part of international law, but because they were part of French values. The public identified these values and their promotion abroad as part of France's national identity and therefore allowed decision makers to participate in a campaign that might otherwise have been unpopular due to its targeting a sovereign country and former ally, Serbia, and its lack of a Security Council mandate.

The argument for preserving civilization against barbarity laid the philosophical groundwork for a compromised or conditional notion of national sovereignty for Serbia for the French. That is, leaders like Slobodan Milosevic, who grossly abuse human rights, were to be considered barbarians and therefore to lie outside the boundaries of international society in which the entitlement to full sovereignty exists.

While the spreading of French values as universal is prima facie an idealist approach, and while the combining of these ideas with the use of force represents hard idealism, the concept was so closely tied to the realist aims of promoting France's influence and maintaining its interests abroad that it fell in the seam between aggressive realism and hard idealism. Three years later, this would be the approach of American neoconservatives who advocated for intervention in Iraq. The irony in the French case is that this took place at a time when the country was grappling with relinquishing some of its Gaullist foreign policy due to the demands of European integration, and at the same time making bold pronouncements against U.S. unilateralism and setting itself up as the leader of a European counterweight based upon multilateralism. While there was no consensus within French policy-making circles to support an entirely multilateral agenda, France's foreign policy continued to be shaped by these competing voices, due to the facts of post–cold war geopolitics and globalization as well as the Gaullist legacy.

CONCLUSION: THE NATURE OF OBLIGATION IN THE CASE OF KOSOVO

None of the four nations declared it had a legal obligation to intervene in Kosovo. Leaders certainly did express some moral obligation, the British most prominently, but each in accordance with its interest. This occurred in the context of other nations who made more clear-cut arguments about moral obligation, nations that did not have the high stakes of sending soldiers to war. For example, Argentina's UN representative claimed that an "obligation to protect" fell to everyone, and Bosnia and Herzegovina's representative said he believed there existed a "legal obligation to confront ethnic cleansing and war crime abuses" as well as a "moral obligation."[124] The president of the EU at the time, a German, likewise claimed that European countries were "under a moral obligation."[125] NATO secretary general Javier Solana said that NATO had a "moral duty" to stop repression,[126] and Spain's foreign minister acknowledged a "moral necessity to intervene" in cases of intractable humanitarian emergencies.[127] But when Bonn, London, Paris, and Washington proposed a moral duty, it was a very different argument for each nation. For the French, there was an obligation to defend civilization against barbarity, and it was a matter of national mission to promote the values in society. The British shared this reasoning but conceived of it not as a mandate to spread British culture, but more as a duty to uphold the standards of international behavior that they believed right. Both of these nations grappled with their statist, sovereigntist foreign policy legacies and the policies required by European integration. Britain had just "brought home" European human rights law, and the British people were accepting of integrationist policies.

Americans weighed the plight of the Kosovar Albanians with many other pressing obligations requiring American military leadership. German officials, like the Americans, had to use arguments with their public that showed a credible national interest at stake before securing support for intervention. While human rights and humanitarian arguments were not entirely persuasive with Americans, they were effective with Germans, especially among the left in parliament. Whereas the Americans' experience in Somalia, Haiti, and Bosnia convinced them of the need to maintain a certain degree of operational control, the Germans' military history led them to believe that multilateralism was in their best interest. Likewise, support for human rights and an aversion to a humanitarian catastrophe near their border was sufficient to override antimilitarist sentiment.

Does the Kosovo case lend credibility to Tony Blair's assertion that, in the case of humanitarian intervention, "ideas are becoming globalized"?[128] Not in the way proponents of a new norm of intervention sometimes propose. Each nation rendered moral arguments for war, but there was not a common norm commonly understood. Rather, each shared common Western values of human rights and human dignity, the defense of which policy makers and publics worked to reconcile with the serious nature of war. And while no binding custom of protection emerged from the Kosovo decision, its cumulative effect was to pave the way—in politics, law, and values—for the Bush administration's campaign to liberate the Iraqi people from Saddam Hussein.

CHAPTER 7

Debating the Iraq War: The Trouble with Mixed Motives

Truly it is more honorable to avenge the wrongs of others rather than one's own.

—Hugo Grotius, *The Law of War and Peace*, 1625

Witnessing the ongoing insurgency in Iraq, a bitter debate persists over the motives for the war and the reasons for the transatlantic antipathy it engendered. There are those who argue that the moral talk the United States used to justify the war represented only a fig leaf for realpolitik, a change in tactics after the failure to find evidence of Saddam Hussein's weapons of mass destruction. Why had president George W. Bush and prime minister Tony Blair, both known for their moral personal philosophies and foreign policies, relied primarily on legal and threat-based justifications?[1] Why did they leave until the eleventh hour the moral argument about Saddam's brutish behavior toward the Iraqi people? Did the timing of various justifications belie their validity?

The Iraq war, like the 1999 Kosovo campaign, was launched without a United Nations Security Council resolution explicitly authorizing it. Some say this unhinged the international legal order, that all moral talk must be expunged from intervention discourse to pave the way for a new legal order, based solely on power and law.[2] But the moral dimension of the Iraq debate is far more pervasive than these critics care to admit. In fact, it was integral to the political and legal cases each nation made, whether or not that nation supported the war. What is more, the prominence of the moral dimension in policy is on the rise, for better and for worse.

The transatlantic relationship was strained by disagreement about the authorization and justification for the Iraq war, and those wishing to promote anti-American and anti-Western sentiment took advantage of the dispute. The national motivations, indeed, were fundamentally mixed, and skeptics and supporters alike see that as a problem. Yet motives in international politics are invariably mixed. Why then the rancor?

The case shows that in the wake of the humanitarian intervention debates of the 1990s, there was a shift in the normative landscape, a radicalization of moral, legal, and political arguments for and against war. That is, moral arguments were not confined to debates about humanitarian necessity or the responsibility to protect civilian victims of grave human rights abuses. In fact, the Iraq case shows how those issues were crowded out of public debates by countervailing arguments against war—ideological arguments about international law and order.

After the debates about humanitarian intervention in the 1990s, culminating in the Kosovo crisis, there were growing expectations among many that war waged strictly for national interests had lost legitimacy.[3] Thus there was alarm when the Bush administration announced that threats of terrorism required a rethinking of the meaning of preemptive war in the modern era.[4] Many scholars and practitioners who had come to believe that only the UNSC has the authority to wage war argued that the use of force outside those boundaries was "unilateral." Some went so far as to equate "unilateral" and "preemptive" uses of force with "immoral" and "illegal" international action even though the UN Charter provides for both unilateral and preemptive action under certain circumstances. A close examination of the way nations behaved during the Iraq debate and the context in which the four countries made their cases for and against war makes it difficult to support this view, however.

As with the Kosovo intervention, what happened in the Iraq case cannot be fully explained by any one dimension alone—political, legal, or moral.[5] It is better to look at the way states authorize and justify the use of force, satisfying domestic and international political requirements—how in this instance Washington, London, Paris, and Bonn chose to justify their behavior leading up to the Iraq war—using all three dimensions, and then test the accusations against them. By examining three contending imperatives within each state's thinking about intervention—imperatives of interests, multilateralism, and human solidarity—it is possible to understand the decision each government made.

Again, the truth about motives is not to be found in any one of these ways of thinking—political, legal, or moral—but rather in the debate among them. This approach denies us the ability to make satisfying judgments against one side or the other in the Iraq debate. Yet a complete picture of what happened is not possible without it.

THE ROAD TO WAR

The Bush administration began internal debates about the prospect of invading Iraq after the September 11, 2001, terrorist attacks on New York, Washington, D.C., and Pennsylvania. The 1990–91 Gulf War, in which the United States and coalition forces repulsed Iraq from its occupation of Kuwait, left the Iraqi army weakened, but Iraq's tyrannical president, Saddam Hussein, was still considered a menace to regional stability as well as to his own people.[6] Specifically, the Americans were concerned that Iraq was part of an "axis of evil" with North Korea and Iran, one that developed and proliferated weapons of mass destruction that could be used against the United States and its allies and friends. Members of the U.S. Congress from both parties had condemned the dictator's use of chemical weapons against his own people, and it was widely known that they had been deployed during the 1980–88 war with Iran.

After the 1991 Gulf War, the UNSC passed some 17 resolutions aimed at enforcing Iraq's promise to destroy its chemical and biological weapons, without success. Economic sanctions also proved ineffective, eventually leading to an "oil for food" scandal that hurt the credibility of the UN and incited public skepticism of the UN's ability to disarm Iraq. After the war, the UN Special Commission (UNSCOM) had conducted inspections in Iraq to ensure its disarmament, but in 1998 Saddam expelled the inspection team, led by the Swedish diplomat Hans Blix, and stopped all inspections for four years.[7] The Security Council created the UN Monitoring, Verification and Inspection Commission (UNMOVIC) in December 1999 to replace the defunct UNSCOM.

The Bush administration used as evidence the fact that UN weapons inspection programs had failed to find Iraq's nuclear weapons program before the Gulf War to support its claim that inspectors had also missed chemical and biological weapons facilities. Intelligence reports of the facilities were corroborated by Saddam's son-in-law, who had defected from Iraq. With growing consensus within the Bush administration about the need to back Western resolve with the use of force, the U.S. president addressed the UN General Assembly in September 2002, calling for a UNSC resolution to that effect. Meanwhile, the U.S.

Congress gave the president the authority to use force if necessary in an October 2002 vote.[8]

In November, the UNSC unanimously passed UNSCR 1441 recalling all previous UNSC resolutions and statements, invoking Chapter VII of the UN Charter, "deciding that Iraq has been and remains in material breach of its obligations," and deciding that "false statements or omissions" in the future would constitute "further material breach." UNSCR 1441 also stated that the Iraqi government had "failed to comply with its commitments . . . with regard to terrorism" and had failed to "end repression of its civilian population and to provide access by international humanitarian organizations to all those in need of assistance."[9]

In December 2002, Iraq submitted a 12,000-page report about its program, which was dismissed by UN weapons inspectors as unhelpful and American and British officials as false. Weapons inspectors returned to Iraq, and a month later, in January 2003, chief UN weapons inspector Hans Blix and International Atomic Energy Agency (IAEA) chief inspector Mohamed El Baradei delivered mixed reports on the state of Iraq's programs and willingness to disarm. El Baradei's analysis convinced many that Iraq had not been able to reconstitute its nuclear weapons program, but Blix's assessment found that Iraq had not accepted the terms of disarmament and was producing the virulent VX agent (nerve agent), claims immediately denied by Iraq's UN ambassador.[10]

The United States and Britain asserted at the Security Council that Iraq's obfuscation was proof that it was in "further material breach" pursuant to UNSCR 1441. Further evidence emerged that Iraq was producing anthrax, had failed to destroy stocks of mustard gas and other agents, and was hording prohibited missiles and warheads. UNSCOM head Hans Blix gave Iraq until March 1, 2003 to commence destruction of the weapons and demanded Saddam allow reconnaissance aircraft to fly overhead to verify progress.

Meanwhile, German chancellor Gerhard Schroeder had taken a staunch antiwar stance to win a tough reelection race, bringing together the Green Party and socialists while appealing to anti-U.S. sentiment among the electorate. After the September 2002 election, the left wing of those parties kept up pressure on the German leadership not to soften its hard line in the face of U.S. pressure and real fears that if France eventually backed the war, Germany would be isolated and Schroeder would have to resign. In January 2003, Chirac and Schroeder met in Paris to mark the 40th anniversary of the Treaty of Elysee, a pact signed by Charles De Gaulle and Konrad Adenauer that pledged to try to find an "analogous position" on foreign policy. Significantly, they stopped short of saying the two countries would adopt a common position, but when Schroeder said "Germany cannot approve legitimizing war," Chirac added, "It is our common policy."[11]

At a NATO meeting on February 10, France, Germany, and Belgium vetoed a U.S. plan to shore up Turkey's defenses in preparation for a war. At the EU, France and Germany blocked 13 EU candidates from a summit in Brussels to discuss the Iraq situation, because the countries largely sided with the United States on the matter. At the UN, France, Germany, and Russia, which all had material interests in Iraq, formed a line against the introduction of a U.S.-U.K. resolution to authorize war. France's business interests in Iraq were reported to amount to one and a half billion dollars.[12] The two sides worked assiduously to secure the votes of the remaining members of the Security Council, and it happened that Germany had just taken over presidency.

In the Security Council on February 14, 2002, U.S. secretary of state Colin Powell made a dramatic presentation laying out the American case for forceful measures against Iraq. Powell played an audiotape of Iraqi agents conspiring to hide nerve agents from inspectors, which were concealed in mobile laboratories, and offered satellite photos as further evidence. He also presented evidence linking Saddam to Al-Qaeda operatives, which he said were offered safe haven in Iraq. Finally, he summed up the U.S. and British stance: that Iraq was in "material breach" of UNSC resolutions and the use of force was justified to put a stop to Saddam's defiance. France's foreign minister, Dominique de Villepin, returned fire in an impassioned speech arguing that the use of force was "fraught with risks" to regional stability and that weapons inspections were bearing fruit and should be allowed to continue. A coordinated antiwar effort led to massive public demonstrations the following day, primarily throughout Europe.

In March, France, Germany, Russia, and China threatened to veto any UNSC resolution on the use of force. Meanwhile, the United States, Britain, and Spain prepared a resolution declaring Iraq in material breach of 17 previous UNSC resolutions, and President Bush promised to make other council members "show their cards" regarding their stance on the issue.[13] Bush publicly announced on March 6, 2003 that Saddam posed a risk to the American people that he was "not willing to take" and that if it came to war the purpose would be "disarmament," "regime change," and replacing Saddam with "a government that represents the rights of all the people."[14]

When Blix and El Baradei returned to the UNSC the next day, they announced that while the Iraqis were starting to cooperate, there were still many weapons unaccounted for, including anthrax, Scud missiles, and unmanned aerial vehicles for delivering chemical and biological weapons. At this point the United States, Britain, and Spain amended their proposed resolution, setting a deadline of March 17, 2003 for the UNSC to certify Iraqi compliance with previous resolutions. France immediately opposed the resolution and worked to defeat it, and along with Russia threatened to veto it. Prime minister Tony Blair had promised his constituency that he would secure this "second" resolution before resorting to war and worked to amend UNSC resolutions to make them acceptable to both sides.

While the United States and Britain pressed for a vote and both sides lobbied remaining UNSC members, the Americans, British, and Spanish leaders met on March 15, 2003 in the Azores and declared that March 17 was the deadline for the UNSC to agree on a way to enforce UNSC 1441.[15] They ultimately allowed the time to expire without a vote on their proposed resolution. They claimed that the March 10 French threat of a veto was a sort of betrayal to the United States, that it had thus effectively vetoed the move, and that diplomatic routes had therefore been closed.

On March 17, 2003, President Bush gave a televised address issuing Saddam Hussein 48 hours to leave Iraq or else war would ensue. Weapons inspectors were evacuated, and when Saddam ignored the ultimatum, U.S. and British-led coalition forces began air strikes on March 19, 2003.

PERCEPTIONS OF UN AUTHORITY AND AUTHORIZATION FOR THE USE OF FORCE

In a meeting in Berlin in early September 2002, top-level defense officials of Britain, France, Germany, and the United States debated the issue of sovereignty and who had the authority to wage war against Iraq.[16] Beginning the meeting, part of a long-standing series dubbed the "quad talks," the U.S. representative, deputy defense secretary Douglas Feith, argued that "it does not serve the interests of peace and world order for Iraq to use sovereignty as a screen behind which it can develop, unhindered, biological and nuclear weapons."[17] His British counterpart, Simon Webb, while acknowledging the importance that Prime Minister Blair placed on the UN, warned "we should guard against speaking of the UN as a necessary source of legitimacy for action against Iraq."[18] Likewise, the French representative, Marc Perrin de Brichambaut, said that the UN could help with "*political legitimation*" but not "*legal authority*" because "states do not need UN approval to act in their own self-defense."[19] De Brichambaut said that the French position was that the U.S. should act jointly with other nations, and that while France may not send combat troops it could help by relieving troops in other arenas such as the Balkans or Afghanistan. The German position, represented by state secretary of the German Ministry of Defense Walter Stuetzle, stressed the requirement to use the "moral authority" of the UN as well as its competence in international law and security.[20]

The U.S. appeal at the UN was the result of bureaucratic politics in which the venue reflected the views of liberal internationalists in the cabinet, while realists controlled the content of the message. Feith recommended to secretary of defense Donald Rumsfeld that the United States make sure that a new UNSC resolution not be "a test of the legitimacy of US-led efforts to defend the US and the world against Iraqi WMD [weapons of mass destruction], but as a test of the UN's willingness to uphold its own principles."[21] Feith recalls that it was secretary of state Colin Powell who convinced President Bush to choose the UN as the venue in which the United States would make its case for war against Iraq. While Feith and others disagreed with the choice, his realist perspective on how to approach the UN informed the U.S. line of argument on the eve of war: the issue was not whether sovereign states have the authority to wage war but rather whether the UN could retain any authority if Iraq was allowed to ignore 17 UNSC resolutions with impunity.

The decision to go to the UN persuaded many Democrats in the U.S. Senate who were reluctant to give President Bush a "blank check" in going to war with Iraq. In essence, the antiwar voices, led by the late senator Ted Kennedy (D-MA), focused on the issue of international authority (the need for multilateralism) as well as on justification (the need for proof of an imminent threat). Congress debated a resolution to authorize war just weeks before the midterm elections, and Democrats, recognizing that public opinion strongly supported the president's case tying Iraq to the attacks of September 11, 2001, feared the appearance of weakness on national security just weeks before elections and did not want to highlight fissures in their party.

After three days of debate on October 10 and 11, respectively, the House and Senate voted in favor of the war powers resolution by a vote of 296 to 133 in the House and 77 to 23 in the Senate. The Senate's 50 Democrats split 28 in favor, 22 against the measure, while the 49 Republicans and one Independent favored, with one Republican dissenting.[22] Two resolutions brought forward the following January designed to slow down the administration's march to war failed to gain traction: a resolution demanding a second Congressional vote authorizing force proposed by Senator Kennedy, and a resolution demanding a second UNSC resolution brought forward by Senator Robert Byrd (D-WV).[23]

Americans were less convinced than Europeans of the need for UNSC authorization for war, and more convinced that the use of force was necessary to solve the Iraq problem. A survey taken in June 2002 found that 75 percent of Americans favored using force to overthrow Saddam Hussein's government in Iraq, while 21 percent opposed it. Most of these (65%) said the United States should do so only with UN approval and the support of allies.[24] This corresponded closely to British views (69%) and French views (63%). Only 56 percent of Germans believed the United States should invade under such conditions. Answering the question about whether the United States should intervene alone, 20 percent of Americans, 10 percent of British, 6 percent of French, and 12 percent of Germans surveyed believed they should. Meanwhile those saying the United States should not invade Iraq included 13 percent of Americans, 20 percent of British, 27 percent of French, and 28 percent of Germans surveyed.[25] Overall, 60 percent of respondents in six European countries supported a U.S. war on Iraq, but only 10 percent would support it without UN approval and the support of allies.

A year later, in a 2003 survey, views on the legitimacy of the UN had slid precipitously on both sides of the Atlantic. When asked about support for military action against North Korea and Iran, 63 percent of Americans and 34 percent of Europeans thought the United States should go it alone, a dramatic increase from the 20 percent and 10 percent respondents in 2002. Even so, both Americans and Europeans favored international cooperation, either through NATO (73% of Americans and 43% of Europeans) or the UN (74% of Americans and 46% of Europeans).

A more striking difference was found in American and European attitudes about authorization when the question was put in terms of justification. Americans were far more willing to bypass the UN if the war was waged for vital American interests (36% strongly, 21% somewhat) than Europeans (16% strongly, 24% somewhat). Overall, 57 percent of Americans agreed the UN should be bypassed if war was justified, while 53 percent of Europeans disagreed. Thus, when President Bush decided not to pursue a vote on the second UNSC resolution for the use of force in Iraq, he had an easier time with his constituency than Britain and Spain. Likewise, French and German leaders had robust public support to insist on a second resolution. The group that did not want to strengthen the UN and was willing to bypass it was twice as large in the United States (26%) as in Europe (12%).[26]

In France, opposition to the war was not based upon whether a Security Council resolution could be obtained. Rather, there was a strong antiwar sentiment that crossed party lines. At the same time President Chirac was telling the French military to prepare for the eventuality of mobilizing for the intervention, various polls showed both left-wing and right-wing parties and a majority of French opposing the war altogether. In January 2003, *Le Figaro* put resistance at 77 percent and *La Parisien* at 66 percent. The latter said only 15 percent approved of the use of force with a UNSC resolution.[27] France's position at the UNSC did not reflect the strict antiwar posture. Rather, the French position at the UN was that they would not support any intervention without UNSC approval. In what critics called a "diplomatic ambush" of the United States, France used its position of UNSC presidency to call a meeting of foreign ministers to discuss the war on terror and elicit antiwar statements from Russia, China, and Germany just a week before UN weapons inspectors were due to report on the situation in Iraq.[28]

Yet the threat of a veto was tricky for France, because it did not want to drive the United States away from the UNSC—where France wielded some international clout—and thus weaken the Council's legitimacy. When the right wing of Chirac's own party and leading foreign policy analysts put pressure on him to ally with the United States, he did not relent. But at the same time, when U.S. Secretary of Defense Rumsfeld referred to the position of Germany and France as "old Europe," causing French politicians to lash out, Chirac interjected to call for calmer deliberations. Prime minister Jean-Pierre Raffarin also tried to repair the breach, saying the split between Washington and Paris "cannot hurt our links of gratitude, of closeness with the American people. . . . We know what we owe them, they can count on our allegiance."[29] And while Gerhard Schroeder was ruling out any participation in the war, Chirac was leaving the door open to the use of force as a last resort and even sent out the French aircraft carrier *Charles de Gaulle* on an exercise with the U.S. Navy within striking distance of Iraq.[30]

JUST WAR AND JUSTIFICATION
FOR THE USE OF FORCE

In his speech to the UN General Assembly on September 12, 2002, President Bush gave his international audience three rationales justifying the use of force: to preempt the use of weapons of mass destruction; to punish Saddam Hussein for ignoring 17 UNSC resolutions; to put an end to the dictator's violations of human rights of own people. As the just war scholar James Turner Johnson has noted, these three arguments closely mirrored those given with frequency by the Western states during the humanitarian intervention debates of the 1990s.[31]

According to a January 31, 2003 report from the Congressional Research Service, the rationale for war advanced by officials in the Bush administration to members of Congress included the threat posed by lethal weapons, Iraq's ties with terrorists, the need for regime change in Baghdad, significant internal support for intervention inside Iraq, and growing international support for the operation.[32] In his address to the UN General Assembly on September 12, President Bush asked, "Are Security Council resolutions to be honored, or cast aside without consequence?" and again in his State of the Union address he called on the UN to "fulfill its charter and stand by its demand that Iraq disarm."[33] While no positive proof had yet emerged about terrorist ties, secretary of defense Donald Rumsfeld argued that "evolving" intelligence reports showed that Saddam Hussein had given Al Qaeda operatives safe haven. And secretary of state Colin Powell's chief of staff Lawrence Wilkerson recalls that British, French, and German officials all believed to be true the intelligence that Powell presented at the UNSC exposing Iraq's ongoing chemical and biological weapons program.[34]

The American position on the need for regime change spanned political parties, as the Iraq Liberation Act of 1998 demonstrated. Perhaps more importantly, many senior Democrats went on record saying Saddam Hussein must go. These included then secretary of state Madeleine Albright and national security advisor Sandy Berger, as well as Democrats in Congress such as Nancy Pelosi, and, later in 2002–03, prominent Senate Democrats including President Bush's opponent in the upcoming presidential election, senator John Kerry as well as senators Hillary Clinton, Harry Reid, Jay Rockefeller, and the late Ted Kennedy.[35]

The belief that Iraqis would welcome American liberators with open arms also crossed political and national divides. When President Bush was releasing funds to Iraqi opposition groups, international humanitarian activists applauded him. Bernard Kouchner, who championed the notion of a "right of intervention," gave a speech at Harvard University in February 2003 arguing for intervention on humanitarian grounds. He had just returned from Kurdish-occupied areas in the north of Iraq and, while not endorsing a strictly military intervention, said these populations were ready to welcome American liberators.[36] Other evidence of international support came from guarantees of overflight and basing rights, even from Arab nations that were publicly opposing the war.

Critics of the war in the United States primarily argued that war was premature and that it would negatively affect the antiterrorism campaign as well as NATO relations. They also pointed out the operational and logistical difficulties, arguing that it was unlikely that the United States would gain the robust coalition it did during the 1990–91

Gulf War, and that the financial requirements of war, especially a long war, could hurt the American economy. Critics also argued in strategic terms, charging that the war could destabilize the region, and, finally, that the outcome of the war was far from certain. Americans may have to occupy the country for a long time, they asserted, there was no guarantee the next leader of Iraq would be better than Saddam Hussein, the country might devolve into ethnic and religious conflict that could affect NATO allies such as Turkey, and the fragmentation of Iraq could be exploited by its neighbors, even for the purpose of promoting terrorism against the United States and its allies.[37]

President Bush ultimately won the internal U.S. debate over the need for war on Iraq because he had the support of public opinion. Some say this is primarily because his administration successfully linked Saddam Hussein's tyrannical regime to the wider war on terrorism, which was perceived as the top security threat on both sides of the Atlantic.[38] While official positions of the four NATO countries largely reflected public opinion, Britain, as it was in 1999, was a sort of exception.

Whereas Tony Blair's outspoken humanitarian argument for war in 1999 was afforded by the fact that he was the only one of the four leaders who enjoyed a comfortable political position at home, in 2002 he was in trouble with his own party. And while the British public was more willing to use force than were their French and German counterparts, they were less willing than the Americans. Blair won a vote in the House of Commons only narrowly and despite rebellion in his own party after making a strong argument based upon Britain's strategic interests:

Tell our allies that at the very moment . . . when they need our determination that Britain faltered. I will not be party to such a course. . . . This is the time for this House . . . to show that we will confront the tyrannies and dictatorships and terrorists who put our way of life at risk, to show at the moment of decision that we have the courage to do the right thing.[39]

Support for Blair's position increased dramatically as the war drew closer, with resistance to the use of force dropping from 52 percent to 44 percent just before the war began. Meanwhile, support among Britons for President Bush's ability "to make the right decision" rose to 53 percent.[40] Blair's victory was arrived at by internal debate and compromise within his government on the nature of justification. The British attorney general, Lord Peter Goldsmith, released a public statement justifying the use of force as legal under international law, based upon Iraq's breach of three UNSC resolutions.[41] He had released a private and secret memo to Blair 10 days earlier citing three legal grounds for war: self-defense (including collective self-defense); the humanitarian exception (which it had claimed for the Kosovo intervention); and war with a UNSC mandate citing Chapter VII of the UN Charter. With a view to the way the International Criminal Court might find Britain in violation of international law, he argued that the first two did not apply and the third was not universally accepted, and so a second resolution would be best to justify the use of force.[42] Even so, he said resort to justification based upon UNSC resolution 1441 could be used if strong evidence of Iraqi WMD was made manifest.

In addition to reliance on previous UNSC resolutions, Blair made the humanitarian case for war. In February 2003 he said,

Ridding the world of Saddam would be an act of humanity. It is leaving him there that is in truth inhumane. And if it does come to this, let us be clear: we should be as committed to the humanitarian task of rebuilding Iraq for the Iraqi people as we have been to removing Saddam.[43]

In France, officials used several arguments to show that war with Iraq was not justified. The primary argument was that peaceful means had not been exhausted and that weapons inspections should continue. In late February, as the United States and Britain were about to introduce a second UNSC resolution on war, Chirac met in Paris with Spanish Prime Minister Jose Maria Aznar—one of Washington's strongest allies despite his country's antiwar sentiment—and said: "We think there is no reason that justifies going beyond (UN Security Council) Resolution 1441 and so we are opposed to any new resolution."[44] Again in February President Chirac announced, "Today, nothing justifies a war" and effectively ruled out any legitimate circumstance for proceeding with the U.S.-led intervention. The only alternative according to Chirac was disarmament "through the inspections process laid out in Resolution 1441, adopted unanimously" by the UNSC on November 8 and through an alternative Franco-German plan to increase the number of weapons inspectors and UN peacekeepers. Critics wrote off the alternative as a nonplan since the likelihood of Saddam Hussein accepting UN peacekeepers was slim.

In a debate in the French parliament, French prime minister Jean-Pierre Raffarin further laid out the French justifications for its antiwar stance. He warned that "A military intervention today, when all the chances for a peaceful solution have not been explored, would divide the international community," "be perceived as precipitous and illegitimate," and "cause a wave of incomprehension and suspicion." Furthermore, he said, "War would weaken the international coalition against terrorism." Additionally, the criteria of just war had not been met: "The use of force is not justified in the current circumstances because there is a credible and effective alternative to war: disarming Iraq through inspections."[45]

The French also justified their position against war by arguing in strategic terms. French defense minister Michele Alliot-Marie said, "The war represents also a real risk that it would lead to conflict between the Arab-Muslim world and the West," and that it represented "a risk of destabilization of the whole region." This concern involved the fear of upsetting the delicate balance of Muslim relations inside France. France has Europe's largest Muslim population, more than four million, as well as historic ties with the Arab world, and therefore many believed that France would suffer more than other countries from reprisals if France was seen as betraying its connections with those constituencies, both internal and external.[46]

French arguments about justification were also highly moralized. French foreign minister Dominique de Villepin's address to the UNSC captured a similar argument about the universality of French values to the one used four years earlier to justify war on Serbia: "France has always stood upright in the face of history before mankind, faithful to its values, it wants resolutely to act together with all members of the international community. France believes in our ability to build together a better world."[47]

The tough stance of the French leadership against a second resolution for the use of force was supported by rising opposition to the war among the French public. A poll taken on February 15, the day after the French foreign minister's passionate address at the UNSC, some 87 percent were opposed to military intervention in Iraq and 85 percent said they approved of Chirac's position. Only 11 percent said they favored military action against Iraq and 2 percent had no opinion. This was an increase from a similar survey conducted at the beginning of January that put opposition to war 10 percent lower. Seventeen percent of the interviewed said they would approve of war with a UNSC resolution. Forty-seven percent said that in the event of war, they preferred France provide only material and logistic support and not combat troops. Thirty-three percent said they did not want France to join any military operations on Iraq at all. Seventy-one percent believed France should veto any UN resolution for war if UN weapons inspectors' findings were insufficient to justify intervention.[48]

At the same time the German state secretary of defense was arguing in the quad talks that the UN represented a "moral authority" for intervention, chancellor Gerhard Schroeder stated that he ruled out any German role in the U.S.-led war with "no ifs ands or buts," even if backed by a UNSC resolution.[49] Schroeder was taking advantage of German antiwar sentiment since he was trailing badly in the polls during a reelection battle against Christian Democrat Edmund Stoiber.[50] While he would eventually allow the thousands of U.S. troops on German soil to use their German bases and airways in the war, Schroeder refused to take a position on the matter during the election. He thus reversed the pledge he made just after September 11, 2001 of unlimited solidarity with America. He reversed again after the election in a public appearance with his foreign and defense ministers, pledging to help the U.S.-led war by providing Patriot missile defense systems to protect Israel from an Iraqi attack during the war.[51] Defense minister Peter Struck also said Germany would comply with its NATO obligations, stating that "German planes, primarily AWACS reconnaissance aircraft, are special units of the North Atlantic Alliance and they will carry out their tasks regarding NATO's missions."[52]

During the campaign Stoiber used the argument that Germany must be a faithful ally—the same argument Schroeder had used three years earlier to rally support for the Kosovo campaign. He told Schroeder in a televised debate that he was "damaging German-American relations."[53] This view was seconded by the head of NATO's military committee, General Harald Kujat (also the former chief of the German armed forces military staff) and the U.S. ambassador to Germany, who also said Schroeder's stance was weakening German-U.S. ties.[54] Even the German press argued that while Schroeder would win the election with his intractable "no" to war, it would have long-term consequences for Germany's position. For example, the center-left *Sueddeutsche Zeitung* newspaper lauded President Chirac for finding a middle road in the war debate, while lamenting with "astonishment" that Paris had become the mediator between Berlin and Washington.[55]

One reason Stoiber failed and Schroeder was undeterred in his stance was the fact that Germans believed they had already done enough for the alliance. In a poll taken around the time of the election, 76 percent of the respondents said that Germany had no obligations vis a vis the United States to participate in a campaign against Iraq, and that 71 percent did not fear that Berlin's relations with Washington would deteriorate if Germany refused to participate in a war.[56] Likewise, Schroeder's reversal of his proalliance stance of 1999 was backed by 57 percent of viewers of the televised debate, who held an antiwar outlook compared to 28 percent backing Stoiber's foreign policy. Two Nobel Prize–winning authors and other celebrities backed Schroeder publicly, as both candidates worked hard to sway the one-third of the population that was yet undecided.[57] The fact that the two German candidates had ruled out a "grand coalition" of Social Democrats and Christian Democrats put their foreign policies in terms of an either–or proposition to the voting public. One poll put antiwar sentiment at 80 percent, and the BBC reported it at 90 percent.[58]

German antiwar attitudes were representative of a significant trans-Atlantic difference in attitudes about the just use of force, and this helps account for the divergence in policy in 2002–03. In a 2002 poll, responding to the idea that "under some conditions, war is necessary to obtain justice," some 84 percent of Americans agreed (55% strongly), with 74 percent of British (35% strongly), and only 39 percent of French and Germans (12% strongly) in concurrence. Here the difference in the intensity of these beliefs is also worth noting.[59] Yet despite the standoff in policy, Americans and Europeans saw eye-to-eye on the hierarchy of international threats. Topping the list was international terrorism (91% of Americans, 65% of Europeans), followed by Iraq developing WMD (86% Americans, 58% Europeans), with Islamic fundamentalism in fourth place (61% Americans, 49% Europeans).[60] The results, however, show more intensity on the part of Americans and explain why U.S. officials made ties to terrorism and WMD the focus of their argument for war in Iraq. Humanitarian emergencies and human rights abuses were not on the list of top foreign policy concerns on either side of the Atlantic, and this also helps explain why these issues were less important to leaders formulating arguments for the use of force in 2002–03.

THE MISSING DEBATE ABOUT OBLIGATION ON HUMANITARIAN GROUNDS

During the 2002 debates about intervention in Iraq, the humanitarian and human rights violations of Saddam Hussein's regime were an important part of American and British justifications for the use of force to their international audiences. Yet most critics and the media largely ignored these justifications and focused on the question of how imminent a threat was posed by Iraq's nuclear, chemical, and biological weapons programs and whether a UNSC resolution was required or obtainable. The humanitarian argument thus eventually disappeared from the broader debate, and many critics accounted for these justifications as merely cover for the prerogatives of power.[61]

Pope John Paul II argued against intervention on the grounds that it would create more humanitarian crises than it would solve. In the main, however, religious leaders not only chose to ignore the proposed humanitarian grounds for intervention, but on both sides of the Atlantic they worked assiduously against the intervention on political grounds.

The Catholic bishops of Germany called the war "morally not permissible" and said a country could only go to war to defend itself from an armed attack or to prevent grave crimes against humanity.[62] The American bishops sent a letter to President Bush that essentially ignored Saddam's long history of human rights abuses against the Iraqis and their current plight, but expressed "serious questions about the moral legitimacy of any preemptive, unilateral use of military force to overthrow the government of Iraq."[63] The French bishops opposed the war, arguing that it might give rise to a wider Christian–Muslim conflict. Anglican Bishop Peter Price of Bath and Wells addressed an antiwar rally in London's Hyde Park in September 2002, saying that a unilateral preemptive strike against Iraq would be "illegal, immoral and unwise."[64]

Former champions of humanitarian intervention were thus absent from the discussion about international responsibility to protect the Iraqi people. In a critique of the responses from world religious leaders, Rev. James Schall of Georgetown University noted, "The 'humanitarian' war advocates of recent years have often made every effort to suggest that it is our 'obligation' to intervene in extreme cases, any place in the world. We have been blamed mostly for inaction. Now, these same voices demand inaction."[65] What is more, moral authorities chose to focus on matters of international law and international authority rather than the humanitarian aspects of the war decision, injecting a highly idealized version of these political aspects of the debate but downplaying issues that called for moral judgment. Some just war scholars concluded that the lack of robust public debate about moral obligation to intervene was related to a general turn to a consequentialist version of the just war doctrine. George Weigel argued at the time that:

The just war tradition does not "begin," theologically, with a "presumption against war." Rather, classic just war thinking begins with moral *obligations:* the obligation of rightly-constituted public authorities to defend the security of those for whom they have assumed responsibility, and the obligation to defend the peace of order in world affairs. That is one reason why Aquinas put his discussion of just war within the *Summa*'s treatise on charity: public authorities are morally obliged to defend the good of *concordia*—the peace of order—against the threat of chaos.[66]

Testimony to the paucity of serious debate about the moral responsibilities to the Iraqi people in 2003 is a collection of essays published in 2005 by a group of intellectuals offering humanitarian arguments for war in Iraq, which included sharp critiques of the intellectual left, especially the European left. The authors argued that "the antiwar position was, in fact, something of a conservative one in that it aimed to preserve a regime of intolerable cruelty in order to preserve the deeply flawed system of international law that give both tyrants and democratically elected leaders equal seats at the table of international justice."[67] They also critiqued the evolution of a consequentialist version of the just war doctrine that has emerged in the last decade, one that "judges actions based on their outcomes rather than the intentions and motivations of the actors involved."[68] In summary, they pondered: "if the war had been waged by a liberal Democratic American president rather than a Republican one (who is objectively and universally loathed by almost all liberals around the world), whether more moral support for the war among liberals would have been the consequence."[69]

THE IRAQ AND KOSOVO DECISIONS COMPARED

The Iraq case shows that the ethical dimension was influenced by two contending agendas for the future of international order. Even though the Americans and British on one side, and the French and Germans on the other, differed on justification and authorization, both viewed Iraq, as they had Kosovo, in the context of a struggle between "civilization" and "barbarity." Their visions of civilization, however, were sharply at variance. The American and British leaders saw a struggle between human liberty and oppression, between democracy and dictatorship; the French and Germans saw a contest between multilateralism and unilateralism, between collective responsibility and superpower prerogative.[70]

Ethical determinations regarding authorization and justification were shaped by these contending viewpoints, just as these lenses continue today to color judgments on the decisions of early 2003. One such judgment is that important moral dimensions were not taken account of at the time; in particular, there was insufficient frank discussion of the humanitarian costs of the alternatives of war and of continued coercive diplomacy and containment.

The November 2002 vote on Security Council Resolution 1441 was viewed as a referendum on war with Iraq. France insisted that its vote in favor of the resolution was meant to "strengthen the role of the UN;"[71] just as in the Kosovo crisis this insistence reflected France's interest in strengthening its own international position as a permanent member of the Security Council. The United States and Britain saw UNSCR 1441 as fulfilling the last-resort principle; France and Germany disagreed, countering that "the conditions for using force against Iraq are not fulfilled."[72] In March 1999, NATO leaders had eventually agreed that they had exhausted diplomatic means after three Security Council resolutions and negotiations convened under threat of coercion had failed to resolve the crisis of Serb "ethnic cleansing" of ethnic Albanians in Kosovo.[73] Each nation found a combination of political, legal, and moral grounds that overcame resistance to the decision to intervene, whereas in Iraq they did not achieve consensus. Even so, the thinking behind each nation's decision was strikingly similar in both cases. What is more, unresolved questions about proper authority, justification, and the obligation to intervene remained unresolved.

Germany

In 1999, Germany and France initially demanded a UNSC mandate, insisting that without it the war would be illegal under international law. They later reversed their positions, for different reasons. Germany was reacting to a tension within the legalist tradition that pitted its post–World War II commitment to international law and multilateralism against its strong wish to be a responsible, reliable international partner.[74] The German position also revealed a tension within its moralist constituencies: its left-leaning coalition government was torn between a tradition of pacifism and a desire to uphold human rights and humanitarianism. In the end, the commitments to reliable international partnership and to humanitarian values overcame pacifism and insistence upon multilateralism. The result was a watershed event: the German aircrews participating in NATO's Operation Allied Force air campaign against Serbia were the first German military personnel ordered to participate in offensive military operations since 1945.[75] And, the decision had been made without a UNSC mandate.[76]

In 2003, the Germans again insisted that "the unity of the [UN Security] Council is of central importance" and, in light of that imperative, argued for a continuation of containment, sanctions, and no-fly zones.[77] Nonproliferation regimes had not, Bonn felt, been fully exploited; the Germans held that "peaceful means have therefore not been exhausted," that the Security Council was "crucial to world order" in the future, and that war should be avoided.[78] Absent in 2003 was the moral imperative of ongoing human rights abuses that had overcome Germany's pacifist tradition and misgivings about unilateralism. The argument that Germany should intervene in order to be a good NATO ally thus did not persuade the public. The humanitarian case was paid little attention in the case the government made against the Iraq war, a case that was largely shaped by domestic political concerns during an uphill reelection battle. The German case in 1999, then, was essentially a tension between elements of the legal and idealist traditions, in which the moral component tipped the scales toward intervention. 1n 2003, the German approach was also legalist, and because it allowed no military option at all, it was also idealist. Thus Germany's approach was idealized multilateralism, just as it was in 1999.

France

President Chirac also took an idealized stance during the Iraq debates regarding the necessary source of authority for war. He maintained that the UN was "the only legitimate framework for building peace, in Iraq and elsewhere" and that France would advance its principles through collective action.[79] Other French officials, meanwhile, were arguing that adherence to international law was a moral obligation, that only such law could legitimate the use of force, and that France must advance the idea of collective responsibility.[80] At home, Jacques Chirac's popularity soared in proportion to the anti-American nature of his stance.[81]

France's stance on Iraq closely mirrored its arguments in the Kosovo debates, in which its attitude toward proper authorization reflected a desire to bolster its position as a veto-bearing member of the Security Council; it thus rested authority solely on the authority of previous council resolutions.[82] Just as in the Iraq case, France had insisted upon a separate resolution authorizing war but in 1999 did not believe its international position was strong enough, or America's position weak enough, to press the issue as far as it did in 2003.[83] To reverse his stance on the UN mandate, president Jacques Chirac declared that "the humanitarian situation constitutes a ground that can justify an exception to a rule, however strong and firm it is."[84]

The insistence on a separate UNSC resolution reflected long-standing reservations about American dominance of NATO and European security affairs, and France's aspiration to a leadership role on the continent.[85] Throughout the Kosovo crisis, French officials expressed concern about "a new American unilateralism."[86] In January 1999, Prime Minister Jospin announced, "We're confronted with a new problem on the international scene. The United States often behaves in a unilateral manner and has difficulty in assuming the role it aspires to as organizer of the international community."[87] In February 1999, foreign minister Hubert Vedrine described the United States as a "hyperpower" that had to be counterbalanced. In an interview with *Liberation*, Vedrine suggested five steps to countering American power: solid nerves; perseverance; methodical widening of the bases of agreement among Europeans; cooperation at each stage with the United States, combining friendship and the will to be respected, while defending in all circumstances organized multilateralism and the prerogatives of the Security Council; preparation—politically, institutionally, and

mentally—for the moment when Europe has the chance to go farther.[88]
The French deemed 1999 too soon to defy the United States, but by
2003 they had clearly revised that estimate.

In both cases France framed its arguments in just war terms—in
particular, the fulfillment of the principle of last resort and just cause.
Whereas in 1999 France argued that NATO had just cause in the face
of Milosevic's barbarous crimes and continued recalcitrance, Saddam
Hussein's barbarity received comparatively little attention. The French
justification of the Kosovo campaign was as moral as it was legal, not
just because of humanitarian aims but in its sense of spreading French
values as universal norms, especially the "matter of human rights on
our continent."[89] Three years later, talk about spreading French values
continued, not in the form of human rights, but rather the need for
multilateralism in world order. The French approach in both cases was
thus essentially a hybrid of realpolitik and idealist thinking, with multilateralism supporting both.

Britain

The British insisted upon a sound legal basis for intervention in Iraq,
just as they had for the Kosovo campaign. In 1999, they had claimed
the existence of a "humanitarian exception" to the authority of the
Security Council and cited previous resolutions as a legal basis.[90] The
British attorney general declared that military action would not violate international law, though other lawyers insisted on the opposite.[91]
The British people insisted on either proof of the existence of weapons
of mass destruction or issuance of a UN mandate.[92] Politicians called
for a separate Security Council mandate for the reconstruction of Iraq,
in order to avoid a postwar occupation situation; the prime minister,
for domestic political purposes, persuaded the Americans to seek a second Security Council resolution for intervention. Yet the British stance
was as moral as it was legal. In 1999, Prime Minister Blair declared,
"This is a just war, based not on any territorial ambitions but on values.
We cannot let the evil of ethnic cleansing stand. . . . We have learned
twice before in this century that appeasement does not work. If we
let an evil dictator range unchallenged, we will have to spill infinitely
more blood and treasure to stop him later."[93] Blair further framed the
crisis as a fight between the forces of order and "a disintegration into
chaos and disorder" in which "many regimes . . . are undemocratic and
engaged in barbarous acts."[94]

Echoing his approach in 1999, Blair couched the threat in Iraq as
"disorder and chaos" that jeopardized other foreign policy aims such
as the alleviation of poverty, protection of the environment, and the

promotion of international health. The threat, he held, was embodied in states and groups that "hate our way of life, our freedom, our democracy."[95] As in the Kosovo case, the struggle was not with the people of the Iraqi nation but with "barbarous rulers" who defied collective norms and laws.[96] Thus the British argument, like the German position, was a combination of strong legalist and idealist approaches. Whereas the Germans saw tension between values and interests, Britons accepted what Blair called a "subtle blend of mutual self interest and moral purpose" in which "the spread of our values makes us safer."[97]

The United States

During debates within the U.S. government leading to both war decisions, justification was framed in terms of the national interest. By the end of the 1990s, the administration believed it had exhausted Congressional patience with requests for troops where vital national interests were not at stake. The Bush administration had run for office on a campaign promising a return to foreign policy based upon the national interest. Interest-based arguments resonated with the American people, as did emphasis on U.S. rather than UN authorization to act.

That said, the United States relied on legal arguments among its international constituency, namely on previous Security Council resolutions, to authorize intervention in Iraq. This way of thinking was also apparent in American just war arguments. Washington interpreted UNSCR 1441 and subsequent inspections as giving Saddam his last chance, beyond which lay force, the last resort. Secretary Powell later recalled, "We gave diplomacy every chance. . . . [W]e could wait no longer." The Americans made clear, however, that this was about power: "The United States of America has the sovereign authority to use force in assuring its own national security."[98] Legal justification formed the basis of American justification of the Kosovo campaign as well, and in that case, too, they relied upon previous Security Council resolutions. In both cases, the United States cited the threat to peace and regional stability as justifications. The impending humanitarian emergency was far more prominent in 1999 than in 2003. The fracas surrounding the evidence of Iraq's possession of weapons of mass destruction cast a shadow on humanitarian arguments.

It has become common to hear that the Americans employed international legal arguments to support a nakedly realist approach to the authorization for war. However, the roles of both law and power had their limits. While legal advisers suggested that the American presence in Iraq was technically an occupation, the moral imperative of "liberation" was more important. The president made Iraqi liberation the centerpiece of his 2003 Captive Nations Week address.[99] Stating his case in the UN General Assembly before the war, the president emphasized solidarity with the Iraqi people, who had, he said, "suffered too long in silent captivity." He explained, "Liberty for the Iraqi people is a great moral cause, and a great strategic goal."[100] Finally, the whole approach was couched as a great struggle for human liberty. The idea of liberation is central to idealist thinking, since ideas are seen as justifying revolution in international affairs.

In his well-known June 2002 West Point graduation speech, the president spoke of the American "commanders who [had] saved a civilization."[101] In his speech at the end of the initial invasion, he likened the American posture to Franklin D. Roosevelt's Four Freedoms, the Truman Doctrine, and Ronald Reagan's "evil empire" doctrine.[102] Clearly, Bush saw the state of the world as a struggle between the civilized forces of democracy and human liberty, on one side, and the barbaric forces of oppression on the other.[103] The American position in Kosovo and Iraq, like that of the French, was thus an idealized version of realism. Like the Germans and British, they had similar approaches but reached opposite conclusions on intervention. Likewise the German and French reached the same conclusion from different motives.

The three traditions—realism, internationalism, and idealism—were thus clearly present in the decision making of each of the four countries, and in very similar ways, from 1999 though 2003. All three dimensions had to be accommodated to make consensus possible. The lesson of the Kosovo case is that diverging attitudes can be reconciled if decision makers satisfy the demands of all three imperatives. It also points to an upswing in the power of moralist arguments, which forcefully challenged both strictly power-based calculations of national interest and attachment to international law.

Decision makers did not reach agreement on intervention in Iraq, as they had four years earlier, and policy and diplomacy have suffered thereby. In particular, the Iraqi people and the men and women of the coalition forces have lost the benefits that could have accrued from increased international cooperation. Western leaders continue to wrestle with the political and legal limitations of the current international system when trying to hurdle ever greater humanitarian emergencies and security dilemmas. It is not too late to recognize the lessons that the Kosovo and Iraq decisions offer.

CHAPTER 8

Conclusion

Whereas disregard and contempt for human rights have resulted in barbarous acts which have outraged the conscience of mankind....
Whereas it is essential, if man is not to be compelled to have recourse, as a last resort, to rebellion against tyranny and oppression, that human rights should be protected by the rule of law....
—Universal Declaration of Human Rights, 1948

Some say the Kosovo crisis was seen as a turning point for international politics, but was it a death knell for the international legal order? Can states take steps to heal the breach? The lesson of the collective Kosovo decision of the NATO nations was that if the demands of three contending imperatives—the fundamental, underlying "mixed motives"—are met, diplomacy benefits and consensus emerges. In 2003, in contrast, decision makers on both sides of the intervention debate showed disappointing unwillingness to recognize the lessons of the Kosovo campaign, and in this sense Iraq was an opportunity lost. The structural deficiencies that exacerbate discord may never be resolved, but if the underlying disputes on the implications of these structural realities are addressed, cohesive policy is possible. Even before then, there are some practical steps that states can take.

IN THE FUTURE, THE DISAGREEMENT OF 2003 IS
MORE LIKELY THAN THE CONSENSUS OF 1999
IF THINGS REMAIN THE SAME

The context of the Kosovo consensus was a period of great-power peace after the fall of the Berlin Wall. Many in Western liberal democracies eagerly expected, even demanded, the "peace dividend" in the form of waging war to make peace rather than in pursuit of naked national interest. The Atlantic alliance, having accomplished the purpose of its founding, sought new roles and missions, and limited intervention for humanitarian purposes thus figured prominently in its 1999 Strategic Concept. War in the Balkans, NATO's backyard, was another urgent reason why Western nations rallied around the Kosovo campaign. Just two years later, the Al Qaeda terrorists delivered the alliance a geopolitical fait accompli and changed the context in which war would be debated. Alliance countries accepted but did not embrace NATO's leadership role of the Afghanistan war in 2003, and some argue that national leaders have noted the heroism of their fallen men and women in that campaign as more like national sacrifices than contributions to an international campaign against a common enemy.[1]

The diplomatic debacle in the Iraq debate was in an important way the result of unresolved questions about international order made manifest in the debates about humanitarian intervention at the end of the twentieth century. Humanitarian war opened the legal and political door wider than it had been before to the legitimacy of war waged with moral purpose and without a Security Council mandate. But after the intervention, scholars and policy makers alike failed to resolve in a practicable way diverging views on international authority, views which led to diverging positions on proper justification for the use of force. This book exposes those underlying unresolved issues and in so doing shows how the positions the allies took in the Kosovo debate was consistent with the arguments they made in the Iraq debate, despite very different outcomes.

Today the UN Security Council and the governments in Washington, London, Paris, and Bonn in particular face the gathering storm in Iran. Tehran, where the leadership recently revealed a secret uranium enrichment plant, continues its invective against Israel and the West and threatens increased support for the insurgency against coalition forces in Iraq as well as for international terrorism and weapons proliferation. Meanwhile in Sudan, the leadership continues to outfox U.S. and European attempts to hold it accountable for the atrocities committed against its own people. The European pursuit of justice through the International Criminal Court has proven not only illusive but counter-effective.[2] The Obama administration's Sudan strategy seems to look a lot like its predecessor's by acknowledging this, despite its campaign rhetoric extolling it as a court of first resort.[3] Meanwhile at the Security Council, Russia will continue to push back at Western policies, especially in the case of Iran. China, which has expanded its national interests to Africa, where humanitarian intervention is most likely to be considered, will be more assertive in wielding its UNSC veto, as the case of Darfur demonstrates. In Europe, the post–World War II generation, embracing pacifism and rigid multilateralism in its worldview, will remain influential in the decades to come, and this will perpetuate tensions, such as between German foreign and domestic policies.[4] Washington, London, Bonn, and Paris, which have allied again to resolve the Iranian and other international crises, now do so without a full accounting of fundamental differences regarding what steps they can take to resolve them.

NEW RULES ARE NOT NEEDED FOR A GLOBAL GAME THAT NATIONS ARE NOT PLAYING

One misreading of the Kosovo war is that agreement about intervention was part of a broader transformation of international order into a transnational mindset. This was not the case, but neither did the Iraq war cause the world to revert, after four short years, to soulless realpolitik. Voices of transnationalism were indeed evident in the Kosovo decision, as they were in the Iraq debate. But none of the allies adopted such thinking as its primary motivation. The United States and France, as the foregoing chapters demonstrate, relied mostly on realist arguments, with international law adduced in support. Britain rested its case primarily on law, and so did Germany. The idealist notion that universal values or elite-inspired international norms trumped sovereignty was useful only as far as it went to help make the broader case for and against war. To the contrary, the role of national culture was evident in the way norms were employed. Rather than obeying human rights norms as imposed from outside the state, France promoted them as "French values" and Germany weighed them against the competing norm of pacifism before making its choice for war in Kosovo.[5] Hence, values entered through the democratic political process and not just through elite discourse. Nor did moral imperatives, even when shared among nations and cultures, necessarily result in similar policy choices.

This book identifies reliance upon older legal and moral frameworks in each nation's quest for legitimacy, when hard law such as the UN Charter, treaty law, or custom fails to provide. As one scholar recently noted, "There are by now no clear criteria for determining

how the intervention norm of the UN Pact should be interpreted, neither among politicians nor among legal scholars,"[6] and this was best
articulated by British defense secretary George Robertson, who said in
1999, "The principles of international law—indeed, international law
itself—did not start with the UN. International law preceded the UN,
and these principles are there whatever the UN charter says."[7] The
status of a UNSC mandate may have been undermined by the decision
in the case of Kosovo, which many scholars now argue was legitimate
even without a mandate. But so was it diminished by the Iraq decision when Germany and for a time France argued the war would have
been illegitimate even if it had a UN mandate. In both cases, moral
arguments offered an alternative form of legitimacy. In Kosovo, the
human rights and humanitarian imperative offered the alliance legitimacy in the form of justification for the war, allowing them to mollify
constituencies who would have preferred a mandate. In the Iraq case,
the moral argument for regime change to bring democracy lent legitimacy to the American and British cause, and a moralized argument
for a UN mandate galvanized opposition to the Iraq war among the
French and Germans. All of the leaders appealed to their constituencies by portraying the campaigns as struggles to save civilization from
barbarity. Sometimes they were in concert about who represented the
new barbarians: men like Slobodan Milosevic and Saddam Hussein
who abused their people were outside the boundaries of civilization
and were not entitled to the protections accorded by sovereignty. Yet
leaders sometimes went too far, such as claiming that war without a
UNSC mandate represents a new barbarity.

An important reason for disagreement about the justness of the Iraq
war, and a reason why world leaders now bitterly dispute the notion
of a "responsibility to protect," is that there is no one version of human
rights or humanitarian imperative. And there is no objective standard
by which states can measure rights violations. Enthusiasm for human
rights could be its undoing if steps are not taken to better define its
boundaries. The meaning of human rights has rapidly expanded even
to include highly controversial social policies, for example, and the
concept has become highly politicized and litigious in the last half century.[8] As a result, a barrier to agreement on a "responsibility to protect"
is not only due to disputes about enforcement, but also about the very
nature of the concept.[9] Already, activists have proposed a responsibility to protect a whole host of social groups and special interests.[10]

SOVEREIGNTY IS ALIVE AND WELL

A closer examination of what actually happened in the Kosovo decision shows that even though Serbian sovereignty was not a barrier to

their aerial campaign, the intervening powers articulated support for a traditional understanding of the concept of sovereignty. Not the least important was their assertion that the intervention was not a prelude to political sovereignty for Kosovo, a promise that was eventually broken in February 2008 when with UN and EU backing Kosovo declared independence from Serbia.

Popular sovereignty, a sort of forgotten aspect of modern debates about the concept of sovereignty, influenced the decision-making process throughout the debates in 1999 and 2003. The fact that Germans would not intervene in Iraq even with a UNSC mandate shows that public sentiment was more powerful than the duty of a sovereign nation to obey international law. French sentiment in 2003 allowed their leaders to make the daring international play at rebuking the United States on the world stage. And Americans and British publics in the case of Iraq, and all four nations in the case of Kosovo, wrestled with and eventually assented to the absence of a UN mandate. While scholars continue to refine their own versions of what sovereignty has become—conditional, individual, pooled—for the liberal democracies studied in these cases, sovereignty embodied preexisting norms of self-determination and liberty upon which a host of civil and political rights rest.[11] Sovereignty was thus weighed in the scales of decision making along with the newer norms of enforcing human rights and the humanitarian imperative—and it proved its value.

Scholars of international norms contend that a norm first emerges through powerful proponents or "entrepreneurs," is codified institutionally, then internalized in society. A norm of humanitarian intervention has trouble every step of the way. First, its promoters exhibited reservations, and even avid proponents have backed away in the post–September 11, 2001 era. Second, the attempt to codify the R2P norm in the World Summit 2005 document resulted in weak compromise language ascribing no "international" responsibility and thus no real change from the status quo, in which it is sovereign states that are responsible for protecting human rights. Third, a norm is said to be "internalized," that is, established as a new international norm, when the public stops debating it.[12] This book demonstrates that there is still a very contentious debate surrounding many aspects of humanitarian intervention.

Conversely, publics do not generally engage in debates about the meaning of sovereignty. Hence even if advocates for a new norm of humanitarian intervention or "responsibility to protect" rest their case in part on the belief that the nature of sovereignty had fundamentally changed in the 1990s, the evidence does not support it. Instead, the claim seems to be the result of focusing on a legalistic view of sovereignty rather than a more comprehensive view that includes national or cultural aspects of modern states. Certainly the humanitarian imperative and the democracy imperative show how far from the short-hand version of Westphalian sovereignty the world has come. That original idea, in which the ruler had no obligations to international law, is a far cry from the debates over intervention in Kosovo and Iraq. Neither Slobodan Milosevic nor Saddam Hussein abused their people or threatened regional stability with impunity when the resolve of the great powers was sufficient. Conversely, the old notion seems vindicated when one looks at Burma today, or North Korea or Sudan, where repeated attempts at nonmilitary international intervention have failed to alleviate the burden the people suffer from their leaders.

HUMANITARIAN AND HUMAN RIGHTS ENTHUSIASTS WHO SCATTERED AFTER THE IRAQ WAR SHOULD RECONVENE BUT REEVALUATE THEIR ASSUMPTIONS THAT NEW NORMS MUST BE CODIFIED IN LAW

Enthusiasts of humanitarian intervention engaged in robust debates in the 1990s about these issues. Witnessing the unity of the allies in March 1999, many believed the world was ushering in a new era in which powerful states would be duty-bound to rescue victims of mass atrocities and humanitarian emergencies. With few exceptions, these advocates fell silent in 2002–03 when George W. Bush proposed humanitarian goals in the Iraq war.[13] Proponents of human rights and humanitarianism were disappointed not only that President Bush would claim humanitarian motives for a war primarily waged for national interest, but also that he would claim such a war could be just. Some erstwhile interventionists reversed their positions in disillusionment. Some, like Bernard Kouchner when he was first a humanitarian activist and then a UN representative, believed that transforming the rules of war could transform the international order. Kouchner as France's foreign minister has since backed down from this high rhetoric and adopted a more realist worldview.[14]

The belief that the humanitarian wars of the 1990s hailed the transformation of war from self-interest to rescue is also a misreading of the case. While the French in 1999 advanced a world order based on "collective sovereignty," they did so not out of idealist adherence to transnationalism, but rather because of realist calculations of power: the desire to balance against the American *hyperpuissance*. Similarly, when France invoked moral reasons for intervention, they did so not out of universalist aims but rather to advance national interests. As French president Jaques Chirac said in 1999, "These are universal values of our republican tradition that we are defending."[15]

A related point is that proponents of human rights and humanitarianism today tend to conflate the just war doctrine with humanitarian intervention when critiquing the Iraq War. Ken Roth, the executive director of the human rights goliath Human Rights Watch, relied solely on a just war framework for determining that the war in Iraq did not qualify as humanitarian intervention.[16] As noted in chapters 3 and 7, many contemporary scholars like Roth have adopted a consequentialist approach to the just war tradition, and use the just war doctrine in support of an essentially pacifist position. These manipulations of the doctrine are not its original intent nor consistent with its logic, as the just war scholar James Turner Johnson has pointed out, and contributed to the fact that humanitarian considerations did not get a full hearing during the public debates before the Iraq war.[17] It is important to note that each of the four countries relied heavily on the just war ethic in its most traditional form: proper authority, just cause, and right intention. It is these three most basic tenets of the doctrine that helped nations consider, in turn, the three questions of authorization, justification, and obligation.

Another purpose for the new norms is the desire to create human rights enforcement mechanisms. The purpose would be to force the great powers, through international institutions, to intervene even when their publics do not share moral outrage, in the absence binding treaty obligations, or when national interests conflict. But this ignores another message from Kosovo. As Secretary Albright said, "Kosovo carries another lesson: political will is more important than additional institutional structures. The problem in Kosovo before we acted together was not the lack of appropriate institutions; it was the lack of agreement to use the institutions we have."[18] Recognizing this, world leaders did not assent to an "international" responsibility to protect in 2005, though some enthusiasts seem to believe so.

The authors of the 2001 report on "Responsibility to Protect" say that the norm's primary purpose is to shift emphasis from the right of powerful states to intervene in the right of citizens to be protected by their governments. But the term "international responsibility to protect" in the 2001 report is absent from the 2005 World Summit document national leaders negotiated, so there is no basis for claiming international consensus on this point. Even if consensus were achievable, using the U.N. system to hold states accountable for human-rights violations is problematic. The demise of the U.N. Human Rights Commission and the disrespect that nations show for the Human Rights Council that replaced it are well known. Less transparent but perhaps more insidious is the way U.N. human-rights treaty experts and U.N. special rapporteurs have been complicit in the abuse by reinterpreting treaty documents with a host of controversial new rights and undermining the credibility of the U.N. human-rights system.[19] Thus, while consensus built around a UN mandate can be an important political tool, and to some extent an emblem of moral right, leaders should be cautious about according the organization its own "moral authority."

Another reason for new binding rules is to hedge not against a lack of moral outrage, which has been evident whether or not allies chose to intervene, but of "political will." The way elites define political will deserves scrutiny, however. The United States and its allies are party to a binding treaty against genocide, yet none of them has concluded that the treaty is extraterritorial. Therefore the allies did not ignore binding treaty obligations due to a lack of political will. Rather, they interpreted their obligations and found that no legal obligation existed in 1994 during the Rwanda genocide, nor do they argue today that the Genocide Convention obligates intervention in the case of Darfur. The failure to act in Rwanda was, as Samantha Power has ably demonstrated, a lack of will on the part of leadership and the people. Public sympathy for the cause of war is essential to creating political will in liberal democracies where sovereignty rests with the people. Thus it is doubtful that the codification of a new norm, even if it had consensus among the elite human rights community, would overcome political resistance to war.

Proponents of new norms of intervention and protection should consider the possibility that the rise of the humanitarian imperative as practiced in the interventions of the 1990s is a temporary phenomenon, propelled by a surge in the popularity of human rights at a time after the end of the cold war when great power war was improbable and a "new world order" seemed imminent. Many seem to perceive the world in progressive terms, such that through human effort it can be improved and eventually perfected. Martin Wight noted that this strain of idealism (what he called revolutionism) has come and gone throughout modern history in waves, while realist and legalist thinking have remained steady streams since the Renaissance. There is no irrefutable reason to believe that the current upswing moralization propelled by transnational thinking will not run its course as well, but scholars and practitioners should beware of undermining traditionally accepted concepts of international legitimacy in the meantime. Rejecting the need for codification of moral norms into new laws or custom does not mean one opposes the notion that people must be protected from grave human rights abuses, or even that the task of protection sometimes falls to other nations. Rather, it is an effort to preserve those aspects of international legitimacy upon which nations can engage in mutual endeavors for international peace and security.

Opposing the proliferation and enforcement of new norms is part of a broader effort for getting states to act morally by fostering subsidiarity, whereby moral decisions are left up to the people of each nation and the leaders who represent them. It is an imperfect solution, but neither has the existence of codified law guaranteed that states will act morally when the time comes to do so.

One man trying to reconvene the debate is the UN secretary general's special assistant on R2P matters, Edward Luck, who is working assiduously to repackage the R2P idea and undermine its opposition. Speaking before the 64th General Assembly in September 2009, Luck seemed to recognize the lessons of Kosovo, especially the excesses of enthusiasm for new norms and a transformation of international law. "This is not 1999," he said, referring to the last time the General Assembly took up the question about humanitarian intervention and found it wanting. He assured them R2P "is a political, not a legal, concept based on well-established international law and the provisions of the UN Charter," that it seeks "to discourage unilateralism, military adventurism, and an overdependence on military responses to humanitarian need." Finally, he tried to allay the opposition of states big and small by assuring world leaders that the R2P and national sovereignty "are mutually reinforcing principles."[20] The intellectual embers of humanitarian intervention are still smoldering, and there are signs the debates can begin again with the benefit of hindsight.

In most need of the lessons of Kosovo is president Barack Obama. In his Nobel Prize acceptance speech, Obama said, "I believe that force can be justified on humanitarian grounds, as it was in the Balkans." This seems straightforward enough, but he immediately pointed to the mixed moral and political motives behind his belief: "Inaction tears at our conscience and can lead to more costly intervention later." Finally, he touched upon the hazards of diverging perspectives on proper authorization. While not offering a specific solution such as a UN mandate, he nonetheless argued that "if we refuse to follow [the rules] ourselves . . . our action can appear arbitrary, and undercut the future of intervention—no matter how justified." Like his predecessors, Obama is influenced by, but has not reconciled, the competing perspectives on waging humanitarian war. It is promising that President Obama is advised by human rights and humanitarian experts who have vowed "never again."[21] This bodes well for a reinvigorated debate in the future about the human costs for and against intervention.[22] On the other hand, he has staffed his administration with transnationalists as well. The combination could be a cocktail for reverting to the old reading of 1999 as "the beginning of the new age of human rights enforcement" as a means to transform international society through

international law.[23] Such a repeating of old thinking about 1999 must
be resisted.

STATESMEN SHOULD BE MORE RESPONSIBLE IN WHAT THEY SAY ABOUT PROPER AUTHORITY, JUSTIFICATION, AND OBLIGATION FOR THE USE OF FORCE AND AVOID HYPER-MORALIZATION OF ARGUMENTS ABOUT MULTILATERALISM

Policy makers can accept the dilemma of mixed motives and resist
temptations to exploit seeming inconsistencies in policy to their political advantage. They can instead ratchet down the rhetoric and accept,
as Michael Walzer urges, the fact that "the lives of foreigners don't
weigh that heavily in the scales of domestic decision making. So we
shall have to consider the moral significance of mixed motives."[24] In
both the Kosovo and Iraq cases, there existed neither strictly realpolitik nor purely legal, cooperative positions. Leaders can help publics
recognize the dilemma of diverging moral imperatives, just as they
acknowledge contending interests and varying, even conflicting, legal
interpretations.

Disagreements about what constitutes international legitimacy were
shaped by calculations of power on one hand and moral imperatives
on the other. One finding is that France's blocking the United States at
the UNSC in 2003 was explicitly articulated by French officials as early
as 1999. In the Kosovo case, France initially opposed plans for a U.S.-
led intervention in Kosovo but found that they had too weak a hand
to call the Americans on their lack of a UN mandate. The French reas-
sessed their position in 2003 and believed that due to various international circumstances, including the opportunity of German solidarity
presented by election politics, the time was right to oppose the United
States and consolidate French leadership internationally. French president Nicholas Sarkozy later offered a diplomatic apology for his predecessor's exploitation of the Iraq crisis, but the damage was done and
transatlantic relations remain strained.

As NATO nations begin to rework their Strategic Concept in 2010,
they should recognize, as they did in 1999 on the eve of the Kosovo
campaign, that the alliance cohesion hangs in the balance during fra-
cases about intervention. They should strive not to allow disagreements
about rules to undermine the enduring utility of the organization as
both a political and military arrangement with international authority.
If alliance leaders continue to take the organization for granted and pursue divisive rhetoric at the expense of long-term goals, the support of
their people for the organization will not be there when they need it.

The fact that the United States and other NATO nations brought their cases for war to the UN Security Council demonstrates that they believe the body to be an important tool of diplomacy. That no consensus was reached on explicit authorization for the uses of force shows that nations cannot always rely on UNSC authority. Further, both cases highlight the political usefulness of the UNSC while underscoring its legal or legislative weakness. Resort to the UNSC has its risks as well. The American decision to take their case for war with Iraq to the council, along with France's threat of a veto on a second resolution for war, undermined UN authority and meant the coalition forces went to war "under a cloud of diplomatic defeat."[25] What is more, the French threat had the opposite effect of the one they publicly claimed—to stop a war and advance multilateralism—by promoting action outside the UNSC, what many consider unilateralism, and sidelining those in the Bush administration who called for more deliberations.[26] During debates on Kosovo, the Russians made it clear that they would veto the action if brought to the UNSC but would be onboard if authority rested outside the UN. Thus Secretary of State Albright advised against seeking a separate UNSC resolution. This lesson was not internalized by the Bush administration or by prime minister Tony Blair, who urged President Bush to go to the UN in 2003.

Thus, appeal to the UNSC may have done more harm than good by endangering great power equipoise.[27] As the brewing crisis regarding Iran's emerging nuclear weapons program gains steam, the allies should keep in mind the cautionary lessons of Kosovo and Iraq. For their part, European leaders should not repeat the overly enthusiastic insistence that a UNSC mandate is required for the use of force, and drop the notion that a lack of UNSC mandate is somehow "illegal" or "immoral" as they did in the Kosovo and Iraq crises. While polling data suggest that most Europeans believe this, it is equally true that populations in the rest of the world, most notably in the United States, do not. Nor do the leaders of Russia and increasingly assertive China seem willing to authorize the use of force for causes that the United States and Europe deem morally justifiable, such as humanitarian emergencies. In such cases, a Security Council mandate should be approached as an important tool, but not the sole means of legitimacy. While some regional arrangements are subject to the UNSC, NATO is not and offers an equally legitimate and legal venue for action.

The just war criteria reemerged in the 1990s as a framework for moral arguments about the use of force and an important tool for testing the legitimacy of motives for and against war. In 2003, it at least made the language of proper authority, just cause, and right intention central in public pronouncements. In part, the ethic was popular with governments because it gave them general and persuasive norms to which to appeal, rather than specific and possibly binding laws. That such words resonate with publics, however, is no doubt the main reason leaders use them. Decision makers should continue to refine their understanding of just war principles as they apply to various situations, such as rogue states possessing WMD, reducing the temptation to wield just war doctrine solely as a political tool, and thus enhancing its usefulness in general.

Finally, governments should make the humanitarian and human rights case even if it is not central to the argument for or against war. One of the casualties of the trend toward polarization between the war on terror and the multilateral imperative was the thorough discussion of humanitarian considerations.

HUMAN RIGHTS EXPERTS AND HUMANITARIAN ADVOCATES SHOULD RENDER A FULL HEARING OF HUMANITARIAN CONSIDERATIONS FOR FUTURE WARS EVEN WHEN THEY DISAGREE WITH THE POLICIES OF THE GOVERNMENTS WHO PURSUE THEM

The United States and Britain produced reports regarding Saddam Hussein's abuses but did not refer to them extensively. Human rights and humanitarian officials were surprisingly absent from the debates. The French/German side argued for disarmament rather than regime change, whereas the American/British coalition called for the use of force. The human rights/humanitarian argument for the removal of Saddam Hussein but against the use of force was not fully heard, and this was a missed opportunity. First, the suffering of the Iraqi people, concealed for years by limited access, could have been more fully exposed. Second, such arguments would have resonated with publics and citizens, who deserved but did not see an open and careful weighing of the human costs and benefits of either containment or military intervention. Third, such an argument, convincingly made, would have increased pressure on regional regimes to censure Saddam Hussein. Finally, a full accounting of the humanitarian costs of intervening vs. failing to intervene may have, as some have argued, convinced Americans not to press toward war. Even if after a thorough consideration of humanitarian considerations, the coalition decided to wage war, such deliberation would have given the campaign added international legitimacy.

There is another, more cynical way to view the absence of the humanitarian voice in 2003, and that is that human rights activists were deliberately silent about the suffering of the Iraqi people because their voices may have lent credibility to the Bush argument for war. Such politicization of human rights is not new, as human rights activists have been accused, for example, of championing women's rights in the West, but ignoring the plight of other women, such as the Chinese women subjected to their government's brutal one-child policy. Ironically, it is the human rights advocate who often accuses governments of selectivity, such as intervening on behalf of Europeans in Kosovo but not for Africans in Rwanda. Yet this cuts both ways. Human rights advocates cannot pick and choose which people they defend just because they do not like the regime that chooses to defend them or the admixture of motives behind that action. Such politicization of human rights undermines the entire ethic, abetting skepticism from would-be advocates on one hand and providing excuses for national leaders who ignore the legitimate rights of their people and instead abuse them with impunity.

*   *   *

The moral dimension played an important role in the political and legal debates about authorization and justification of intervention in Kosovo and Iraq. The moral element was not merely "tacked on" or secondary; rather, it informed legal and political considerations, overcoming objections to the use of force in Kosovo and causing a standoff among NATO allies with regard to Iraq. The lesson is that, of the three imperatives that influence international behavior, recourse to moral imperatives will be increasingly important in the decades ahead, but that laws and institutions have not caught up to the social reality. This is nothing new. In the nineteenth century, the dominance of the realist tradition stimulated bilateral international relations and brought an institutionalized balance of power. In the twentieth century, the internationalist approach prevailed in the aftermath of two World Wars, and multilateralism and international institutions proliferated. Entering the twenty-first century, the moral imperative and its concomitant appeal to worldwide human solidarity is on the rise, fostered by transnational movements, the democratization of information technology, and other trends. Current political and legal structures are inadequate to address this increasingly collective consciousness, on one hand, and increasing transborder threats, state failure, and poverty on the other. Disputes over the legitimacy of unilateralism and multilateralism injected bitter dissent in an otherwise unprecedented period of great-power peace. The need is to move beyond ideological condemnation of unilateralism and seek multilateral diplomacy that integrates—by addressing them simultaneously—the persistence of realism, the embedded nature of international legal structures, and the reemergence of the idealist imperative.

A way to begin is to identify and bolster the elements of the old order that nations hold most dearly and in common. Norms of humanitarian intervention, protection, and prevention of WMD proliferation have all been proposed as ripe for codification, but states continue to resist engaging the matter. A decade and a half after the Rwanda genocide, decision makers have yet to develop criteria for responding to such crises, and this belies the promise that law, positive or customary, is the solution. Rather than seeking to create new norms for emerging threats, nations should give existing universal values a chance. Western intellectuals are often the quickest to question the universality of norms, such as those in the Universal Declaration of Human Rights.[28] They can do so only by ignoring the fact that the declaration had international authorship and offers international benefits. Likewise, critics may continue to argue that the trend away from United Nations mandates means that all talk of right and wrong should be expunged from the law and replaced by state practice. The Kosovo and Iraq decisions, however, show that moral talk *is* state practice. The reason is that, despite significant legal and political disagreements surrounding authorization and justification for forcible intervention, fundamental freedoms, to those who do not yet possess them, remain more than rhetorical.

It is a shame that what is lost in contentious debates about intervention is the very frame of reference at the center of them: the unique dignity of each human person. By learning the lessons that past debates about war waged to make peace have to offer, national leaders and their publics, scholars, and human rights advocates alike can balance the contending imperatives of foreign policy better prepared to protect and promote the value of human life and human dignity.

Notes

CHAPTER 1

1. See Conor Foley, *The Thin Blue Line: How Humanitarianism Went to War* (New York: Verso, 2008), 155–65.

2. David Rieff, "The Conversion of Bernard Kouchner," *The Daily Star,* August 3, 2007.

3. Interview with Edward Luck, special assistant to United Nations secretary general Ban Ki-moon, November 13, 2007.

4. Madeleine K. Albright, "The End of Intervention," *New York Times,* June 11, 2008.

5. James Turner Johnson, "Humanitarian Intervention after Iraq: Just War and International Law Perspectives," *Journal of Military Ethics* 5, no. 2 (2006): 114–27.

6. *National Security Strategy of the United States,* September 2002. http://georgewbush-whitehouse.archives.gov/nsc/nss/2002/.

7. Tony Capaccio, "Bush Preemptive Strike Doctrine under Review, May Be Discarded," *Bloomberg.com* October 16, 2009, http://www.bloomberg.com/apps/news?pid=newsarchive&sid=aw4BqFAVbkf8#.

8. For a discussion of the ethical dimensions of humanitarian intervention, see Terry Nardin and Melissa S. Williams, eds., *Humanitarian Intervention* (New York: New York University Press, 2006); for a political science critique see Thomas G. Weiss, *Humanitarian Intervention: War and Conflict in the Modern World* (Malden, Mass.: Polity, 2007); for a historical approach, see Gary J. Bass, *Freedom's Battle: The Origins of Humanitarian Intervention* (New York: Alfred A. Knopf, 2008); for an international legal perspective see Ellery Stowell, *Intervention in International Law* (Washington, D.C.: John Byrne & Co., 1921); and Michael Byers, *War Law: Understanding International Law and Armed Conflict* (New York: Grove Press, 2005).

9. Philip Alston and Euan MacDonald, eds., *Human Rights, Intervention, and the Use of Force* (Oxford: Oxford University Press, 2008), 10.

CHAPTER 2

1. James Holmes, "Myanmar Disaster: The dangers of Gunboat Compassion," *The Providence Journal,* May 21, 2008, http://www.projo.com/opinion/contributors/content/CT_holmes21_05–21–08_U3A5T20_v7.39c3136.html. For "Monroe Doctrine" in the Indian Ocean see James Holmes and Toshi Yoshihara, "Strongman, Constable, or Free-Rider? India's 'Monroe Doctrine' and Indian Naval Strategy," *Comparative Strategy,* Vol. 28, No. 4 (September 2009): 332–48.

2. Madeleine K. Albright, "The End of Intervention," *New York Times,* June 11, 2008.

3. Edward Luck, special assistant to the UN secretary general, interview with the author, November 13, 2007. See also Edward Luck, Remarks to the 64th General Assembly, September 1, 2009, http://www.ipacademy.org/news/general-announcement/98-general-assembly-passes-resolution-on-responsibility-to-protect.html.

4. For "Global Sheriff," see Richard N. Haass, *The Reluctant Sheriff: The United States After the Cold War* (New York: Council on Foreign Relations, 1997).

5. Ban Ki-moon, "Secretary-General's Message to United Nations University—International Crisis Group Conference on the Prevention of Mass Atrocities," New York, October 10, 2007.

6. *The Economist,* "An Idea Whose Time Has Come—and Gone?" July 23, 2009, http://www.economis.com/world/international/PrinterFriendly.cfm?story_id=14087788.

7. Statement by General Assembly president Miguel D'Escoto Brockmann at the Opening of the Thematic Dialogue of the General Assembly on the Responsibility to Protect, July 23, 2009, http://www0.un.org/ga/president/63/statements/openingr2p230709.shtml.

8. Ibid.

9. Steven Groves, "The U.S. Should Reject the U.N. 'Responsibility to Protect' Doctrine," *Heritage Foundation Backgrounder* #2130, May 1, 2008, http://www.heritage.org/Research/InternationalOrganizations/bg2130.cfm.

10. Peter Berkowitz, "Laws of Nations," *Policy Review,* April/May 2005. 71–81.

11. Ibid., 71–81.

12. Mohamed Sahnoun, *Somalia: The Missed Opportunities* (Washington, D.C.: United States Institute of Peace, 1994), 45.

13. Ibid., 46–47.

14. Javier Perez de Cuellar, quoted in Mohamed Sahnoun, *Somalia: The Missed Opportunities,* 49.

15. Boutros Boutros-Ghali, quoted in Mohamed Sahnoun, *Somalia: The Missed Opportunities,* 49.

16. Kofi Annan, "Peacekeeping and National Sovereignty," in *Hard Choices: Moral Dilemmas in Humanitarian Intervention"* Jonathan Moore, ed. (New York: Rowman and Littlefield, 1998), 56–57.

17. Gareth Evans and Mohamed Sahnoun, "The Responsibility to Protect," *Foreign Affairs,* November/December 2002.

18. Report of the International Commission on Intervention and State Sovereignty: XI, December 2001, http://www.dfait-maeci.gc.ca/iciss-ciise/menu-en.asp.

19. Kofi Annan, quoted in UN Press Release SG/SM/7136, GA/9596, "Secretary General Presents His Annual Report to General Assembly," September 20, 1999, http://www.un.org/News/Press/docs/1999/19990920.sgsm7136.html.

20. Kofi Annan, Secretary General's Annual Report to the General Assembly, September 20, 1999, Press Release SF/SM/7136/GA/9596, quoted in Nicholas Wheeler, *Saving Strangers: Humanitarian Intervention in International Society*, (Oxford: Oxford University Press, 2000), 285.

21. Anne Marie Slaughter, lecture at Brown University, March 31, 2003.

22. J. L. Holzgrefe and Robert O. Keohane, eds., *Humanitarian Interventions: Ethical, Legal, and Political Dilemmas* (Cambridge: Cambridge University Press, 2003), quoted in Conor Foley, *The Thin Blue Line: How Humanitarianism Went to War* (London: Verso, 2008), 155.

23. J. Bryan Hehir, interview by the author, March 21, 2001.

24. J. Bryan Hehir, "Military Intervention and National Sovereignty," in *Hard Choices: Moral Dilemmas in Humanitarian Intervention*, ed. Jonathan Moore (Lanham, Md.: Rowman & Littlefield, 1998), 30.

25. Michael Walzer, *Just and Unjust Wars: A Moral Argument with Historical Illustrations* (New York: Basic Books, 1977), 108.

26. Ibid., 101–2.

27. See for example David Chandler, *From Kosovo to Kabul: Human Rights and International Intervention* (London: Pluto, 2002). Ian Brownlie notes that humanitarian intervention began in the nineteenth century as a vague doctrine employed when it served the interest of the intervening state. He remarks that a possible genuine humanitarian intervention was France's occupation of Syria and policing the coast in 1860–61 to protect Maronite Christians. Ian Brownlie, *International Law and the Use of Force by States* (Oxford: Oxford University Press, 1963), 568.

28. Cited in Chandler, *From Kosovo to Kabul*, 165.

29. Gary J. Bass, *Freedom's Battle: The Origins of Humanitarian Intervention* (New York: Alfred A. Knopf, 2008), 41.

30. Martin Wight, *International Theory: The Three Traditions* (New York: Holmes and Meier, 1992), 7–24.

31. Ibid., 258.

32. In reference to Thomas Hobbes (1588–1679, English philosopher), Hugo Grotius (1583–1645, Dutch jurist and statesman), and Immanuel Kant (1724–1804, German philosopher). Stewart Patrick, "Beyond Coalitions of the Willing: Assessing U.S. Multilateralism," in *Strategy and Force Planning*, 4th ed., ed. Security, Strategy, and Forces Faculty (Newport, R.I.: Naval War College, 2004), 589–602.

33. Jaane Haaland Matlary, "The Legitimacy of Military Intervention: How Important Is a UN Mandate?" *Journal of Military Ethics* 3, no. 2 (2004): 129–41.

34. Hedley Bull, *The Anarchial Society: A Study of Order in World Politics*, (New York: Columbia University Press, 1977); Paul R. Viotti and Mark V. Kauppi, *International Relations Theory: Realism, Pluralism, Globalism and Beyond*, (Boston: Allyn and Bacon, 1999); Stewart Patrick, "Beyond Coalitions of the Willing: Assessing U.S. Multilateralism," *Ethics & International Affairs* 17, no. 1 (Spring 2003): 37–46; Jaane Haaland Matlary, "The Legitimacy of Military Intervention: How Important is a UN Mandate?" *Journal of Military Ethics* 3, no. 2 (2004): 129–41; Euan MacDonald and Philip Alston, "Sovereignty, Human Rights, Security," in *Human Rights, Intervention, and the Use of Force*, ed. Philip Alston and Euan MacDonald (Oxford: Oxford University Press, 2008), 6–7.

35. Carl von Clausewitz, *On War*, edited and translated by Michael Howard and Peter Paret (Princeton: Princeton University Press, 1976), 605.

36. *International Theory: The Three Traditions*, edited by Gabriele Wight and Brian Porter (London: Leicester University Press for the Royal Institute of International Affairs, 1991; London and New York: Continuum for the Royal Institute of International Affairs, 2002), 16 [emphasis in the original].

37. Martin Wight, "An Anatomy of International Thought," in *Four Seminal Thinkers in International Theory: Machiavelli, Grotius, Kant and Mazzini*, edited by Gabriele Wight and Brian Porter (London: Oxford University Press, 2005), 145.

38. Martin Wight, *Power Politics*, ed. by Hedley Bull and Carsten Holbraad (London: Leicester University Press for the Royal Institute of International Affairs, 1978), 293.

39. Henry Kissinger, *Diplomacy* (New York: Simon & Schuster, 1994), 761.

40. Martha Finnemore and Kathryn Sikkink define "sovereignty" not as a norm but as an institution, which is a collection of norms. Martha Finnemore and Kathryn Sikkink, "International Norm Dynamics and Political Change," *International Organization* 52, no. 4 (Autumn 1998): 891.

41. Francis Fukuyama, *America at the Crossroads: Democracy, Power, and the Neoconservative Legacy* (New Haven: Yale University Press, 2006), 48–49.

42. John Fonte, "Global Governance v. the Liberal Democratic Nation State," *Family Security Matters*, June 18, 2008.

43. Wight, *Power Politics*, 101. Wight believed that the most extraordinary example of this was the signing of the 1928 Kellogg Briand Pact midway between the two World Wars, which was to outlaw the use of aggressive armed force.

44. Fukuyama, *America at the Crossroads*, 48–49.

45. von Clausewitz, *On War*, 606–7.

46. The "unipolar moment" was articulated by the columnist Charles Krauthammer in 1990 to explain the period immediately after the fall of the Soviet Union in which the United States was the sole superpower. Charles Krauthammer, "The Unipolar Moment," *Foreign Affairs* (Winter 1990/91): 22–33; Charles Krauthammer, "The Unipolar Moment Revisited," *The National Interest* (Winter 2002/2003): 5–17.

47. Right to intervene or "right of interference": see, for example, Bernard Kouchner, "The Future of Humanitarianism," 23rd annual Morgenthau Memorial Lecture on Ethics and Foreign Policy, Carnegie Council on Ethics and International Affairs, March 2, 2004, http://www.cceia.org/media/23%20MML.pdf. Doctrine of limited preemption: George W. Bush, *The National Security Strategy of the United States of America 2002* (Washington, D.C.: September 2002), 15. http://georgew bush-whitehouse.archives.gov/nsc/nss/2002/nss5.html.

CHAPTER 3

1. The Independent International Commission on Kosovo, *Kosovo Report: Conflict, International Response, Lessons Learned* (Oxford: Oxford University Press, 2000).

2. Kofi Annan, *Preventing War and Disaster: A Growing Global Challenge* (New York: 1999 Annual Report on the Work of the Organization, 1999), 20, quoted in Nicholas Wheeler, *Saving Strangers: Humanitarian Intervention in International Society* (Oxford: Oxford University Press, 2000), 294.

3. Ibid.

4. Kofi A. Annan, "Two Concepts of Sovereignty," *The Economist*, September 18, 1999, 49.

5. For a look at NATO's expanding role see David Yost, *NATO Transformed: The Alliance's New Roles in International Security* (Washington, D.C.: United States Institute for Peace, 1998). For a look at the evolution of the relationship between the Security Council and NATO, see N. D. White, *Keeping the Peace* (Manchester: Manchester University Press, 1997).

6. Lawrence S. Kaplan, *NATO and the United States: The Enduring Alliance* (Boston: Twayne Publishers, 1988), 36. See also Kaplan, *NATO's First Fifty Years* (Westport, Conn.: Praeger, 1999), 4.

7. See also David Yost, *Nato and International Organizations* (Rome: NATO Defense College, 2007), 32.

8. Willem Van Eekelen, *The Security Agenda for 1996: Background and Proposals*, CEPS Paper No. 64 (Brussels: Centre for European Policy Studies, 1995).

9. James B. Steinberg, U.S. deputy assistant to the president for national security affairs, April 25, 1999, in *NATO and Southeastern Europe: Security Issues for the Early 21st Century*, ed. Dimistris Keridis and Robert L. Pfaltzgraff (Dulles, Va.: Brassey's, 2000), 49.

10. *NATO Handbook* (Brussels: NATO Office of Information Press, 1999), 68.

11. David Yost, *NATO Transformed*, 256–57.

12. Ibid.

13. Peter Anderson, "Airstrike: NATO astride Kosovo," in *The Kosovo Crisis: The Last American War in Europe?*, ed. Tony Weymouth and Stanley Henig (London: Reuters, 2001), 199.

14. The NATO handbook states that, "The North Atlantic Treaty of April 1949—which is the legal and contractual basis for the Alliance—was created within the framework of Article 51 of the United Nations Charter, which reaffirms the inherent right of independent states to individual or collective defence." *NATO Handbook*, 23.

15. Lawrence Kaplan, *The Long Entanglement: NATO's First Fifty Years* (Westport, Conn.: Praeger, 1999), 4.

16. North Atlantic Council, Strategic Concept, para. 10, November 7, 1991, quoted in Yost, *NATO Transformed*, 191.

17. North Atlantic Council, The North Atlantic Treaty, Article 5, April 4, 1949, http://www.nato.int/docu/basictxt/treaty.htm.

18. Ibid.

19. General Sir Michael Rose, House of Commons testimony, February 3, 1999, http://www.parliament.the-stationery-office.co.uk/pa/cm/cmhansrd.htm.

20. Annan, "Two Concepts of Sovereignty," 49.

21. David Yost, *NATO Transformed*, 254.

22. Wesley Clark, *Waging Modern War* (New York: Public Affairs, 2001), xxiii.

23. Conor Foley, *The Thin Blue Line: How Humanitarianism Went to War* (London: Verso, 2008), 36.

24. Ibid., 32.

25. See also David Rieff, *At the Point of a Gun: Democratic Dreams and Armed Intervention* (New York: Simon & Schuster, 2005).

26. Foley, *The Thin Blue Line*, 36.

27. Ibid., 119.

28. Angela Merkel, Remarks at NATO 60th Anniversary, March 26, 2009, http://natomonitor.blogspot.com/2009/04/let-strategic-concept-debate-begin.html.

29. Nicholas Wheeler, *Saving Strangers: Humanitarian Intervention in International Society* (Oxford: Oxford University Press, 2000), 4. Wheeler cites Martin Wight's essay, "International Legitimacy," in *System of States*, ed. H. Bull, as one of the earliest considerations of the subject of international legitimacy, and credits Inis Claude with the conclusion that power and legitimacy are complimentary.

30. See for example Byron York, "President of the World," *National Review Online*, July 25, 2008, http://article.nationalreview.com/?q=ZTJkNzIwZWQ5MTU3OWY2ODM2OWRkZjczYjVjMGU4Yjg=

31. Martin Wight, *Power Politics*, ed. Hedley Bull and Carsten Holbraad (New York: Holmes & Meier, 1978), 95.

32. Michael Walzer, *Just and Unjust Wars: A Moral Argument with Historical Illustrations* (New York: Basic Books, 1977), 107.

33. Ibid., 107.

34. *Charter of the United Nations* (New York: United Nations, 1945), Article 2 paragraph 4.

35. Thomas M. Franck and Nigel S. Rodley, "After Bangladesh: The Law of Humanitarian Intervention by Military Force," cited in Walzer, *Just and Unjust Wars*, 106.

36. Ellery Stowell, *Intervention in International Law* (Washington, D.C.: John Byrne and Co., 1921), 103.

37. Lionel Jospin, French prime minister, Speech to the National Assembly, Paris, March 26, 1999.

38. Jacques Chirac, speech, March 26, 1999.

39. Madeleine Albright, October 8, 1998, Department of State transcript.

40. Steny H. Hoyer (Democrat—Maryland).

41. Wight, *Power Politics*, 96–98.

42. Tony Blair, Economic Club of Chicago, April 22, 1999, reprinted in *Strategy and Force Planning*, 3rd ed., ed. Security, Strategy, and Forces Faculty (Newport, R.I.: U.S. Naval War College Press, 2000), 588.

43. Paul Ramsey, *The Just War: Force and Political Responsibility* (New York: Charles Scribner's Sons, 1968), 30.

44. Thomas Aquinas, *Summa Theologica*, in *Aquinas: Selected Political Writings*, ed. A. P. D'Entreves. Translated by J. G. Dawson (Oxford: Basil Blackwell, 1954), 159–61.

45. Michael Walzer, *Just and Unjust Wars*, 106.

46. James F. Childress, "Just-War Theories: The Bases, Interrelations, Priorities, and Functions of Their Criteria," in *War, Morality and the Military Profession*, ed. M. M. Wakin (Boulder, Co.: Westview Press, 1986), 427–45.

47. Philip Alston and Euan MacDonald, *Human Rights, Intervention, and the Use of Force* (Oxford: Oxford University Press, 2008).

48. Jack Goldsmith and Eric Posner, "Moral and Legal Rhetoric in International Relations: A Rational Choice Perspective," University of Chicago Law & Economics, Olin Working Paper 108, November 2000.

49. Ibid.

50. Anthony Lake and Roger Morris, "The Human Reality of Realpolitik," *Foreign Policy*, Fall 1971, 157–62.

51. Margaret Thatcher, TV interview with London Weekend Television, *Weekend World*, January 6, 1980.

52. Wight, *Power Politics*, 292.

53. Ibid., 291–92.

54. For example, see the ICRC publication *Hard Choices: Moral Dilemmas in Humanitarian Intervention*, ed. Jonathan Moore (Lanham, Md.: Rowman and Littlefield, 1998).

55. Joel Rosenthal, lecture at the Fletcher School of Law and Diplomacy, November 2001.

56. Wight, *Power Politics*, 293.

57. Ibid.

58. Ibid.

59. Caroline Moorehead, *Dunant's Dream: War, Switzerland and the History of the Red Cross* (London: Harper Collins, 1998), 25.

60. Ibid., 29.

61. Mary Ann Glendon, *A World Made New: Eleanor Roosevelt and the Universal Declaration of Human Rights* (New York: Random House, 2001).

62. Ibid., 170.

63. Ibid., 87.

64. Ibid., 176.

65. Glendon notes that after its approval, the document was attacked as "pink" in the United States and as an Anglo-American interference with national sovereignty in the Soviet Union. Smaller states felt a growing resentment toward the United States linked to a perceived racism, and dissent rose in Britain to oppose observance of the declaration. Politics in France also prevented the embracing of the declaration. For Rene Cassin, the French Republic was a revolution, but for its leader, President de Gaulle, France was a fortress, and human rights were not central to France's foreign and security policy. Thus, from the beginning the contest with sovereignty, self-determination of peoples, and economic, racial, and religious issues was at the center of the debate about universal human rights. Also in contest was the Anglo-American perspective that accords primacy to individuals, vs. the European, Latin American, and Asian traditions that acknowledge the needs of the community when acknowledging personal rights.

66. Ibid., 217.

67. Samuel P. Huntington, *The Clash of Civilizations and the Remaking of World Order* (New York: Simon & Schuster, 1996).

68. Martin Wight, *International Theory: The Three Traditions* (London: Holmes & Meier, 1992), 61.

69. Ibid., 62.

70. In Britain, vehicles for propaganda included the Department for Enemy Propaganda, as well as the Political Intelligence Department in the Foreign Office, the BBC, and the Political Warfare Executive. The Soviets used the agitprop department of the central committee for propaganda at home, working with the 7th Department of Political Administration of the Red Army for enemy propaganda. The U.S. Office for War Information was established in 1942, including an office in London. The Psychological Warfare Division was set up at Supreme Headquarters of the Allied Expeditionary Forces in Europe (PWD/SHAEF). Whereas the Anglo-American propaganda effort was ad hoc, the German system, established by Dr. Joseph Goebbels in 1926 in order to bring Hitler to power, was highly

centralized. See Zybnek Zeman, *Selling the War: Art and Propaganda in World War II* (New York: Exeter, 1982).

71. Zeman, *Selling the War.*

72. One Italian poster depicted an American pilot as a gangster, standing with his machine gun over a bullet-riddled, lifeless child; another showed an African American soldier desecrating a church. One American "This is the enemy" poster showed Hitler's image in the smoke and fire behind a child, weeping in a pool of blood, holding the hand of his dead mother, who lay impaled in a mass open grave. A UK poster juxtaposed a bombed British city with a fist-shaking Hitler delivering his own words of 1933, "One is either a German or a Christian . . . you cannot be both." Germans equated Bolshevism and Judaism and depicted a Jewish-featured Josef Stalin ravaging the civilization of "Fortress Europe." See Zeman, *Selling the War.*

73. See, for example, Hansard debates of March 25, 1999. George Galloway tied reaction to media images to hypocrisy and limited resources, saying, "There are conflicts or humanitarian catastrophes . . . all over the globe and the Queen does not have enough soldiers to address every one of them. If we are to deal only with those that are thought televisual enough to make it on to the transitory editorial choices of the British or other media, we will be drawn into a very selective use of international force." http://www.publications.parliament.uk/cgi-bin/semaphore server?DB=semukparl&FILE=search.

74. See for example Michael Ignatieff, "The Stories We Tell: Television and Humanitarian Aid," in *Hard Choices: Moral Dilemmas In Humanitarian Intervention* (Lanham, Md.: Rowman and Littlefield, 1998), 287–302; Larry Minear, Colin Scott, and Thomas Weiss, *The News Media, Civil War and Humanitarian Action* (Boulder, Co.: Lynne Rienner Publications, 1996); Susan D. Moeller, *Compassion Fatigue: How the Media Sell Disease, Famine, War and Death* (New York: Routledge, 1998).

75. Eric Burman, "Innocents Abroad: Western Fantasies of Childhood and the Iconography of Emergencies," *Disasters* 18, no. 3 (1994): 238–53.

76. Mark Duffield, "The Symphony of the Damned: Racial Discourse, Complex Political Emergencies and Humanitarian Aid," *Disasters: The Journal of Disaster Studies and Management* 20, no. 3 (1996): 178.

77. Martin Wight, *Systems of States,* ed. Hedley Bull (London: Leicester University Press, 1977), 153.

78. Samantha Power, *A Problem From Hell: America and the Age of Genocide* (New York: Harper Collins, 2003); and Norman Podhoretz, *World War IV: The Long Struggle against Islamofascism* (New York: Doubleday, 2007).

79. National Security Strategy of the United States 2002, section V, http://georgewbush-whitehouse.archives.gov/nsc/nss/2002/nss5.html.

80. Critics of NATO's aerial campaign in Kosovo have sometimes openly accused the West of racism for intervening to save the European Kosovars after having refused to intervene to save Africans in Rwanda in 1994. The accusation is reminiscent of the one Wight recounts from the *Middle East Journal* in 1955, which stated that, "Most Indians actually believe that the US dropped the atom-bomb on the Japanese rather than the Germans because she wanted to spare white Europeans but did not care about killing Asians. This also, they believe, is why the US tests the H-bomb only in the Pacific." Wight, *International Theory: The Three Traditions,* 87.

CHAPTER 4

1. Thomas F. Walsh III, "Operation Allied Force: Setting a New Precedent for Humanitarian Intervention?" (Masters thesis, Naval Postgraduate School, Monterey, Calif., 2000).

2. The term *unilateral* is used here to mean a single sovereign state. Louis Henkin argues that for the purposes of the international legal order, the NATO intervention was unilateral because it was exercised without a UNSC mandate. See Louis Henkin, "Kosovo and the Law of 'Humanitarian Intervention,'" *American Journal of International Law* 93, no. 4 (October 1999): 824–28.

3. William Cohen, PBS *Frontline* interview, http://www.pbs.org/wgbh/pages/frontline/shows/Kosovo/interviews/choen.html.

4. See Henkin, "Kosovo and the Law of 'Humanitarian Intervention'"; and Catherine Guicherd, "International Law and the War in Kosovo," *Survival* 41, no. 2 (Summer 1999): 19–34.

5. Report of the International Commission on Intervention and State Sovereignty, December 2001, http://www.dfait-maeci.gc.ca/iciss-ciise/report2-en.asp. See also Gareth Evans and Mohamed Sahnoun, "The Responsibility to Protect," *Foreign Affairs* (November/December 2002); and Gareth Evans, "The Responsibility to Protect," *NATO Review* (Winter 2002).

6. For an account of the political party debates see Peter Rudolf, "Germany and the Kosovo Conflict," in *Alliance Politics, Kosovo, and NATO's War: Allied Force or Forced Allies?*, ed. Pierre Martin and Mark R. Brawley (New York: Palgrave, 2000), 135.

7. NATO Web site, http://www.nato.int/kosovo/history.htm#2.

8. Alex J. Bellamy, *Kosovo and International Society* (New York: Palgrave, 2002), 76.

9. For further analysis of the role of the UNSC in the Kosovo conflict see David Travers, "The UN: Squaring the Circle," in *The Kosovo Crisis: The Last American War in Europe?*, ed. Tony Weymouth and Stanley Henig (London: Reuters, 2001), 246–77.

10. Ibid., 254–55.

11. North Atlantic Assembly, *NATO in the 21st Century*, October 2, 1998, cited in Richard Caplan, "Humanitarian Intervention: Which Way Forward?" *Ethics & International Affairs* 14 (2000): 31.

12. For perspectives on strategic culture see Colin S. Gray, *Nuclear Strategy and National Style* (Lanham, Md.: Hamilton Press, 1986); and Alastair Iain Johnston, "Strategic Culture: A Critique," in *Cultural Realism: Strategic Culture and Grand Strategy in Chinese History* (Princeton, N.J.: Princeton University Press, 1995.

13. William Cohen, *Lehrer NewsHour* interview, June 18, 1998, http://www.pbs.org/newshour/bb/europe/jan-june98/cohen_6–18.html.

14. Ibid.

15. Sandy Berger, Online *NewsHour* interview, October 2, 1998, http://www.pbs.org/newshour/bb/europe/july-dec98/berger_10-2.html.

16. Ibid.

17. Jamie Rubin press conference, U.S. Department of State, October 7, 1998, http://www.hri.org/docs/statedep/1998.

18. Richard Holbrooke, quoted in Bellamy, *Kosovo and International Society*, 93.

19. Confidential interview with the author.

20. Madeleine Albright, Newshour with Jim Lehrer interview, February 18, 1999. http://www.pbs.org/newshour/bb/europe/jan-june99/albright_2-18.html.

21. Charles Kupchan, "Kosovo and the Future of U.S. Engagement in Europe," in Martin and Brawley, *Alliance Politics, Kosovo, and NATO's War*, 76.

22. *Democrats voting "yes" included:* Akaka, Hawaii; Baucus, Mont.; Bayh, Ind.; Biden, Del.; Boxer, Calif.; Breaux, La.; Bryan, Nev.; Byrd, W.Va.; Cleland, Ga.; Conrad, N.D.; Daschle, S.D.; Dodd, Conn.; Dorgan, N.D.; Durbin, Ill.; Edwards, N.C.; Feinstein, Calif.; Graham, Fla.; Harkin, Iowa; Inouye, Hawaii; Johnson, S.D.; Kennedy, Mass.; Kerrey, Neb.; Kerry, Mass.; Kohl, Wis.; Landrieu, La.; Lautenberg, N.J.; Leahy, Vt.; Levin, Mich.; Lieberman, Conn.; Lincoln, Ark.; Mikulski, Md.; Moynihan, N.Y.; Murray, Wash.; Reed, R.I.; Reid, Nev.; Robb, Va.; Rockefeller, W.Va.; Sarbanes, Md.; Schumer, N.Y.; Torricelli, N.J.; Wellstone, Minn.; Wyden, Ore. *Democrats voting "no" were:* Bingaman, N.M.; Feingold, Wis.; Hollings, S.C. *Republicans voting "yes" were:* Abraham, Mich.; Chafee, R.I.; DeWine, Ohio; Hagel, Neb.; Hatch, Utah; Jeffords, Vt.; Lugar, Ind.; Mack, Fla.; McCain, Ariz.; McConnell, Ky.; Roth, Del.; Shelby, Ala.; Smith, Ore.; Snowe, Maine; Specter, Pa.; Warner, Va. *Republicans voting "no" were:* Allard, Colo.; Ashcroft, Mo.; Bennett, Utah; Bond, Mo.; Brownback, Kan.; Bunning, Ky.; Burns, Mont.; Campbell, Colo.; Collins, Maine; Coverdell, Ga.; Craig, Idaho; Crapo, Idaho; Domenici, N.M.; Enzi, Wyo.; Fitzgerald, Ill.; Frist, Tenn.; Gorton, Wash.; Gramm, Texas; Grams, Minn.; Grassley, Iowa; Gregg, N.H.; Helms, N.C.; Hutchinson, Ark.; Hutchison, Texas; Inhofe, Okla.; Kyl, Ariz.; Lott, Miss.; Murkowski, Alaska; Nickles, Okla.; Roberts, Kan.; Santorum, Pa.; Sessions, Ala.; Smith, N.H.; Stevens, Alaska; Thomas, Wyo.; Thompson, Tenn.; Thurmond, S.C.; Voinovich, Ohio. Republican not voting: Cochran, Miss.

23. Charles Kupchan, "Kosovo and the Future of U.S. Engagement in Europe," 76.

24. "When You've a Moment, Bill," *The Economist*, September 24, 1998, http://findarticles.com/p/articles/mi_hb5037/is_199809/ai_n18283606/.

25. Ibid.

26. Ibid.

27. Bellamy, *Kosovo and International Society*, 87.

28. See Wesley Clark, *Waging Modern War* (New York: Public Affairs, 2001).

29. Lawrence Kaplan, *The Long Entanglement: NATO's First Fifty Years* (Westport, Conn.: Praeger, 1999), 191.

30. Charles Kupchan, "America and Europe: From Pacifier to Partner," in Dimitris Keridis and Robert L. Pfaltzgraff Jr., eds., *NATO and Southeastern Europe: Security Issues for the Early 21st Century* (Dulles, Va.: Brassey's, 2000), 34.

31. Dana Rohrabacher, Online *NewsHour* interview, March 11, 1999.

32. Bellamy, *Kosovo and International Society*, 87.

33. Louise Richardson, "A Force for Good in the World? Britain's Role in the Kosovo Crisis," in Martin and Brawley, *Alliance Politics, Kosovo, and NATO's War*, 154.

34. Bellamy, *Kosovo and International Society*, 87.

34. Ibid., 154.

36. Foreign Broadcast Information Service (FBIS) Daily Report, March 29, 1999.

37. Anthony Weymouth, "Why War, Why NATO," in Weymouth and Henig, *The Kosovo Crisis*, 3.

38. Richardson cites a phrase often quoted by Blair and Robin Cook, Britain's foreign secretary, that Britain was a "force for good" in the world. They used the same expression describing the United States. Richardson, "A Force for Good in the World?" 159.

39. Tony Blair, *Frontline* interview, http://www.pbs.org/wgbh/pages/front line/shows/kosovo/interviews/blair.html.

40. Ibid.

41. George Robertson, House of Commons testimony, March 24, 1999, http://www.parliament.the-stationery-office.co.uk/pa/cm199900/cmselect/cmdfence/347/34707.htm.

42. General Sir Michael Rose, House of Commons testimony, February 3, 1999, http://www.parliament.the-stationery-office.co.uk/pa/cm199900/cmselect/cmdfence/219/21908.htm.

43. Adrian Hyde-Price, "Berlin Republic Takes to Arms," *The World Today*, June 1999, 13, quoted in Martin and Brawley, *Alliance Politics, Kosovo, and NATO's War*, 131.

44. Bellamy, *Kosovo and International Society*, 75.

45. Joschka Fischer, quoted in "Germany: Green's Leader Warns against Ignoring UN in Kosovo Intervention," BBC Worldwide Monitoring, October 3, 1998.

46. Quoted in Bellamy, *Kosovo and International Society*, 93.

47. Nicholas Wheeler, *Saving Strangers: Humanitarian Intervention in International Society* (Oxford: Oxford University Press, 2000), 262.

48. "Germany May Not Participate in Possible Intervention in Kosovo," *Xinhua News Agency*, October 8, 1998.

49. Rudolf, "Germany and the Kosovo Conflict," 134.

50. Ibid., 135.

51. Ibid., 137.

52. Manfred Woerner, quoted in David Yost, *NATO Transformed: The Alliance's New Roles in International Security* (Washington, D.C.: United States Institute for Peace, 1998), 189–90.

53. Rudolf, "Germany and the Kosovo Conflict," 134–35.

54. Sabrina P. Ramet and Phil Lyon, "Germany: The Federal Republic, Loyal to NATO," in Weymouth and Henig, *The Kosovo Crisis*, 91.

55. Ibid., 94.

56. Ibid., 93.

57. Ministere des Affaires Etrangeres Dossiers d'archive, "Legal Basis of the Action Undertaken by NATO (Paris, March 25, 1999)," http://www.france.diplomatie.fr/actual/ dossiers/kossovo/kossovo.html.

58. Craig R. Whitney, "French are Gearing up to Join in Dousing the Flames in Kosovo," *The New York Times*, January 25, 1999, A6.

59. Ibid.

60. David Yost, *NATO Transformed*, 253.

61. Hubert Vedrine, quoted in Craig Whitney, "Western Officials Say Accord on Kosovo Seems Uncertain," *The New York Times*, July 4, 1998, A6.

62. Ibid.

63. Alex Macleod, "Kosovo: France and the Emergence of a New European Security," in Martin and Brawley, *Alliance Politics, Kosovo, and NATO's War*, 113.

64. Ibid.

65. Bernard Lamizet and Sylvie Debras, "France: Questions of Identity," in Weymouth and Henig, *The Kosovo Crisis*, 107.

66. Ibid., 117.

67. Macleod, "Kosovo: France and the Emergence of a New European Security," 116.

68. Keridis and Pfaltzgraff, *NATO and Southeastern Europe*; and Fraser Cameron, *The Foreign and Security Policy of the European Union Past, Present and Future* (Sheffield: Sheffield Academic Press, 1999).

69. The author participated in negotiations between the United States and Europe regarding sanctions under the Helms Burton Act from 1996–97 as an assistant to the under secretary of commerce for international trade.

70. "That Awkward Relationship," *The Economist*, May 14, 1998.

71. Macleod, "Kosovo: France and the Emergence of a New European Security," 125.

72. *Le Monde*, April 9, 1999, quoted in Lamizet and Debras, "France: Questions of Identity," 115.

73. Bellamy, *Kosovo and International Society*, 93.

74. Francisco Suarez, S.J. (1548–1617).

75. Martin Wight, *International Theory: The Three Traditions.*, 39.

76. Ibid., 40.

77. Rudolf, "Germany and the Kosovo Conflict," 136.

78. Tony Blair, April 14, 1999, quoted in Stanley Henig, "Britain: To War for a Just Cause," in Weymouth and Henig, *The Kosovo Crisis*, 49.

79. Wesley Clark, interview with the author, November 19, 2002.

CHAPTER 5

1. NATO launched a sustained air strike campaign, *Operation Deliberate Force*, beginning on August 30, 1995, against Bosnian Serb military targets in response to a Bosnian Serb mortar attack on civilians in Sarajevo.

2. Michael Glennon, *Limits of Law, Prerogatives of Power: Interventionism after Kosovo* (New York: Palgrave, 2001), 25.

3. Leon Feurth, national security advisor to Vice President Gore, 1993–2000, and member of Principals and Deputies committee meetings on the Kosovo crisis, interview with the author, Tufts University, March 13, 2003.

4. William Clinton, letter to Senate leaders, October 6, 1998, Congressional Record—Senate S11899.

5. President William J. Clinton, February 4, 1999. Papers of the William J. Clinton Administration, http://ftp.resource.org/gpo.gov/papers/1999/1999_vol1_163.pdf.

6. *Charter of the United Nations*, Article 51.

7. Yoram Dinstein, The 13th Waldemar A. Solf Lecture in International Law, *Military Law Review* 166 (2000): 93–108.

8. Legal counsel staff to the chairman, Joint Chiefs of Staff 1999, interview with the author, August 20, 2001.

9. William J. Clinton, "Remarks at a North Atlantic Treaty Organization Commemorative Ceremony," April 23, 1999, in *Public Papers of the Presidents of the United States, William J. Clinton, 1999, Book I—January 1 to June 30, 1999* (Washington, D.C.: United States Government Printing Office, 2000).

10. Legal counsel staff to the Chairman, Joint Chiefs of Staff 1999, interview with the author, August 20, 2001.

11. General Wesley Clark, interview with the author, Tufts University, November 19, 2002.

12. National Security Council legal counsel staff 1999, interview with the author, August 9, 2001, Naval War College.

13. Legal counsel staff to the Chairman, Joint Chiefs of Staff 1999, interview with the author, August 20, 2001.

14. Madeleine Albright, October 8, 1998, Department of State transcript.

15. Madeleine Albright, policy address on Kosovo, February 4, 1999, Department of State transcript.

16. Bob Dole, Senator (Republican-Kansas), speech to the International Republican Institute, September 22, 1998, http://www.fas.org/man/dod-101/ops/docs/s980923-kosovo2.htm.

17. Senator Sam Brownback, Congressional Record, Senate, p. S3110 March 23, 1999, http://thomas.loc.gov/r106/r106.html.

18. Senator Strom Thurmond, S3114, March 23, 1999.

19. Senator Kay Bailey Hutchinson, October 7, 1998 hearing, U.S. Senate.

20. Senator John Kerry, S3118, March 23, 1999.

21. Senator Robert Byrd, S3115, March 23, 1999.

22. Rep. John Lewis (D-Georgia) cited a moral obligation to use force to stop the killing of innocent Kosovar Albanians, Congressional Record, House, p. H1664, March 24, 1999, http://thomas.loc.gov/r106/r106.html.

23. Senator John Warner, S118, March 23, 1999.

24. Senator Carl Levin, S3112, March 23, 1999.

25. Senator John Warner and Senator Joseph Lieberman, interviews of October 1, 1998, PBS *NewsHour* Online.

26. Senator Joseph Biden, "Kosovo: A Test for NATO," delivered at The Atlantic Council of the United States, Washington, D.C., March 25, 1999, http://Biden.senate.gov/press/speeches/atlantic.htm.

27. Jonathan Landay, "Kosovo, Next Balkan Boilover?" *The Christian Science Monitor International*, March 6, 1998, http://www.csmonitor.com/durable/1998/03/06/intl/intl.4.html.

28. Senator Frank Lautenberg, S115, March 23, 1999.

29. Senator John McCain, S10796, September 23, 1998.

30. Ibid. See the Melian Dialogue in Thucydides, *History of the Peloponnesian War* (London: Penguin, 1972), 400–408.

31. Senators who had traveled to Kosovo and who cited personal antipathy for Milosevic included Joseph Biden (D-Delaware) and Christopher Dodd (D-Connecticut), S2203, March 18, 1998.

32. Senator Joseph Biden (D-Delaware), S10582, September 18, 1998.

33. George Robertson, *Hansard,* March 25, 1999.

34. S/PV.3988, March 24, 1999.

35. Robertson, *Hansard,* March 25, 1999.

36. Adam Roberts, "NATO's Humanitarian War over Kosovo," *Survival,* Autumn 1999, 106.

37. Tony Blair, "Doctrine of the International Community," speech delivered at the Economic Club of Chicago, April 22, 1999, in *Strategy and Force Planning,* 3rd ed. (Newport: U.S. Naval War College Press, 2000), 588.

38. Ibid.

39. Ibid.

40. Robertson, *Hansard,* March 25, 1999.

41. S/PV.3937, October 24, 1998.

42. Prime Minister Tony Blair, "Chaos and Disorder," House of Commons, March 23, 1999.

43. Robin Cook, House of Commons, March 25, 1999, http://www.parliament.the-stationery-office.co.uk/pa/cm199899/cmhansrd/vo990325/debindx/90325-x.htm.

44. Ibid.

45. General Sir Michael Rose, House of Commons, February 3, 1999, http://www.parliament.the-stationery-office.co.uk/pa/cm199899/cmhansrd.

46. Ibid.

47. Ibid.

48. Peter Nonnenmacher, "Dragon-Slayer in the Heart of Europe," *Main Frankfurter Rundschau*, March 24, 1999, FBIS-WEU-1999–0323.

49. Stefan Klein, "With a Brave Yes," *Munich Sueddeutsche Zeitung*, March 24, 1999, FBIS-WEU-1999–0324.

50. Maartje Rutten, "From St. Malo to Nice: European Defence: Core Documents," *Institute for Security Studies of the WEU 2001*, http://www.iss-eu.org/chaillot/chai47e.html#p.

51. Tony Blair, October 25, 1998 press conference, quoted in Rutten, "From St. Malo to Nice."

52. Madeleine Albright, December 7, 1998, *Financial Times*, quoted in Rutten, "From St. Malo to Nice."

53. German troops had participated in earlier crisis management operations in the 1990s, including service in Somalia, Cambodia, and Bosnia. See David Yost, *NATO Transformed: The Alliance's New Roles in International Security* (Washington, D.C.: United States Institute for Peace, 1998), 189.

54. Gregor Schöllgen, University of Erlangen, "Putting Germany's Post-Unification Foreign Polity to the Test," *NATO Review* 41, no. 2 (1993). http://www.nato.int/docu/review/rev93-2.htm.

55. Karl Kaiser and Klaus Becher, cited in Yost, *NATO Transformed*, 266.

56. Spyros Economides and Paul Taylor, in *The New Interventionism 1991–1994: United Nations Experience in Cambodia, former Yugoslavia and Somalia*, ed. James Mayall (Cambridge: Cambridge University Press, 1996), 82–83.

57. *Decisions of the Bundesverfassungsgericht—Federal Constitutional Court—Federal Republic of Germany Vol. 1/I and 1/II International Law and Law of the European Communities, 1952–1989* (Baden-Baden: Nomos Verlagsgessellschaft, 1992).

58. Rainer Baumann and Gunther Hellman, "Germany and the Use of Military Force: 'Total War', the 'Culture of Restraint', and the Quest for Normality," *German Politics* 10, no. 1 (April 2001), http://www.frankcass.com/jnls/gp_v10.htm.

59. Basic Law for the Federal Republic of Germany (Grundgesetz, GG), Preamble, http://www.iuscomp.org/gla/statutes/GG.htm#Preamble.

60. Rudolf Scharping, interview with Richard Meng, Main Frankfurter Rundschau, March 27, 1999, FBIS-WEU-1999–0327.

61. Gerhard Schroeder, March 24, 1999, quoted in Alexander Weinlein, "Friedliche Losung mit militarischen Mitteln 24 Marz 1999: Erster Kampfeinsatz der Bundeswehr," http://www.das-parlament.de/2001/10/Titelseite/2001_10_001_4751.html.

62. Hans Christian Stroebele (Alliance90/Greens), March 26, 1999, Bundestag proceedings, http://www.bundestag.de/aktuell/bp/1999/bp9901/9901034b.html.

63. "Majority of Greens Support NATO Air Strikes in Serbia," *Main Frankfurter Rundschau*, FBIS-WEU-1999–0324.

64. "PDS Suit Challenging NATO Operation Dismissed," *German News* (English Edition), March 25, 1999, http://www.mathematik.uni-ulm.de/de-news/1999/03/2522.html.

65. Minutes of the meeting between Gerhard Schroeder and President Clinton, August 4, 1998, quoted in Andreas Zumach, "Rambouillet, ein Jahr danach," http://www.blaetter.de/kommenta/zuma0300.htm.

66. Gerhard Schroeder, "German Security Policy at the Threshold of the 21st Century," presented at the Conference for Security Policy, Munich, February 6, 1999, http://www.byndesregierung.de.

67. Rudolf Scharping, interview with Richard Meng, *Main Frankfurter Rundschau*, Internet version, March 27, 1999, FBIS-WEU-1999–0327.

68. Baumann and Hellmann, "Germany and the Use of Military Force."

69. S/PV.3868, March 31, 1998.

70. Ibid.

71. Basic Law for the Federal Republic of Germany (Grundgesetz, GG) article 25, available at http://www.iuscomp.org/gla/statutes/GG.htm#25

72. "Jurists Question NATO's Kosovo Deployment," *Main Frankfurter Rundschau*, March 29, 1999, FBIS-EEU-1999–0328.

73. "Volmer: Milosevic Counts on Greens' Pacifism against NATO," *Main Frankfurter Rundschau*, March 27, 1999, FBIS-WEU-1999–0327.

74. Scharping, interview with Richard Meng, *Main Frankfurter Rundschau*, March 27, 1999, FBIS-WEU-1999–0327.

75. "Volmer: Milosevic Counts on Greens' Pacifism against NATO."

76. Jacques Chirac, Press Conference at Palazzo Vecchio, Florence, October 6, 1998, cited in Ivo H. Daalder and Michael E. O'Hanlon, *Winning Ugly: NATO's War to Save Kosovo* (Washington, D.C.: Brookings Institution, 2000), 44.

77. S/PV.3937, October 24, 1998.

78. S/PV.3868, March 31, 1998.

79. *PBS Frontline*, "War in Europe," http://www.pbs.org/wgbh/pages/front line/shows/kosovo/etc/cron.html.

80. Hans-Georg Ehrhart, "France and NATO: Change by Rapprochement? Asterix' quarrel with the Roman Empire," paper of January 2000, Hamburg, Germany, http://edoc.vifapol.de/opus/volltexte/2008/563/pdf/hb121.pdf.

81. Eric Rouleau, "French Diplomacy Adrift in Kosovo," *Le Monde Diplomatique*, December 1999, 5, http://mondediplo.com/1999/12/04rouleau.

82. Jaques Chirac, statement in Berlin, March 24, 1999, French Ministry of Foreign Affairs, http://www.france.diplomatie.fr/actual/dossiers/kossovo/ko ssovo.gb.html.

83. See Lionel Jospin, speech of the prime minister to the National Assembly, Paris, March 26, 1999.

84. Schöllgen, "Putting Germany's Post-Unification Foreign Policy to the Test."

85. Available at French Embassy in the United States Web site, http://www. info-france-usa.org/.

86. Ehrhart, "France and NATO."

87. Ibid.

88. See Rouleau, "French Diplomacy Adrift in Kosovo."

89. Jospin, March 26, 1999.

90. S/PV.3868, March 31, 1998; S/PV.3937, October 24, 1998.

91. Chirac, March 24, 1999.

92. Jospin, March 26, 1999.

93. Lionel Jospin, March 30, 1999.

94. Lionel Jospin, March 31, 1999.

95. Jospin, March 30, 1999.

96. Chirac, March 24, 1999.

97. Hubert Vedrine, March 29, 1999.

98. Jospin, March 26, 1999.

99. Hubert Vedrine, March 25, 1999.

100. Ibid.

101. S/PV.3988, March 23, 1999.

102. S/PV.3989, March 26, 1999.

103. Jospin, March 26, 1999.

104. Chirac, March 24, 1999.

105. Jacques Chirac, March 26, 1999.

106. Ibid.

107. Jospin, March 26, 1999.

108. Ibid.

109. Jospin, March 31, 1999.

110. Ibid.

111. Ibid.

112. Hubert Vedrine, quoted in Rouleau, "French Diplomacy Adrift in Kosovo," *Le Monde Diplomatique*, December 1999, http://mondediplo.com/1999/12/04rouleau.

113. John Vinocur, "Going It Alone, U.S. Upsets France; So Paris Begins a Campaign to Strengthen Multilateral Institutions," *International Herald Tribune*, February 3, 1999, 1.

114. Lionel Jospin, quoted in John Vinocur, "Going It Alone, U.S. Upsets France; So Paris Begins a Campaign to Strengthen Multilateral Institutions," *International Herald Tribune*, February 3, 1999, 1.

115. Hubert Vedrine, quoted in John Vinocur, "Going It Alone, U.S. Upsets France; So Paris Begins a Campaign to Strengthen Multilateral Institutions," *International Herald Tribune*, February 3, 1999, 1.

116. Ibid.

117. Jacques Chirac, quoted in John Vinocur, "Going It Alone, U.S. Upsets France; So Paris Begins a Campaign to Strengthen Multilateral Institutions," *International Herald Tribune*, February 3, 1999, 1.

CHAPTER 6

1. Tony Blair, "Doctrine of the International Community," speech at the Economic Club of Chicago, April 22, 1999, in *Strategy and Force Planning*, 3rd ed., ed. Strategy and Force Planning Faculty (Newport, Rhode Island: U.S. Naval War College Press, 2000), 587–97.

2. William J. Clinton, press conference, March 19, 1999.

3. Ibid.

4. William J. Clinton, *Statement by the President to the Nation*, March 24, 1999. Office of the Press Secretary transcript.

5. Russel Frank Weigley, *The American Way of War: A History of United States Military Strategy and Policy* (Bloomington: Indiana University Press, 1977).

6. Max Boot, *The Savage Wars of Peace: Small Wars and the Rise of American Power* (New York: Basic Books, 2002).

7. The doctrines, articulated by secretary of defense Caspar Weinberger and later chairman of the Joint Chiefs of Staff General Colin Powell, called for clear objectives, overwhelming force, and an exit strategy before committing U.S. troops to an operation.

8. Mary Kaldor, *New and Old Wars: Organized Violence in a Global Era* (Stanford, Calif.: Stanford University Press, 1999).

9. Richard Haass, *Intervention* (Washington, D.C.: Carnegie Endowment, 1994).

10. Among these classical strategists, Haass includes Clausewitz, Mahan, Hart, Fuller, Douhet, and Mitchell. He argues that the just war doctrine was adapted to the cold war nuclear environment of self-restrained limited war by defense thinkers such as Henry Kissinger, Bernard Brodie, Morton Halperin, Thomas Schelling and Robert Osgood.

11. Examples include Iran, Guatemala, and the Dominican Republic, as well as the failed "Bay of Pigs" intervention into Cuba.

12. Concerning when to use force, secretary of defense Caspar Weinberger set out six rules: "1) U.S. or allies' interests at stake; 2) use all necessary forces to win; 3) clear political and military objectives; 4) be ready to change the commitment if the objectives change; 5) support from American people and Congress; and 6) commit U.S. forces only as a last resort." See Colin Powell, *My American Journey* (New York: Random House, 1995), 303.

13. Ibid.

14. President Clinton, quoted in William Durch, ed., *UN Peacekeeping, American Policy, and the Uncivil Wars of the 1990s* (New York: St. Martin's Press, 1996), 56.

15. David Malone, *Decision Making in the UN Security Council: The Case of Haiti, 1990–1997* (Oxford: Clarendon Press, 1998), 180.

16. Durch, *UN Peacekeeping, American Policy, and the Uncivil Wars of the 1990s*, 47.

17. Mary Ann Glendon, "Rights Babel: Thoughts on the Approaching 50th Anniversary of the Universal Declaration of Human Rights," lecture at De Sales University, 1996, http:www4desales.edu/~philtheo/Glendon.html.

18. In *A Problem from Hell: America and the Age of Genocide* (New York: HarperCollins, 2003), Samantha Power analyzes the reticence with which the United States ratified the 1948 Convention on the Prevention and Punishment of the Crime of Genocide (Genocide Convention). Similar situations have occurred with the International Criminal Court (ICC), the Convention on the Rights of the Child, and the Convention on the Elimination of All Forms of Discrimination against Women (CEDAW). Several reasons have been given for resistance to ratification, including lack of domestic consensus on the contents of conventions signed by American officials. For example, the U.S. military has expressed concern that the ICC will be used by opponents to bring unjustified suits against American military and civilians. Another controversy is that CEDAW has been promoted by its advocates in the UN as a means of forcing governments to legalize abortion, which has been labeled as a "reproductive right" guaranteed by the convention. See Doulas Sylva and Susan Yoshihara, "Rights by Stealth: The Role of UN Human Rights Treaty Bodies in the Campaign for an International Right to Abortion," *National Catholic Bioethics Quarterly* 7, no. 1 (Spring 2007): 97–128. http://www.c-fam.org/docLib/20080425_Number_8_Rights_By_Stealth.pdf Governments may claim exceptions to certain articles of some conventions when signing them, in the form of reservations or less formal explanations of position.

19. Alberto Coll, "Kosovo and the Moral Burdens of Power," in *War over Kosovo: Politics and Strategy in a Global Age,* ed. Andrew J. Bacevich and Eliot Cohen (New York: Columbia University, 2001), 126.

20. For a critical view of the Clinton administration's "pragmatic Wilsonianism" see Stanley Hoffman, "The Crisis of Liberal Internationalism," *Foreign Policy* 98 (1995).

21. Staff, office of peacekeeping and humanitarian assistance, Department of Defense, first Clinton administration, interview with the author, April 6, 2001, Cambridge, Mass.

22. "The Clinton Administration's Policy on Reforming Multilateral Peace Operations," May 1994, 3. http://www.grandslacs.net/doc/2280.pdf

23. Martin L. Cook, "'Immaculate War:' Constraints on Humanitarian Intervention," *Ethics & International Affairs* 14 (2000): 61.

24. The author is grateful to Samantha Power for this point.

25. *Declarations and Reservations by the United States of America Made upon Ratification, Accession or Succession of the Genocide Convention.* http://www.prevent genocide.org/law/convention/reservations/

26. Holly Burkhalter, Physicians for Human Rights, argued on April 9, 1999, that the Serb campaign throughout 1998 and 1999 was genocide. See "Statement on Kosovo Genocide," http//www.glypx.com/balkanwitness/genocide.htm. After the start of the air campaign, British defense secretary George Robertson said, "We are confronting a regime which is intent on genocide," in "NATO, British Leaders Allege 'Genocide' in Kosovo," March 29, 1999, CNN.com, http://www.cnn.com/WORLD/europe/9903/29/refugees.01/. In September 2001, a United Nations court ruled that genocide had not taken place in Kosovo. See "Kosovo Assault Was Not Genocide," BBC, September 7, 2001, http://www.globalpolicy.org/security/issues/kosovo1/2001/0907genocide.htm.

27. Senate Joint Resolution authorizing air strikes on Serbia, February 23, 1999.

28. U.S. Code; Chapter 50A; Section 1091.Genocide, http://www.preventgeno cide.org/law/domestic/uscode.htm.

29. Charles Krauthammer argues that there is an inherent contradiction in the practice of humanitarian intervention: "Humanitarian war requires means that are inherently inadequate to its ends," and he therefore claims that President Clinton did not miscalculate the effect of coercion without casualties on the "blood averse" American public. The lesson for Clinton, rather, was that Americans were tolerant of losses for first-tier interests. Americans accepted the loss of 146 troops in the Gulf War with little complaint. Loss of life for humanitarian emergencies was not as acceptable. Charles Krauthammer, "The Short, Unhappy Life of Humanitarian War," *The National Interest,* Fall 1999, 5–8.

30. Ian Johnstone, "Security Council Deliberations: Justification and Persuasion on the Basis of Law," unpublished paper, The Fletcher School of Law and Diplomacy, 2002.

31. Legal staff to secretary of state Madeleine Albright, interview with the author, July 23, 2001.

32. Confidential interview by the author, February 20, 2001.

33. Leon Fuerth, interview by the author, March 13, 2003.

34. Ibid.

35. Ibid.

36. For one analysis of the institutional resistance to human rights policy, see Albert O. Hirschman, *The Rhetoric of Reaction: Perversity, Futility, Jeopardy* (Cambridge, Mass.: Belknap, 1991).

37. Confidential interview with the author, February 23, 2001. The official referred to the reluctant sector of the population as "Jacksonians," referring to Walter Russell Mead's article, "The Jacksonian Tradition," which claims that the most influential constituency among the American voting public are philosophical descendants of Andrew Jackson: unwilling to use force unless a convincing national interest argument is made, and then desirous of using overwhelming force to defeat the enemy. See Walter Russell Mead, "The Jacksonian Tradition and American Foreign Policy," *The National Interest,* Washington, D.C. *1999/2000.*

38. James A. Baker, III, *The Politics of Diplomacy: Revolution, War & Peace 1989–1992* (New York: Putnam, 1995), 480.

39. Richard Holbrooke, October 14, 1998 interview, PBS *NewsHour with Jim Lehrer.*

40. Richard Holbrooke stated that Serbs were imposing a paraffin test on the Albanians that they said helped them catch KLA "terrorists" by determining whether they had fired weapons. These tests were allegedly administered at sites where Serbs were distributing rebuilding materials to the Kosovar Albanians. Holbrooke interview on PBS *Frontline,* October 14, 1998.

41. Sandy Berger, PBS *Frontline* interview, October 23, 1998.

42. Cited in David Chandler, *From Kosovo to Kabul: Human Rights and International Intervention* (London: Pluto Press, 2002), 165.

43. Jack Straw, "Strategic Priorities for British Foreign Policy," http://www:fco. gov.uk.

44. William Wallace, "Foreign Policy and National Identity in the United Kingdom," *International Affairs* 67, no. 1 (1991), 65–80.

45. See references to parliamentary debates during the campaign against the spreading influence of the European Court of Human Rights in William Wallace, "What Price Interdependence? Sovereignty and Interdependence in British Politics," *International Affairs* 62, no. 3 (Summer 1986): 382–85. See also Kenneth Younger, "Britain in Europe: The Impact on Foreign Policy," *International Affairs* 48, no. 4 (1972): 579–92.

46. William Wallace, "Foreign Policy and National Identity in the United Kingdom," 69.

47. J.C.D. Clark, "The Strange Death of British History? Reflections on Anglo-American Scholarship," *The Historical Journal* 40, no. 3 (1997): 806.

48. "Rights Brought Home: The Human Rights Bill," http://www.archive. official-documents.co.uk/document/hoffice/rights/chap1.htm.

49. See Mary Ann Glendon, *A World Made New: Eleanor Roosevelt and the Universal Declaration of Human Rights* (New York: Random House, 2001); and Andrew Moravcsik, "Explaining the Emergence of Human Rights Regimes: Liberal Democracy and Political Uncertainty in Postwar Europe," Weatherhead Center for International Affairs, Harvard University, December 1998, http://www.ciaonet. org/wps/moa02/.

50. Moravcsik, "Explaining the Emergence of Human Rights Regimes," para. 1.14.

51. Available at http://www.leeds.ac.uk/law/hamlyn/echr.htm.

52. Tony Blair, Preface to British government green paper, "Rights Brought Home," 1997.

53. Iain McLean, review of W. L. Miller, A. M. Timpson, and M. Lessnoff, *Political Culture in Contemporary Britain: People and Politicians, Principles and Practice* (Oxford: Clarendon Press, 1996), in *The British Journal of Sociology* 48, no. 3 (September 1997): 533–34.

54. Tony Blair, "Doctrine of the International Community.".

55. MORI poll in *Mail on Sunday*, http://www.mori.com/polls/1999/ms990327.shtml.

56. Ibid.

57. Michael Howard, *Hansard*, March 25, 1999. http://hansard.millbank systems.com/commons/1999/mar/25/kosovo#S6CV0328P0_19990325_HOC_184.

58. Michael Howard and Tony Lloyd, both in *Hansard*, March 25, 1999.

59. Ken Livingston, *Hansard*, March 25, 1999.

60. Donald Anderson, *Hansard*, March 25, 1999.

61. George Robertson, *Hansard*, March 25, 1999.

62. Tony Blair, "Doctrine of the International Community."

63. Tony Benn, *Hansard*, March 25, 1999.

64. Alan Clark, *Hansard*, March 25, 1999.

65. Tony Blair, "Doctrine of the International Community."

66. Bowen Wells and Frank Cook, both in *Hansard*, March 25, 1999.

67. See John Duffield, *World Power Forsaken: Political Culture, International Institutions, and German Security Policy* (Stanford, Calif.: Stanford University Press, 1998). Duffield points out the errors of John Mearsheimer, Kenneth Waltz, and others who predicted Germany's rearmament and withdrawal from NATO following reunification.

68. Harmut Mayer, "Early at the Beach and Claiming Territory? The Evolution of German Ideas on a New European Order," *International Affairs* 73, no. 4 (1997): 722.

69. Ibid., 725.

70. Wolfgang Schauble, "Die christliche Identitat Europas—Erbe und Auftrag" ("The Christian Identity of Europe"), speech delivered on May 6, 1994 to Christian entrepreneurs, translated by and quoted in Mayer, "Early at the Beach and Claiming Territory?" 726.

71. Ibid., 729.

72. Ibid.

73. Tamar Hermann, "Contemporary Peace Movements: Between the Hammer of Political Realism and the Anvil of Pacifism," *The Western Political Quarterly* 45, no. 4 (December 1992): 877.

74. For a survey of the internal dynamics of the Greens and their place among German political parties, see Library of Congress country studies at http://country studies.us/germany/163.htm.

75. "A Green Light for NATO: German Foreign Minister Joschka Fischer Wins His Party's Support for Backing the War in Kosovo," *Time International*, May 24, 1999, 1.

76. *The New York Times*, June 15, 1999, 1.

77. Harald Mueller and Thomas Risse-Kappen, "Origins of Estrangement: The Peace Movement and the Changed Image of America in West Germany," *International Security* 12, no. 1 (Summer 1987): 59.

78. Members of the Greens also likened presidents Ronald Reagan, George H. W. Bush, and George W. Bush to Hitler. See Mueller and Risse-Kappen, 84.

79. See Steve Breyman, *Movement Genesis: Social Movement Theory and the West German Peace Movement* (Boulder, Colo.: Westview, 1998).

80. Ibid., 84.

81. Joyce Marie Mushaben, *From Post-War to Post-Wall Generations: Changing Attitudes toward the National Question and NATO in the Federal Republic of Germany* (Boulder, Colo.: Westview, 1999).

82. Ibid., 6.

83. Hans Christian Stroeble, Alliance 90/Greens, Bundestag meeting of March 26, 1999.

84. Joschka Fischer, speech at the 54th Session of the UN General Assembly, September 22, 1999.

85. Ibid.

86. "Principles and Objectives of Germany's Human Rights Policy," *Auswartiegs Amt*, http://www.auswaertiges-amt.de.

87. Moravcsik, "Explaining the Emergence of Human Rights Regimes: Liberal Democracy and Political Uncertainty in Postwar Europe," 17.

88. Glendon, *A World Made New.*

89. "German Political Parties," Library of Congress country studies, http://countrystudies.us/germany/163.htm.

90. Wolfgang Thierse, Social Democratic Party, meeting of the Bundestag, March 26, 1999.

91. Gernot Erler, SPD, Bundestag meeting of March 26, 1999.

92. James Mayall, ed., *The New Interventionism: United Nations Experience in Cambodia, Former Yugoslavia and Somalia* (Cambridge: Cambridge University Press, 1996).

93. Angela Stent, *Russia and Germany Reborn: Unification, the Soviet Collapse, and the New Europe* (Princeton, N.J.: Princeton University Press, 1999).

94. Brian Rathbun, "Partisan Lenses and Historical Frames: Ideology and the Politics of Humanitarian Intervention in Britain and Germany," paper delivered at the American Political Science Association, http://apsaproceedings.cup.org/site/search.htm.

95. The SPD platform, revised in 1991, allowed for the use of force only with consent of the UNSC. Their support of German participation in the Kosovo campaign clearly violated their stated platform.

96. Rathbun, "Partisan Lenses and Historical Frames," 47.

97. Ibid., 56.

98. Joschka Fischer, speech of September 22, 1999.

99. Hubert Vedrine, *Le Monde Diplomatique*, December 2000, http://mondediplo.com/2000/12/14foreignpolicy.

100. P. Terrence Hopmann, "French Perspectives on International Relations after the Cold War," *Mershon International Studies Review* 38 (1994): 86–87.

101. See Alex MacLeod, "Kosovo: France and the Emergence of a New European Security," in *Alliance Politics, Kosovo, and NATO's War: Allied Force or Forced Allies?* (New York: Palgrave, 2000).

102. See Patrick McCarthy, ed., *France-Germany, 1983–1993: The Struggle to Cooperate* (London: Macmillan, 1994).

103. Hopmann, "French Perspectives on International Relations after the Cold War," 86.

104. The government's 2003 statement on foreign policy begins with the language of rights, stating that "France's foreign policy is based on certain fundamental principles: the right of peoples to self-determination, respect for human rights and democratic principles, respect for the rule of law and cooperation among nations. These principles underlie France's twofold concern to preserve its national independence while at the same time working to foster regional and international solidarity." French Embassy document, http://www.ambafrance-il.oreg/english/politics.htm.

105. See, for example, Pierre Hassner, "L'Amérique et le monde," *Etudes* 389, no. 4 (October 1998): 293–304.

106. Hopmann, "French Perspectives on International Relations after the Cold War," 71.

107. Claire Auplat, "The Commonwealth, the Francophonie and NGOs," *The Round Table* 368, no. 1 (January 2003): 53.

108. Shaun Gregory, "France and Missions de Souverainete," *Defense Analysis* 16, no. 3 (2000): 329.

109. Jacques Chirac, quoted in Gregory, "France and Missions de Souverainete," 329.

110. Sandi E. Cooper, "Pacifism in France, 1889–1914: International Peace as a Human Right," *French Historical Studies* 17, no. 2 (Fall 1991): 359–86.

111. Jan William Duyvendak, *The Power of Politics: New Social Movements in France* (Boulder, Colo.: Westview, 1995), 127.

112. See Sunil Khilnani, *Arguing Revolution: The Intellectual Left in Postwar France* (New Haven, Conn.: Yale University Press, 1993).

113. See Philip Gordon, *A Certain Idea of France: French Security Policy and the Gaullist Legacy* (Princeton, N.J.: Princeton University Press, 1993).

114. "Center-Left Still Trying to Redefine Its Mission: Third Way Conference Brings Leaders to London," ZENIT News Agency, July 19, 2003, http://www.zenit.org.

115. See Liesbet Hooghe, Gary Marks, and Carole Wilson, "Does Left/Right Structure Party Positions on European Integration?" *Comparative Political Studies* 35, no. 8 (October 2002): 965–89.

116. Simon Duke, Hans-Georg Ehrhart, and Matthias Karadi, "The Major European Allies: France, Germany, and the United Kingdom," in *Kosovo and the Challenge of Humanitarian Intervention*, ed. Albrecht Schnabel and Ramesh Thakur (New York: The United Nations University Press, 2000), 130.

117. Richard Holbrooke was quoted saying that he made the final deal at Dayton "while Europe slept." He claims he meant this literally, since the deal was finalized late in the morning hours, but he does not disagree with the European interpretation that the United States saw itself handling what the Europeans could not—in Europe's back yard. See Richard Holbrooke, *To End a War* (New York: Random House, 1998).

118. Pierre Lefevre, *Le Soir,* February 2, 1999.

119. See previous chapter.

120. See BVA poll of French public opinion, http://www.bva.fr/fr/archives/kosovo9920.html.

121. Duke, Erhart, and Karadi, "The Major European Allies," 132.

122. Nicholas Wheeler, *Saving Strangers: Humanitarian Intervention in International Society* (Oxford: Oxford University Press, 2000), 236.

123. Glendon, *A World Made New,* 209.

124. S/PV.3989, March 26, 1999.

125. S/PV.3988, March 24, 1999.

126. Javier Solana, statement of March 23, 1999, USIS Washington file, http://www.fas.org/man/dod-101/ops/docs99/99032313_tlt.htm.

127. Abel Matutes, October 6, 1998, quoted in Foreign Broadcast Information Service (FBIS) report FBIS-WEU-98–279.

128. Tony Blair, "Doctrine of the International Community."

CHAPTER 7

1. Daniel Casse, "The War of Ideas: A Look at the Men and Women Who Shape Bush's Bold Foreign Policy," *Wall Street Journal,* March 10, 2004, http://www.opinionjournal.com/forms/printThis.html?id=110004795.

2. Michael Glennon, "Why the Security Council Failed," *Foreign Affairs,* May/June 2003, 32.

3. See for example Jean-Marc Coicaud, *Beyond the National Interest: The Future of UN Peacekeeping and Multilateralism in an Era of U.S. Primacy* (Washington, D.C.: United States Institute of Peace Press, 2007).

4. *Security Strategy of the United States,* September 2002, http://georgewbush-whitehouse.archives.gov/nsc/nss/2002/nss5.html.

5. For a realist-based explanation of the French and British positions as a contest for leadership on the European continent, see John O'Sullivan, "The British-French Duel," *United Press International,* March 24, 2003. For a strictly economic argument explaining the American position as a contest for control of Iraqi oil fields, see Jeffrey Sachs, "Saudi Arabia Was Real Target in Iraq War," *Financial Times,* August 12, 2003, http://www.globalpolicy.org/security/issues/iraq/justify/2003/0812target.htm. For a human rights perspective, see Kenneth Roth, "War in Iraq: Not a Humanitarian Intervention," *Human Rights Watch,* http://hrw.org/wr2k4/3.htm. For a just war analysis supporting the war, see George Weigel, "Iraq and Just War, Revisited," *The Catholic Difference,* April 21, 2004, http://www.catholicexchange.com/vm/PFarticle.asp?vm_id=2&art_id=23364&sec_id=44806.

6. The following timeline of the events is based on the synopsis of intelligence found in, "Iraq War: Prelude to War (The International Debate Over the Use and Effectiveness of Weapons Inspections)," *Intelligence Encyclopedia,* The Gale Group, 2004. http://www.answers.com/topic/iraq-war-prelude-to-war-the-international-debate-over-the-use-and-effectiveness-of-weapons-inspections.

7. UNMOVIC was created by UNSC 1284, December 1999.

8. "Iraq War," *Intelligence Encyclopedia.*

9. UN Security Council Resolution 1441 (November 8, 2002), S/RES/1441 (2002).

10. "Iraq War," *Intelligence Encyclopedia.*

11. Lisa Bryant, "Iraq War Should Be Only Last Resort, Agree France and Germany," *Voice of America News,* January 22, 2003.

12. Keith Miller, "French Poll Shows More Than Three Out of Four Oppose US War with Iraq," *NBC Nightly News,* January 24, 2003.

13. "Iraq War," *Intelligence Encyclopedia.*

14. President George W. Bush, *PBS Online Newshour,* http://www.pbs.org/newshour/bb/white_house/jan-june03/news_conference_3–6.html.

15. "Iraq War," *Intelligence Encyclopedia.*

16. Douglas J. Feith, U.S. deputy secretary of defense, *War and Decision: Inside the Pentagon at the Dawn of the War on Terrorism* (New York: Harper Collins, 2008), 305.

17. Ibid., 306.

18. Simon Webb, British defense ministry official, quoted in Feith, *War and Decision,* 306.

19. Marc Perrin, French defense ministry official, quoted in Feith, *War and Decision,* 306. Emphasis original.

20. German state secretary of the German Ministry of Defense Walter Stuetzle, quoted in Feith, *War and Decision,* 306.

21. Feith, *War and Decision.*

22. "US Congress gives Bush Authority to Go to War against Iraq," *Agence France Presse,* October 11, 2002.

23. Dan Robinson, "War Powers Debated in Congress," *Voice of America News,* January 31, 2003.

24. Worldviews 2002 Survey of American and European Attitudes and Public Opinion on Foreign Policy, http://www.worldviews.org/key_findings/us_911_report.htm.

25. The German Marshall Fund of the United States and The Chicago Council on Foreign Relations, ibid.

26. Transatlantic Trends 2003, http://www.transatlantictrends.org/trends/.

27. "Surveys Show Overwhelming Majority of French Oppose War with Iraq," *Deutsche Presse-Agentur,* January 9, 2003.

28. Nick Spicer, "France States They Are Not Prepared to Support Any UN Security Council Resolution That Would Authorize War with Iraq," *NPR Morning Edition,* January 21, 2003.

29. French prime minister Jean-Pierre Raffarin, quoted in Marc Burleigh, "France Sees No Need for UN Veto, Firms Up Resistance to War Resolution," *Agence France Presse,* February 26, 2003.

30. Julio Godoy, "Chirac Resists Right Wing Pressure to Back War," *IPS Interpress Service,* February 6, 2003.

31. James Turner Johnson, "Humanitarian Intervention after Iraq: Just War and International Law Perspectives," *Journal of Military Ethics* 5, no. 2 (2006), 114.

32. Alfred B. Prados, "Iraq: Divergent Views on Military Action," *Congressional Research Service Report for Congress,* January 31, 2003.

33. Ibid., 2.

34. Norman Podhoretz, *World War IV: The Long Struggle against Islamofascism* (New York: Doubleday, 2007), 150–51.

35. Ibid., 153–58.

36. Bernard Kouchner, lecture at the Center for European Studies, Harvard University, February 2003.

37. Prados, "Iraq: Divergent Views on Military Action," 4–6.

38. On the link of Iraq to 9/11: Amy Gershkoff and Shana Kushner, "Shaping Public Opinion: The 9/11-Iraq Connection in the Bush Administration's Rhetoric," *Perspectives on Politics* 3, no. 3 (September 2005), 525–37. For American and European perceptions of security threats see "Worldviews 2002 Survey of American and European Attitudes and Public Opinion on Foreign Policy."

39. Tony Blair, quoted in Fawn Vrazo, "Blair Manages a Vote of Support; A House of Commons Majority Backed a War Role. But Blair's Own Party Signaled Distaste," *The Philadelphia Inquirer*, March 19, 2003.

40. Vrazo, "Blair Manages a Vote of Support."

41. Conor Foley, *The Thin Blue Line: How Humanitarianism Went to War* (London: Verso, 2008), 145.

42. Ibid., 146.

43. British prime minister Tony Blair, quoted in Foley, *The Thin Blue Line*, 148.

44. Burleigh, "France Sees No Need for UN Veto."

45. Nathalie Schuck, "France Warns Iraq Would Divide World," Associated Press, February 26, 2003.

46. Joe Ray, "The View from France: War with Iraq Looks a Lot Different from the French Perspective," *The Gazette (Canada)*, March 19, 2003.

47. French foreign minister Dominique de Villepin, quoted in Nick Spicer, "Leading Role the French Have Taken against a War in Iraq," *NPR Morning Edition*, March 2, 2003.

48. "Most French Oppose War on Iraq," *Xinhua General News Service*, February 17, 2003.

49. Tony Czuczka, "Shroeder, Stoiber Debate Iraq on TV," *Associated Press Online*, September 8, 2002.

50. David Crossland, "Schroeder's Anti-War Talk Boosts His Poll Numbers: Chancellor Moves Campaign Focus away from Economy," *National Post (Canada)*, September 11, 2002.

51. Jeevan Vasagar, "Schroeder Makes U-Turn on Iraq: Chancellor Will Allow US to Use German Bases in Event of War," *The Guardian London*, November 28, 2002.

52. Andrei Urban, "Germany to Fulfil Obligations in Case of War with Iraq—Minister," *TASS*, December 13, 2002.

53. Edmond Stoiber, quoted in David Crossland, "Schroeder's Anti-War Talk Boosts His Poll Numbers."

54. "Germany Isolated over Iraq War Rejection," *Deutsche Presse-Agentur*, September 10, 2002.

55. Ibid.

56. "Over 90 Percent of Germans Opposed to War against Iraq—Poll," *BBC Monitoring Europe*, October 2, 2002. The Hamburg-based GEWIS Institute carried out the survey for the television program "TV Hoeren und Sehen" among 1,051 Germans aged 16 to 65 between September 26 and 29.

57. Czuczka, "Shroeder, Stoiber Debate Iraq on TV."

58. "Germany Isolated over Iraq War Rejection."

59. Transatlantic Trends 2003. It is interesting to note that by 2004, support for just war had increased throughout the alliance countries, including 89 percent of Americans, 69 percent of British, 33 percent of French, and 31 percent of Germans. See Transatlantic Trends 2004, http://www.transatlantictrends.org/trends/.

60. Americans and Europeans shared similar views on the remaining top threats: global warming (third), the Israel/Arab conflicts, illegal immigration, the India/Pakistan tension, globalization, the rise of China, U.S.–European economic competition, and political turmoil in Russia. The German Marshall Fund of the United States and The Chicago Council on Foreign Relations, http://www.world views.org/key_findings/us_911_report.htm.

61. Johnson, "Humanitarian Intervention after Iraq," 115.

62. "Germany Clergy Warn against Iraq War in Christmas Statements," *Associated Press Worldstream,* December 25, 2002.

63. Bishop Wilton D. Gregory, president of the U.S. Conference of Catholic Bishops, letter to President George W. Bush, September 13, 2002, http://www.usccb.org/sdwp/international/bush902.shtml.

64. Gill Donovan, "Bishop: War with Iraq Illegal, Immoral and Unwise," *National Catholic Reporter,* October 11, 2002.

65. James V. Schall, S.J. "The Pious & The War: Iraq and Justice," *National Review Online,* February 13, 2003, http://article.nationalreview.com/?q=NTZjYWRhMzg3Y2Q2MDA1OTkwYTc0Nzc3YjM4MDNjYzM=.

66. George Weigel, "The Just War Case for the War," *America,* March 31, 2003, http://www.americamagazine.org/content/article.cfm?article_id=2879.

67. Thomas Cushman, ed., *A Matter of Principle: Humanitarian Arguments for War in Iraq* (Berkeley: University of California Press, 2005), 4.

68. Ibid., 9.

69. Ibid., 10.

70. During the 1999 Kosovo debates, Chirac offered a plan to counter U.S. "unilateralism"—a proposal made to the French diplomatic corps that the UN General Assembly consider reshaping the international order based upon "collective sovereignty." He listed seven principles, the first (aimed at the unnamed Americans) advocating "collective responsibility" in international action, "excluding unilateral temptations and leading to shared management of the global risks and threats that weigh on our peoples." John Vincour, "Going It Alone, U.S. Upsets France; So Paris Begins a Campaign to Strengthen Multilateral Institutions," *International Herald Tribune,* February 3, 1999.

71. *NewsHour with Jim Lehrer,* November 8, 2002.

72. "Battle of the Rival Texts," *Guardian Unlimited,* http://www.guardian.co.uk/Iraq/Story/0,2763,902543,00.html.

73. The UN Security Council resolutions were UNSCR 1160 of March 31, 1998, calling upon Belgrade and the Kosovo Albanian leaders to enter into meaningful dialogue with international involvement, for the return of refugees and a solution to the political problems in Kosovo, and an understanding that the territorial integrity of Yugoslavia should be maintained and the rights of the Kosovo Albanians respected; UNSCR 1199 of September 23, 1998, calling for a cessation of hostilities, endorsement of international monitoring, and the establishment of Kosovo Diplomatic Observer Mission (KDOM); and UNSCR 1203 of October 24, 1998, endorsing the agreements between Yugoslavia and the Organization for Security and Cooperation in Europe (OSCE), inserting an observer mission between Yugoslavia and NATO, and calling for the use of force in Serbia in the form of unarmed aerial observer missions to verify compliance with the cease-fire and refugee returns. Additionally, the Security Council issued, in the form of presidential statements, condemnations of the Racak massacre (January 19, 1999) and Belgrade's declaration of the head of the Kosovo Verification Mission (KVM) as persona non grata (January 29, 1999). It further condemned the barring of the prosecutor of the International Criminal Tribunal for the Former Yugoslavia from Yugoslavia after the Racak massacre, and the shooting of KVM personnel.

74. Article 25 of the German Basic Law states: "The general rules of public international law form part of the Federal law. They take precedence over

the laws and directly create rights and duties for the inhabitants of the Federal territory."

75. Defense Minister Rudolf Scharping declared the Kosovo operation "very clearly . . . a turning point in German foreign policy. . . . [I]n my view, this is a turning point in a certainly positive way." Echoing Gerhard Schroeder, he referred to German responsibility among nations, stating, "For the first time we accept responsibility in such a fundamental matter, and Germany is part of Europe, of the western democracies, and not opposed to them as it was until the end of World War II." Rudolf Scharping, interview with Richard Meng, *Main Frankfurter Rundschau*, March 27, 1999, Federal Broadcast Information Service (FBIS), FBIS-WEU-1999–0327.

76. Adrian Hyde-Price, "Berlin Republic Takes to Arms," *World Today* (June 1999), 13, quoted in Pierre Martin and Mark R. Brawley, eds., *Alliance Politics, Kosovo, and NATO's War: Allied Force or Forced Allies?* (New York: Palgrave, 2000), 131. German troops had participated in earlier crisis-management operations in the 1990s, including service in Somalia, Cambodia, and Bosnia. See David Yost, *NATO Transformed: The Alliance's New Roles in International Security* (Washington, D.C.: U.S. Institute of Peace, 1999), 189.

77. Joschka Fischer, "Statement by Minister for Foreign Affairs of the Federal Republic of Germany, Mr. Joschka Fischer: Public Meeting of the Security Council on the Situation between Iraq and Kuwait, New York, 5 February 2003," http://www.germany-info.org/relaunch/politics/speeches/020503.htm.

78. Ibid.

79. Jacques Chirac, March 20, 2003, http://special.diplomatie.fr/imprimer_gb.php3?id_article=191.

80. Dominique de Villepin, "Law, Force and Justice," speech delivered to the International Institute for Strategic Studies, March 27, 2003, http://special.diplomatie.fr/imprimer_gb.php3?id_article=240.

81. Philip Delves Broughton, "Chirac's Tough Stand Wins Friends at Home," *Daily Telegraph*, March 17, 2003, http://www.telegraph.co.uk/core/Content/displayPrintable.jhtml?xml=/news. Sixty percent of French citizens opposed the war with or without a UN mandate, a level of opposition second only to the Spanish in Europe. Support for the war rose significantly in Britain and Germany with the prospect of a separate Security Council resolution, "A Review of Worldwide Support (or Lack of It) for War on Iraq," *Eriposte*, http://www.eriposte.com/war_peace/iraq/iraq_war_worldwide_support.htm.

82. Ministère des Affaires Étrangeres Dossiers d'archive, "Legal Basis of the Action Undertaken by NATO" (Paris, March 25, 1999), http://www.france.diplomatie.fr/actual/ dossiers/kossovo/kossovo.html.

83. Craig R. Whitney, "French Are Gearing Up to Join in Dousing the Flames in Kosovo," *New York Times*, January 25, 1999, A6.

84. Jacques Chirac, Speech to the French People, March 24, 1999, http://www.diplomatie.fr/actual/dossiers/kossovo/kollovo6.gb.html.

85. Throughout the Kosovo crisis, France was engaged in promoting European Security and Defense Policy (ESDP), the purpose of the December 1998 meeting at Saint Malo with prime minister Tony Blair of the United Kingdom and prime minister Lionel Jospin and president Jacques Chirac of France. See Dimitris Keridis and Robert L. Pfaltzgraff Jr., *NATO and Southeastern Europe: Security Issues for the Early 21st Century* (Dulles, Va.: Brassey's, 2000), and Fraser Cameron, *The Foreign*

and Security Policy of the European Union Past, Present and Future (Sheffield, UK: Sheffield Academic, 1999).

86. Vincour, "Going It Alone, U.S. Upsets France," 1. In January 1999, Prime Minister Jospin announced, "We're confronted with a new problem on the international scene. The United States often behaves in a unilateral manner and has difficulty in assuming the role it aspires to as organizer in the international community."

87. Ibid.

88. Ibid.

89. Chirac, Speech to the French People, March 24, 1999.

90. United Nations Security Council S/PV.3988, March 24, 1999, http://www.uu.nl/content/PV-3988.pdf.

91. Clare Short, "Full Text: Clare Short's Statement," *Guardian*, March 18, 2003, http://www.guardian.co.uk/Iraq/Story/0,2763,916678,00.html.

92. Support for the war in Britain was 75 percent with both proof of WMD and a UN mandate, 46 percent with proof alone, 41 percent with a mandate only, and 24 percent with neither. "War with Iraq" (poll), *MORI Social Research Institute*, http://www.mori.com/polls/2003/iraq2 .shtml.

93. Tony Blair, "Doctrine of the International Community," in *Strategy and Force Planning*, ed. Security, Strategy, and Forces Faculty (Newport, R.I.: Naval War College, 2004), 569–79.

94. Tony Blair, "Chaos and Disorder," House of Commons, March 23, 1999, http://www.parliament.the-stationery-office.co.uk/pa/cm199899/cmhansrd/vo990323/debtext/90323–03.htm. Blair, "Barbarous Acts," and "Doctrine of the International Community."

95. Tony Blair, "Britain Has Never Been a Nation to Hide at the Back," *Guardian*, March 21, 2003, http://www.guardian.co.uk/Iraq/Story/0,2763,918661,00.html.

96. Ibid.

97. Ibid.

98. George W. Bush, "War Ultimatum from the Cross Hall in the White House, 18 March 2003," http://www.guardian.co.uk/Iraq/Story/0,2763,916543,00.html.

99. "A Proclamation by the President of the United States: Captive Nations Week, 2003," http://www.whitehouse.gov/news/releases/2003/07. The Captive Nations Week Resolution, signed by President Eisenhower and passed as Public Law 86–90 on July 9, 1959, declared, "Those submerged nations look to the United States, as the citadel of human freedom, for leadership in bringing about their liberation and independence and in restoring to them the enjoyment of their Christian, Jewish, Moslem, Buddhist, or other religious freedoms, and of their individual liberties." Despite its bold wording, successive presidents ignored the law, and liberation theory was often credited more as a domestic political strategy to "roll back" political opposition rather than communism. See, for example, Perry L. Weed, *The White Ethnic Movement and Ethnic Politics* (New York: Praeger, 1973), and John W. Spanier, *American Foreign Policy since World War II*, 11th ed. (Washington, D.C.: CQ Press, 1988). Whereas previously most administrations minimized commemoration of captive nations and liberation theory altogether, the Bush administration, like the Reagan administration before it, seemed willing to act on it.

100. George W. Bush, "President's Remarks at the United Nations General Assembly," September 12, 2002, http://www.whitehouse.gov/news/releases/2002/09/print/20020912–1.html.

101. George W. Bush, quoted in "President Bush Delivers Graduation Speech at West Point," June 1, 2002, http://www.whitehouse.gov/news/releases/2002/06/print/20020601–3.html.

102. George W. Bush, quoted in "President Bush Announces Major Combat Operations in Iraq Have Ended: Remarks by the President from the USS *Abraham Lincoln*," http://www.whitehouse.gov/news/releases/2003/05/iraq/20030501–15.html. The Four Freedoms were those of speech and worship, and from want and fear (declared January 6, 1941 and incorporated in the August 1941 Atlantic Charter); Harry S. Truman declared on March 12, 1947 his determination to extend military and economic aid to any nation threatened by communism; on June 8, 1982 president Ronald Reagan asserted the need to promote and extend freedom in the face of the "totalitarian evil" represented by the Soviet Union.

103. In a half-hour address in November 2003, he used the terms "freedom" and "liberty" 54 times, and "democracy" 30 times, mentioning national interests only once. George W. Bush, "Remarks by the President at the 20th Anniversary of the National Endowment for Democracy," November 6, 2003, http://www.white house.gov/news/releases/2003/11/print/20031106–3.html.

CHAPTER 8

1. Anne Applebaum, "The Slowly Vanishing NATO," *Washington Post*, October 20, 2009.

2. John Bolton, "The Sudan, the ICC and the Obama Administration," *New York Post*, August 6, 2009.

3. Samantha Power, national security campaign advisor to President Obama, "Court of First Resort," *The New York Times*, February 10, 2005.

4. Ibid.

5. David Crossland, "Schroeder's Anti-War Talk Boosts His Poll Numbers: Chancellor Moves Campaign Focus away from Economy," *National Post (Canada)*, September 11, 2002.

6. Jaane Haaland Matlary, "The Legitimacy of Military Intervention: How Important Is a UN Mandate?" *Journal of Military Ethics* 3, no. 2 (2004): 139.

7. George Robertson, *Hansard*, March 25, 1999.

8. See Susan Yoshihara, "The Quest for Happiness: How the UN's Advocacy of Economic, Social and Cultural Rights Undermines Liberty and Opportunity," in *ConUNdrum: The Limits of the United Nations and the Search for Alternatives* Brett D. Schaefer, ed., New York: Roman & Littlefield, 2009), 169–208. http://www.c-fam.org/docLib/20091020_ConUNdrum.pdf.

9. On the changing nature of human rights and their relationship to truth and politics, see Janet Holl Madigan, *Truth, Politics, and Universal Human Rights* (New York: Palgrave, 2007).

10. Edward Luck, special assistant to the UN secretary general (for R2P), interview with the author, November 13, 2007.

11. Martha Finnemore and Kathryn Sikkink define "sovereignty" not as a norm but as an institution, which is a collection of norms. Martha Finnemore and Kathryn Sikkink, "International Norm Dynamics and Political Change," *International Organization* 52, no. 4 (Autumn 1998): 891.

12. Ibid., 895.

13. For a survey of those who supported the Iraq war on its humanitarian merits see Thomas Cushman, ed., *A Matter of Principle: Humanitarian Arguments for War in Iraq* (Berkeley: University of California Press, 2005).

14. David Rieff, "The Conversion of Bernard Kouchner," *The Daily Star,* August 2007. http://www.dailystar.com.lb/article.asp?edition_id=10&categ_id=5&article_id=84284.

15. Jacques Chirac, March 26, 1999.

16. Kenneth Roth, "Was the Iraq War a Humanitarian Intervention," *Journal of Military Ethics* 5, no. 2 (2006): 84–92.

17. James Turner Johnson, "Humanitarian Intervention after Iraq: Just War and International Law Perspectives," *Journal of Military Ethics* 5, no. 2 (2006): 114–27.

18. Madeleine Albright, December 7, 1998, *Financial Times,* quoted in Maartje Rutten, "From St. Malo to Nice: European Defence: Core Documents," *Institute for Security Studies of the WEU 2001,* http://www.iss-eu.org/chaillot/chai47e.html#p.

19. For an examination of the way activists are attempting to create and enforce new reproductive rights using the UN human rights system, see Douglas Sylva and Susan Yoshihara, "Rights by Stealth: The Campaign to Create an International Right to Abortion," *National Catholic Bioethics Quarterly* 7, no. 1 (Spring 2007): 97–128.

20. Edward Luck, Remarks to the 64th General Assembly, September 1, 2009, http://www.ipacademy.org/news/general-announcement/98-general-assembly-passes-resolution-on-responsibility-to-protect.html.

21. Barak Hussein Obama, Nobel Prize acceptance speech. Oslo, Norway, December 10, 2009. http://www.nydailynews.com/news/politics/2009/12/10/2009-12-10_barack_obama_nobel_peace_prize_speech_full_transcript.html.

22. David Weigel, "Obama's Wars," *Reason* 40, no. 5 (October 2008): 16.

23. David Chandler, *From Kosovo to Kabul: Human Rights and International Intervention* (London: Pluto, 2002), 12.

24. Michael Walzer, *Just and Unjust Wars: A Moral Argument with Historical Illustrations* (New York: Basic Books, 1977), 107.

25. David L. Bosco, *Five to Rule them All: The UN Security Council and the Making of the Modern World* (Oxford: Oxford University Press: 2009), 241.

26. Ibid., 230.

27. Ibid., 251. Bosco cites UNSC deliberations about the Congo crisis in the 1960s as the first time that resort to the Council jeopardized great power relations.

28. See Michael Ignatieff, "The Attack on Human Rights," *Foreign Affairs,* September/October 2001.

Bibliography

Albright, Madeleine K. Department of State transcript. October 8, 1998.
———. "The End of Intervention."*New York Times,* June 11, 2008.
———. Newshour with Jim Lehrer interview. October 18, 1999.
———. Policy address on Kosovo, February 4, 1999. Department of State transcript.
Alston, Philip, and Euan MacDonald, eds. *Human Rights, Intervention, and the Use of Force.* Oxford: Oxford University Press, 2008.
"An Idea Whose Time Has Come—and Gone?" *The Economist,* July 23, 2009. http://www.economis.com/world/international/PrinterFriendly.cfm?story_id=14087788.
Anderson, Peter. "Airstrike: NATO Astride Kosovo." *The Kosovo Crisis: The Last American War in Europe?,* ed. Tony Weymouth and Stanley Henig. London: Reuters, 2001.
———. Annual Report to the General Assembly, September 20, 1999, Press Release SF/SM/7136/GA/9596.
Annan, Kofi. "Peacekeeping and National Sovereignty." In *Hard Choices: Moral Dilemmas in Humanitarian Intervention.* Jonathan Moore, ed. New York: Rowman and Littlefield, 1998, 55–70.
———. *Preventing War and Disaster: A Growing Global Challenge.* New York: United Nations, 1999.
———. "Two Concepts of Sovereignty." *The Economist,* September 18, 1999, 49. http://www.un.org/News/ossg/sg/stories/kaecon.html.
———. "Secretary General's Address to the General Assembly." New York, September 23, 2003.
Applebaum, Anne. "The Slowly Vanishing NATO."*Washington Post,* October 20, 2009.
Aquinas, Thomas. *Summa Theologica.* In *Aquinas: Selected Political Writings,* ed. A. P. D'Entreves. Translated by J. G. Dawson. Oxford: Basil Blackwell, 1954, 102–79.

Auplat, Claire. "The Commonwealth, the Francophonie and NGOs." *The Round Table* 368, no. 1 (January 2003): 53.

Baker, James A. *The Politics of Diplomacy: Revolution, War & Peace 1989–1992.* New York: Putnam, 1995.

Ban Ki-moon. "Secretary-General's Message to United Nations University—International Crisis Group Conference on the Prevention of Mass Atrocities." New York, October 10, 2007.

Basic Law for the Federal Republic of Germany (Grundgesetz, GG). http://www.iuscomp.org/gla/statutes/GG.htm#Preamble.

Bass, Gary J. *Freedom's Battle: The Origins of Humanitarian Intervention.* New York: Alfred A. Knopf, 2008.

"Battle of the Rival Texts," *Guardian Unlimited,* February 25, 2003. http://www.guardian.co.uk/world/2003/feb/25/iraq.

Baumann, Rainer, and Gunther Hellman, "Germany and the Use of Military Force: 'Total War', the 'Culture of Restraint', and the Quest for Normality." *German Politics* 10, no. 1 (April 2001). http://www.frankcass.com/jnls/gp_v10.htm.

Bellamy, Alex J. *Kosovo and International Society.* New York: Palgrave, 2002.

Benn, Tony. *Hansard,* March 25, 1999. http://www.publications.parliament.uk/cgi-bin/semaphoreserver?DB=semukparl&FILE=search.

Berger, Sandy. Interview with Online *NewsHour,* October 2, 1998.

———. PBS *Frontline* interview, October 23, 1998. http://www.pbs.org/newshour/bb/europe/july-dec98/berger_10-2.html.

Berkowitz, Peter. "Laws of Nations." *Policy Review* (April/May 2005).

Biden, Joseph. "Kosovo: A Test for NATO." Speech delivered at The Atlantic Council of the United States, Washington, D.C., March 25, 1999.

Blair, Tony. "Britain Has Never Been a Nation to Hide at the Back." *Guardian,* March 21, 2003.

———. "Chaos and Disorder." House of Commons, March 23, 1999.

———. "Doctrine of the International Community." Speech delivered at the Economic Club of Chicago, April 22, 1999. In *Strategy and Force Planning,* 3rd ed., ed. Strategy and Force Planning Faculty, 588. Newport, R.I.: U.S. Naval War College Press, 2000.

———. *Frontline* interview, http://www.pbs.org/wgbh/pages/frontline/shows/kosovo/interviews/blair.html.

Bolton, John. "The Sudan, the ICC and the Obama Administration." *New York Post,* August 6, 2009.

Boot, Max. *The Savage Wars of Peace: Small Wars and the Rise of American Power.* New York: Basic Books, 2002.

Bosco, David L. *Five to Rule them All: The UN Security Council and the Making of the Modern World.* Oxford: Oxford University Press: 2009.

Boutros-Ghali, Boutros. *Somalia: The Missed Opportunities.* Washington, D.C.: United States Institute of Peace, 1994.

Breyman, Steve. *Movement Genesis: Social Movement Theory and the West German Peace Movement.* Boulder, Colo.: Westview, 1998.

Broughton, Philip Delves. "Chirac's Tough Stand Wins Friends at Home," *Daily Telegraph,* March 17, 2003, http://www.telegraph.co.uk/core/Content/displayPrintable.jhtml?xml=/news.

Brownlie, Ian. *International Law and the Use of Force by States*. Oxford: Oxford University Press, 1963.

Bryant, Lisa. "Iraq War Should be Only Last Resort, Agree France and Germany," *Voice of America News*, January 22, 2003.

Bull, Hedley. *The Anarchial Society: A Study of Order in World Politics*. New York: Columbia University Press, 1977.

Burleigh, Marc. "France Sees No Need for UN Veto, Firms Up Resistance to War Resolution." *Agence France Presse*, February 26, 2003.

Burman, Eric. "Innocents Abroad: Western Fantasies of Childhood and the Iconography of Emergencies." *Disasters* 18, no. 3 (1994): 238–53.

Bush, George W. *PBS Online Newshour*, http://www.pbs.org/newshour/bb/white_house/jan-june03/news_conference_3–6.html.

———. "President's Remarks at the United Nations General Assembly," September 12, 2002, http://www.whitehouse.gov/news/releases/2002/09/print/20020912–1.html.

———. "A Proclamation by the President of the United States: Captive Nations Week, 2003," http://www.whitehouse.gov/news/releases/2003/07.

———. "Remarks by the President at the 20th Anniversary of the National Endowment for Democracy," November 6, 2003.

———. War Ultimatum from the Cross Hall in the White House, March 18, 2003.

Buzan, Barry. *From International to World Society? English School Theory and the Social Structure of Globalization*. Cambridge: Cambridge University Press, 2004.

Byers, Michael. *War Law: Understanding International Law and Armed Conflict*. New York: Grove Press, 2005.

Cameron, Fraser. *The Foreign and Security Policy of the European Union Past, Present and Future*. Sheffield, UK: Sheffield Academic Press, 1999.

Capaccio, Tony. "Bush Preemptive Strike Doctrine under Review, May Be Discarded." *Bloomberg.com*, October 16, 2009, http://www.bloomberg.com/apps/news?pid=newsarchive&sid=aw4BqFAVbkf8#.

Caplan, Richard. "Humanitarian Intervention: Which Way Forward?" *Ethics & International Affairs* 14 (2000): 31.

Casse, Daniel. "The War of Ideas: A Look at the Men and Women Who Shape Bush's Bold Foreign Policy." *Wall Street Journal*, March 10, 2004, http://www.opinionjournal.com/forms/printThis.html?id=110004795.

"Center-Left Still Trying to Redefine Its Mission: Third Way Conference Brings Leaders to London," *ZENIT News Agency*, July 19, 2003, http://www.zenit.org.

Chandler, David. *From Kosovo to Kabul: Human Rights and International Intervention*. London: Pluto, 2002.

Charter of the United Nations. New York: United Nations, 1945.

Childress, James. "Just-War Theories: The Bases, Interrelations, Priorities, and Functions of Their Criteria." *War, Morality and the Military Profession*. Boulder, Colo.: Westview Press, 1986.

Chirac, Jacques. March 20, 2003, http://special.diplomatie.fr/imprimer_gb.php3?id_article=191.

———. Press Conference at Palazzo Vecchio, Florence, October 6, 1998.

———. Speech of March 26, 1999.

———. Speech to the French People, March 24, 1999, http://www.diplomatie.fr/actual/dossiers/kossovo/kollovo6.gb.html.

————. Statement in Berlin, March 24, 1999, French Ministry of Foreign Affairs, http://www.france.diplomatie.fr/actual/dossiers/kossovo/kossovo.gb.html.

Clark, Alan. *Hansard,* March 25, 1999. http://www.publications.parliament.uk/cgi-bin/semaphoreserver?DB=semukparl&FILE=search.

Clark, J.C.D. "The Strange Death of British History? Reflections on Anglo-American Scholarship." *The Historical Journal* 40, no. 3 (1997): 806.

Clark, Wesley K. *Waging Modern War.* New York: Public Affairs, 2001.

Clausewitz, Carl von. *On War.* ed. and trans. Michael Howard and Peter Paret. Princeton: Princeton University Press, 1976.

Clinton, William J. Letter to Senate leaders, October 6, 1998, Congressional Record—Senate S11899.

————. Press conference, March 19, 1999.

————. "Remarks at a North Atlantic Treaty Organization Commemorative Ceremony," April 23, 1999. In *Public Papers of the Presidents of the United States, William J. Clinton, 1999, Book I—January 1 to June 30, 1999.* Washington, D.C.: United States Government Printing Office, 2000.

————. "Statement by the President to the Nation." March 24, 1999. Office of the Press Secretary transcript.

Cohen, William. *Lehrer NewsHour* interview, June 18, 1998, http://www.pbs.org/newshour/bb/europe/jan-june98/cohen_6–18.html.

————. PBS *Frontline* interview, http://www.pbs.org/wgbh/pages/frontline/shows/Kosovo/interviews/choen.html.

Coicaud, Jean-Marc. *Beyond the National Interest: The Future of UN Peacekeeping and Multilateralism in an Era of U.S. Primacy.* Washington, D.C.: United States Institute of Peace Press, 2007.

Coll, Alberto. "Kosovo and the Moral Burdens of Power." *War over Kosovo: Politics and Strategy in a Global Age,* ed. Andrew J. Bacevich and Eliot Cohen. New York: Columbia University, 2001, 124–54.

Cook, Frank, *Hansard,* March 25, 1999. http://www.publications.parliament.uk/cgi-bin/semaphoreserver?DB=semukparl&FILE=search.

Cook, Martin L. " 'Immaculate War': Constraints on Humanitarian Intervention." *Ethics & International Affairs* 14 (2000): 61.

Cook, Robin. House of Commons, March 25, 1999, http://www.parliament.the-stationery-office.co.uk/pa/cm199899/cmhansrd/vo990325/debindx/90325-x.htm.

Cooper, Sandi E. "Pacifism in France, 1889–1914: International Peace as a Human Right." *French Historical Studies* 17, no. 2 (Fall 1991): 359–86.

Crossland, David. "Schroeder's Anti-War Talk Boosts His Poll Numbers: Chancellor Moves Campaign Focus away from Economy." *National Post (Canada),* September 11, 2002.

Cushman, Thomas, ed. *A Matter of Principle: Humanitarian Arguments for War in Iraq.* Berkeley: University of California Press, 2005.

Czuczka, Tony. "Shroeder, Stoiber Debate Iraq on TV." *Associated Press Online,* September 9, 2002. http://www.highbeam.com/doc/1P1-67242655.html.

Daalder, Ivo H., and Michael E. O'Hanlon, *Winning Ugly: NATO's War to Save Kosovo.* Washington, D.C.: Brookings Institution, 2000.

Decisions of the Bundesverfassungsgericht—Federal Constitutional Court—Federal Republic of Germany Vol. 1/I and 1/II International Law and Law of the European Communities, 1952–1989. Baden-Baden: Nomos Verlagsgesellschaft, 1992.

D'Escoto Brockmann, Miguel. Statement of General Assembly President at the Opening of the Thematic Dialogue of the General Assembly on the Responsibility to Protect, July 23, 2009, http://www0.un.org/ga/president/63/statements/openingr2p230709.shtml.

De Villepin, Dominique. "Law, Force and Justice." Speech delivered to the International Institute for Strategic Studies, March 27, 2003, http://special.diplomatie.fr/imprimer_gb.php3?id_article=240.

Dinstein, Yoram. "The 13th Waldemar A. Solf Lecture in International Law." *Military Law Review* 166 (2000): 93–108.

Dole, Robert. Speech to the International Republican Institute, September 22, 1998, http://www.fas.org/man/dod-101/ops/docs/s980923-kosovo2.htm.

Donovan, Gill. "Bishop: War with Iraq Illegal, Immoral and Unwise," *National Catholic Reporter,* October 11, 2002.

Duffield, John. *World Power Forsaken: Political Culture, International Institutions, and German Security Policy.* Stanford, Calif.: Stanford University Press, 1998.

Duffield, Mark. "The Symphony of the Damned: Racial Discourse, Complex Political Emergencies and Humanitarian Aid." *Disasters: The Journal of Disaster Studies and Management* 20, no. 3 (1996): 178.

Duke, Simon, Hans-Georg Ehrhart, and Matthias Karadi. "The Major European Allies: France, Germany, and the United Kingdom." In *Kosovo and the Challenge of Humanitarian Intervention,* ed. Albrecht Schnabel and Ramesh Thakur. New York: The United Nations University Press, 2000, 128–50.

Durch, William, ed. *UN Peacekeeping, American Policy, and the Uncivil Wars of the 1990s.* New York: St. Martin's Press, 1996.

Duyvendak, Jan William. *The Power of Politics: New Social Movements in France.* Boulder, Colo: Westview, 1995.

Ehrhart, Hans-Georg. "France and NATO: Change by Rapprochement? Asteriz' Quarrel with the Roman Empire." Paper of January 2000, Hamburg, Germany.

Evans, Gareth. "The Responsibility to Protect." *NATO Review* (Winter 2002).

———. *The Responsibility to Protect: Ending Mass Atrocity Crimes Once and for All.* Washington, D.C.: Brookings Institution, 2008.

Evans, Gareth, and Mohamed Sahnoun. "The Responsibility to Protect." *Foreign Affairs* 81, no. 6 (November/December 2002): 99–110.

Feinstein, Lee, and Anne-Marie Slaughter. "The Duty to Prevent." *Foreign Affairs* 83, no. 1 (January/February 2004): 136–50.

Feith, Douglas J. *War and Decision: Inside the Pentagon at the Dawn of the War on Terrorism.* New York: Harper Collins, 2008.

Finnemore, Martha, and Kathryn Sikkink. "International Norm Dynamics and Political Change." *International Organization* 52, no. 4 (Autumn 1998): 891.

Fischer, Joschka. Speech at the 54th Session of the UN General Assembly, September 22, 1999.

———. Statement by Minister for Foreign Affairs of the Federal Republic of Germany, Public Meeting of the Security Council on the Situation between Iraq and Kuwait, New York, March 19, 2003, http://www.germany-info.org/relaunch/politics/speeches/020503.htm.

Foley, Conor. *The Thin Blue Line: How Humanitarianism Went to War.* London: Verso, 2008.

Fonte, John. "Global Governance v. the Liberal Democratic Nation State." *Family Security Matters* (June 18, 2008).

French Embassy document, http://www.ambafrance-il.oreg/english/politics.htm.

French Embassy in the United States Web site, http://www.info-france-usa.org/.

Fukuyama, Francis. *America at the Crossroads: Democracy, Power and the Neoconservative Legacy*. New Haven: Yale University Press, 2006.

The German Marshall Fund of the United States and The Chicago Council on Foreign Relations, http://www.worldviews.org/key_findings/us_911_report.htm.

"German Political Parties," Library of Congress Country Studies, http://country studies.us/germany/163.htm.

"Germany Clergy Warn against Iraq War in Christmas Statements." *Associated Press Worldstream*, December 25, 2002.

"Germany: Green's Leader Warns against Ignoring UN in Kosovo Intervention," *BBC Worldwide Monitoring*, October 3, 1998.

"Germany Isolated over Iraq War Rejection,"*Deutsche Presse-Agentur,* September 10, 2002.

"Germany May Not Participate in Possible Intervention in Kosovo," *Xinhua* News Agency, October 8, 1998.

Gershkoff, Amy, and Shana Kushner. "Shaping Public Opinion: The 9/11-Iraq Connection in the Bush Administration's Rhetoric." *Perspectives on Politics* 3, no. 3 (September 2005): 525–37.

Glendon, Mary Ann. "Rights Babel: Thoughts on the Approaching 50th Anniversary of the Universal Declaration of Human Rights." Lecture at De Sales University, 1996, http:www4desales.edu/~philtheo/Glendon.html.

———. *A World Made New: Eleanor Roosevelt and the Universal Declaration of Human Rights*. New York: Random House, 2001.

Glennon, Michael. *Limits of Law, Prerogatives of Power: Interventionism after Kosovo*. New York: Palgrave, 2001.

———. "Why the Security Council Failed." *Foreign Affairs* (May/June 2003): 32.

Godoy, Julio. "Chirac Resists Right Wing Pressure to Back War." *IPS Interpress Service*, February 6, 2003.

Goldsmith, Jack, and Eric Posner. "Moral and Legal Rhetoric in International Relations: A Rational Choice Perspective." University of Chicago Law & Economics, Olin Working Paper 108, November 2000.

Gordon, Philip. *A Certain Idea of France: French Security Policy and the Gaullist Legacy*. Princeton, N.J.: Princeton University Press, 1993.

Gray, Colin S. *Nuclear Strategy and National Style*. Lanham, Md.: Hamilton Press, 1986.

"A Green Light for NATO: German Foreign Minister Joschka Fischer Wins His Party's Support for Backing the War in Kosovo." *Time International*, May 24, 1999.

Gregory, Shaun. "France and Missions de Souverainete." *Defense Analysis* 16, no. 3 (2000): 329.

Gregory, Bishop Wilton D. Letter to President George W. Bush, September 13, 2002. http://www.usccb.org/sdwp/international/bush902.shtml.

Grotius, Hugo. *The Law of War and Peace*. New York: Bobbs-Merrill Co., 1962.

Groves, Steven. "The U.S. Should Reject the U.N. 'Responsibility to Protect' Doctrine." *Heritage Foundation Backgrounder* #2130, May 1, 2008.

Guicherd, Catherine. "International Law and the War in Kosovo," *Survival* 41, no. 2 (Summer 1999): 19–34.

Haass, Richard. *Intervention.* Washington, D.C.: Carnegie Endowment, 1994.
———. *The Reluctant Sheriff: The United States After the Cold War.* New York: Council on Foreign Relations, 1997.
Hassner, Pierre. "L'Amérique et le monde," *Etudes* 389, no. 4 (October 1998): 293–304.
Hehir, J. Bryan. "Military Intervention and National Sovereignty." In *Hard Choices: Moral Dilemmas in Humanitarian Intervention,* ed. Jonathan Moore. Rowman & Littlefield, Lanham, Md.: 1998.
Henkin, Louis. "Kosovo and the Law of 'Humanitarian Intervention.'" *American Journal of International Law* 93, no. 4 (October 1999): 824–28.
Hermann, Tamar. "Contemporary Peace Movements: Between the Hammer of Political Realism and the Anvil of Pacifism." *The Western Political Quarterly* 45, no. 4 (December 1992): 877.
Hirschman, Albert O. *The Rhetoric of Reaction: Perversity, Futility, Jeopardy.* Cambridge, Mass.: Belknap, 1991.
Hoffman, Stanley. "The Crisis of Liberal Internationalism." *Foreign Policy* 98 (1995): 159–77.
Holbrooke, Richard. Interview with PBS *NewsHour with Jim Lehrer,* October 14, 1998.
Holbrooke, Richard. Interview on PBS *Frontline,* October 14, 1998.
Holbrooke, Richard. *To End a War.* New York: Random House, 1998.
Holmes, James. "Myanmar Disaster: The Dangers of Gunboat Compassion."*Providence Journal,* May 21, 2008, http://www.projo.com/opinion/contributors/content/CT_holmes21_05–21–08_U3A5T20_v7.39c3136.html.
Holmes, James. *Theodore Roosevelt and World Order: Police Power in International Relations.* Washington, D.C.: Potomac Books, 2006.
Holmes, James, and Toshi Yoshihara. "Strongman, Constable, or Free-Rider? India's 'Monroe Doctrine' and Indian Naval Strategy." *Comparative Strategy* 28, no. 4 (September 2009): 332–48.
Holzgrefe, J. L., and Robert O. Keohane, eds. *Humanitarian Interventions: Ethical, Legal, and Political Dilemmas.* Cambridge: Cambridge University Press, 2003.
Hooghe, Liesbet, Gary Marks, and Carole Wilson. "Does Left/Right Structure Party Positions on European Integration?" *Comparative Political Studies* 35, no. 8 (October 2002): 965–89.
Hopmann, P. Terrence. "French Perspectives on International Relations after the Cold War." *Mershon International Studies Review* 38 (1994): 86–87.
Howard, Sir Michael. *Hansard,* March 25, 1999. http://www.publications.parliament.uk/cgi-bin/semaphoreserver?DB=semukparl&FILE=search
Huntington, Samuel P. *The Clash of Civilizations and the Remaking of World Order.* New York: Simon & Schuster, 1996.
Hutchinson, Kay Bailey. October 7, 1998 hearing, U.S. Senate.
Hyde-Price, Adrian. "Berlin Republic Takes to Arms." *The World Today,* June 1999, 13.
Ignatieff, Michael. "The Attack on Human Rights," *Foreign Affairs,* September/October 2001.
———. "The Stories We Tell: Television and Humanitarian Aid." In *Hard Choices: Moral Dilemmas in Humanitarian Intervention;* Jonathan Moore, ed. Lanham, Md.: Rowman and Littlefield, 1998, 287–302.
Independent International Commission on Kosovo. *The Kosovo Report: Conflict, International Response, Lessons Learned.* Oxford: Oxford University Press, 2000.

"Iraq War: Prelude to War (The International Debate Over the Use and Effectiveness of Weapons Inspections)." *Intelligence Encyclopedia.* The Gale Group, 2004. http://www.answers.com/topic/iraq-war-prelude-to-war-the-international-debate-over-the-use-and-effectiveness-of-weapons-inspections.

Johnson, James Turner. "Humanitarian Intervention after Iraq: Just War and International Law Perspectives." *Journal of Military Ethics* 5, no. 2 (2006): 114–27.

Johnston, Alastair Iain. "Strategic Culture: A Critique." In *Cultural Realism: Strategic Culture and Grand Strategy in Chinese History.* Princeton, N.J.: Princeton University Press, 1995, 1–31.

Johnstone, Ian. "Security Council Deliberations: Justification and Persuasion on the Basis of Law." Unpublished paper, The Fletcher School of Law and Diplomacy, 2002.

Jokic, Aleksandar, and Burleigh Wilkins. *Lessons of Kosovo: The Dangers of Humanitarian Intervention.* Peterborough, Ontario: Broadview, 2003.

Jospin, Lionel. Speech of the prime minister to the National Assembly. Paris, March 26, 1999.

"Jurists Question NATO's Kosovo Deployment."*Main Frankfurter Rundschau,* March 29, 1999, FBIS-EEU-1999–0328.

Kaldor, Mary. *New and Old Wars: Organized Violence in a Global Era.* Stanford, Calif.: Stanford University Press, 1999.

Kaplan, Lawrence S. *The Long Entanglement: NATO's First Fifty Years.* Westport, Conn.: Praeger, 1999.

———. *NATO and the United States: The Enduring Alliance.* Boston: Twayne Publishers, 1988.

Keridis, Dimistris, and Robert L. Pfaltzgraff. *NATO and Southeastern Europe: Security Issues for the Early 21st Century.* Dulles, Va.: Brassey's, 2000.

Khilnani, Sunil. *Arguing Revolution: The Intellectual Left in Postwar France.* New Haven, Conn.: Yale University Press, 1993.

Kirkpatrick, Jeane J. *Making War to Keep Peace.* New York: Harper Collins, 2007.

Kissinger, Henry. *Diplomacy.* New York: Simon & Schuster, 1994.

Klein, Stefan. "With a Brave Yes." *Munich Sueddeutsche Zeitung,* March 24, 1999, FBIS-WEU-1999–0324.

"Kosovo Assault Was Not Genocide." *BBC,* September 7, 2001, http://www.global policy.org/security/issues/kosovo1/2001/0907genocide.htm.

Kouchner, Bernard. "France Is at an Impasse." *Le Monde,* March 3, 2003.

———. "The Future of Humanitarianism." Twenty-Third Annual Morgenthau Memorial Lecture on Ethics and Foreign Policy. Carnegie Council on Ethics and International Affairs, March 2, 2004.

———. Lecture at the Center for European Studies, Harvard University, February 2003.

Krauthammer, Charles. "The Short, Unhappy Life of Humanitarian War." *The National Interest,* Fall 1999, 5–8.

_____. "The Unipolar Moment." *Foreign Affairs* (Winter 1990/1991): 22–33.

_____. "The Unipolar Moment Revisited." *The National Interest* (Winter 2002/2003): 5–17.

Kupchan, Charles. "America and Europe: From Pacifier to Partner." In *NATO and Southeastern Europe: Security Issues for the Early 21st Century,* ed. Dimitris Keridis and Robert L. Pfaltzgraff Jr. Dulles, Va.: Brassey's, 2000.

Kupchan, Charles. "Kosovo and the Future of U.S. Engagement in Europe." In *Alliance Politics, Kosovo, and NATO's War: Allied Force or Forced Allies?* New York: Palgrave, 2000, 75–90.

Lake, Anthony, and Roger Morris. "The Human Reality of Realpolitik." *Foreign Policy,* Fall 1971, 157–62.

Lamizet, Bernard, and Sylvie Debras. "France: Questions of Identity." In *The Kosovo Crisis: The Last American War in Europe?*, ed. Tony Weymouth and Stanley Henig. London: Reuters, 2001, 106–21.

Landay, Jonathan. "Kosovo, Next Balkan Boilover?" *The Christian Science Monitor International,* March 6, 1998, http://www.csmonitor.com/durable/1998/03/06/intl/intl.4.html.

Pierre Lefevre, *Le Soir,* February 2, 1999.

Library of Congress Country Studies, http://countrystudies.us/germany/163.htm.

Lieberman, Joseph. Interview with *PBS NewsHour* Online, October 1, 1998, http://www.pbs.org/newshour/bb/europe/july-dec98/kosovo_10-1.html.

Livingston, Ken. *Hansard,* March 25, 1999. http://www.publications.parliament.uk/cgi-bin/semaphoreserver?DB=semukparl&FILE=search.

Lloyd, Tony. *Hansard,* March 25, 1999. http://www.publications.parliament.uk/cgi-bin/semaphoreserver?DB=semukparl&FILE=search.

Luck, Edward. Remarks to the 64th General Assembly, September 1, 2009, http://www.ipacademy.org/news/general-announcement/98-general-assembly-passes-resolution-on-responsibility-to-protect.html.

MacDonald, Euan, and Philip Alston. "Sovereignty, Human Rights, Security." In *Human Rights, Intervention, and the Use of Force,* ed. Philip Alston and Euan MacDonald. Oxford: Oxford University Press, 2008.

Macleod, Alex. "Kosovo: France and the Emergence of a New European Security." In *Alliance Politics, Kosovo, and NATO's War: Allied Force or Forced Allies?* New York: Palgrave, 2000, 113–30.

Madigan, Janet Holl. *Truth, Politics, and Universal Human Rights.* New York: Palgrave, 2007.

"Majority of Greens Support NATO Air Strikes in Serbia." *Main Frankfurter Rundschau,* FBIS-WEU-1999–0324.

Malone, David. *Decision Making in the UN Security Council: The Case of Haiti, 1990–1997.* Oxford: Clarendon Press, 1998.

Martin, Pierre, and Mark R. Brawley, eds. *Alliance Politics, Kosovo, and NATO's War: Allied Force or Forced Allies?* New York: Palgrave, 2000.

Matlary, Jaane Haaland. "The Legitimacy of Military Intervention: How Important is a UN Mandate?" *Journal of Military Ethics* 3, no. 2 (2004): 129–41.

Mayall, James, ed. *The New Interventionism: United Nations Experience in Cambodia, Former Yugoslavia and Somalia.* Cambridge: Cambridge University Press, 1996.

Mayer, Harmut. "Early at the Beach and Claiming Territory? The Evolution of German Ideas on a New European Order," *International Affairs* 73, no. 4 (1997): 722.

McCarthy, Patrick, ed., *France-Germany, 1983–1993: The Struggle to Cooperate.* London: Macmillan, 1994.

McLean, Iain. Review of *Political Culture in Contemporary Britain: People and Politicians, Principles and Practice,* W. L. Miller, A. M. Timpson, and M. Lessnoff. Oxford: Clarendon Press, 1996. In *The British Journal of Sociology* 48, no. 3 (September 1997): 533–34.

Mead, Walter Russell. "Deadlier Than War," *Washington Post*, March 12, 2003, A21.
———. "The Jacksonian Tradition and American Foreign Policy." *The National Interest*. Washington, D.C.: 1999/2000.
Merkel, Angela. Remarks at NATO 60th Anniversary, March 26, 2009, http://nato monitor.blogspot.com/2009/04/let-strategic-concept-debate-begin.html.
Miller, Keith. "French Poll Shows More Than Three out of Four Oppose US War with Iraq." *NBC Nightly News*, January 24, 2003.
Minear, Larry, Colin Scott, and Thomas Weiss. *The News Media, Civil War and Humanitarian Action*. Boulder, Colo.: Lynne Rienner Publications, 1996.
Ministere des Affaires Etrangeres Dossiers d'archive. "Legal Basis of the Action Undertaken by NATO." Paris, March 25, 1999, http://www.france.diplo matie.fr/actual/ dossiers/kossovo/kossovo.html.
Moeller, Susan D. *Compassion Fatigue: How the Media Sell Disease, Famine, War and Death*. New York: Routledge, 1998.
Moore, Jonathan, ed. *Hard Choices: Moral Dilemmas in Humanitarian Intervention*. Lanham, Md.: Rowman and Littlefield, 1998.
Moorehead, Caroline. *Dunant's Dream: War, Switzerland and the History of the Red Cross*. London: Harper Collins, 1998.
Moravcsik, Andrew. "Explaining the Emergence of Human Rights Regimes: Liberal Democracy and Political Uncertainty in Postwar Europe." Weatherhead Center for International Affairs, Harvard University, December 1998, http://www.ciaonet.org/wps/moa02/.
MORI poll. *Mail on Sunday*, http://www.mori.com/polls/1999/ms990327.shtml.
"Most French Oppose War on Iraq," *Xinhua General News Service*, February 17, 2003.
Mueller, Harald, and Thomas Risse-Kappen. "Origins of Estrangement: The Peace Movement and the Changed Image of America in West Germany." *International Security* 12, no. 1 (Summer 1987): 59.
Mushaben, Joyce Marie. *From Post-War to Post-Wall Generations: Changing Attitudes toward the National Question and NATO in the Federal Republic of Germany*. Boulder, Colo.: Westview, 1999.
Nardin, Terry, and Melissa S. Williams. *Humanitarian Intervention*. New York: New York University Press, 2006.
National Security Strategy of the United States 2002, http://georgewbush-white house.archives.gov/nsc/nss/2002/nss5.html.
NATO, http://www.nato.int/kosovo/history.htm#2.
"NATO, British Leaders Allege 'Genocide' in Kosovo." March 29, 1999, CNN.com, http://www.cnn.com/WORLD/europe/9903/29/refugees.01/.
NATO Handbook. Brussels: NATO Office of Information Press, 1999.
NewsHour with Jim Lehrer, November 8, 2002.
Nonnenmacher, Peter. "Dragon-Slayer in the Heart of Europe." *Main Frankfurter Rundschau*, March 24, 1999, FBIS-WEU-1999–0323. http://www.fr-online.de/.
North Atlantic Council. *The North Atlantic Treaty*. April 4, 1949, http://www.nato. int/docu/basictxt/treaty.htm.
———. *Strategic Concept*. April 24, 1999.
Obama, Barak Hussein. Nobel Prize acceptance speech. December 10, 2009. http://www.nydailynews.com/news/politics/2009/12/10/2009-12-10_barack_ obama_nobel_peace_prize_speech_full_transcript.html.
O'Sullivan, John. "The British-French Duel." *United Press International*, March 24, 2003.

"Over 90 Percent of Germans Opposed to War against Iraq—Poll," *BBC Monitoring Europe*, October 2, 2002.

Patrick, Stewart. "Beyond Coalitions of the Willing: Assessing U.S. Multilateralism." *Ethics & International Affairs* 17, no. 1 (Spring 2003): 37–46.

"PDS Suit Challenging NATO Operation Dismissed." *German News* (English Edition), March 25, 1999, http://www.mathematik.uni-ulm.de/de-news/1999/03/2522.html.

Perez de Cuellar, Javier. *Somalia: The Missed Opportunities.* Washington, D.C.: United States Institute of Peace, 1994.

Podhoretz, Norman. *World War IV: The Long Struggle against Islamofascism.* New York: Doubleday, 2007.

Powell, Colin. *My American Journey.* New York: Random House, 1995.

Power, Samantha. *Chasing the Flame: Sergio Vieira De Mello and the Fight to Save the World.* New York: Penguin, 2008.

———. "Court of First Resort." *The New York Times,* February 10, 2005.

———. *A Problem from Hell: America and the Age of Genocide.* New York: Harper Collins, 2003.

Prados, Alfred B. "Iraq: Divergent Views on Military Action." *Congressional Research Service Report for Congress,* January 31, 2003.

"President Bush Announces Major Combat Operations in Iraq Have Ended: Remarks by the President from the USS *Abraham Lincoln.*" May 2003, http://www.whitehouse.gov/news/releases/2003/05/iraq/20030501–15.html.

"President Bush Delivers Graduation Speech at West Point." June 1, 2002, http://www.whitehouse.gov/news/releases/2002/06/print/20020601–3.html.

"Principles and Objectives of Germany's Human Rights Policy," *Auswartiegs Amt,* http://www.auswaertiges-amt.de.

Ramet, Sabrina P., and Phil Lyon. "Germany: The Federal Republic, Loyal to NATO." In *The Kosovo Crisis: The Last American War in Europe?,* ed. Tony Weymouth and Stanley Henig. London: Reuters, 2001.

Ramsey, Paul. *The Just War: Force and Political Responsibility.* New York: Charles Scribner's Sons, 1968.

Rathbun, Brian. "Partisan Lenses and Historical Frames: Ideology and the Politics of Humanitarian Intervention in Britain and Germany." Paper delivered at the American Political Science Association, August 28, 2002. http://apsaproceedings.cup.org/site/search.htm.

Ray, Joe. "The View from France: War with Iraq Looks a Lot Different from the French Perspective." *The Montreal Gazette,* March 19, 2003. http://www.joe-ray.com/index.php/JoeT/work/the_view_from_france_war_with_iraq_looks_a_lot_different_from_the_french_pe/.

Report of the International Commission on Intervention and State Sovereignty. December 2001, http://www.dfait-maeci.gc.ca/iciss-ciise/menu-en.asp.

"A Review of Worldwide Support (or Lack of It) for War on Iraq." *Eriposte,* http://www.eriposte.com/war_peace/iraq/iraq_war_worldwide_support.htm.

Richardson, Louise. "A Force for Good in the World? Britain's Role in the Kosovo Crisis." In *Alliance Politics, Kosovo, and NATO's War: Allied Force or Forced Allies?* New York: Palgrave, 2000, 145–64.

Rieff, David. *At the Point of a Gun: Democratic Dreams and Armed Intervention.* New York: Simon & Schuster, 2005.

————. "The Conversion of Bernard Kouchner."*Daily Star,* August 3, 2007.

"Rights Brought Home: The Human Rights Bill," http://www.archive.official-documents.co.uk/document/hoffice/rights/chap1.htm.

Roberts, Adam, "NATO's Humanitarian War over Kosovo,"*Survival,* Autumn 1999, 106.

Robertson, George. *Hansard,* March 25, 1999. http://www.publications.parliament.uk/cgi-bin/semaphoreserver?DB=semukparl&FILE=search.

————. House of Commons testimony, March 24, 1999, http://www.parliament.the-stationery-office.co.uk/pa/cm199900/cmselect/cmdfence/347/34707.htm.

Robinson, Dan. "War Powers Debated in Congress." *Voice of America News,* January 31, 2003.

Rohrabacher, Dana. Interview with Online *NewsHour,* March 11, 1999.

Rose, Sir Michael. House of Commons testimony, February 3, 1999, http://www.parliament.the-stationery-office.co.uk/pa/cm/cmhansrd.htm.

Rosenthal, Joel. Lecture at the Fletcher School of Law and Diplomacy, November 13, 2001.

Roth, Kenneth. "War in Iraq: Not a Humanitarian Intervention." *Human Rights Watch,* http://hrw.org/wr2k4/3.htm.

————. "Was the Iraq War a Humanitarian Intervention." *Journal of Military Ethics* 5, no. 2 (June 2006): 84–92.

Rouleau, Eric. "French Diplomacy Adrift in Kosovo,"*Le Monde Diplomatique,* December 1999, 5, http://mondediplo.com/1999/12/04rouleau.

Rubin, Jamie. Press conference at U.S. Department of State, October 7, 1998, http://www.hri.org/docs/statedep/1998.

Rudolf, Peter. "Germany and the Kosovo Conflict." In *Alliance Politics, Kosovo, and NATO's War: Allied Force or Forced Allies?* New York: Palgrave, 2000, 131–44.

Rutten, Maartje. "From St. Malo to Nice: European Defence: Core Documents." *Institute for Security Studies of the WEU 2001,* http://www.iss-eu.org/chaillot/chai47e.html#p.

Sachs, Jeffrey. "Saudi Arabia Was Real Target in Iraq War." *Financial Times,* August 12, 2003, http://www.globalpolicy.org/security/issues/iraq/justify/2003/0812target.htm.

Sahnoun, Mohamed. *Somalia: The Missed Opportunities.* Washington, D.C.: United States Institute of Peace, 1994.

Scharping, Rudolf. Interview with Richard Meng, *Main Frankfurter Rundschau,* March 27, 1999, FBIS-WEU-1999–0327.

Schöllgen, Gregor. "Putting Germany's Post-Unification Foreign Polity to the Test," *NATO Review* 41, no. 2 (1993). http://www.nato.int/docu/review/1993/9302-4.htm.

Schroeder, Gerhard. "German Security Policy at the Threshold of the 21st Century." Presented at the Conference for Security Policy, Munich, February 6, 1999, http://www.byndesregierung.de.

Schuck, Nathalie, "France Warns Iraq Would Divide World," Associated Press, February 26, 2003.

Security Strategy of the United States, September 2002, http://georgewbush-whitehouse.archives.gov/nsc/nss/2002/nss5.html.

Short, Clare. "Full Text: Clare Short's Statement." *Guardian,* March 18, 2003, http://www.guardian.co.uk/Iraq/Story/0,2763,916678,00.html.

Slaughter, Anne Marie. Lecture at Brown University, March 31, 2003.

Solana, Javier. Statement of March 23, 1999, USIS Washington file, http://www.fas.org/man/dod-101/ops/docs99/99032313_tlt.htm.

Spanier, John W. *American Foreign Policy since World War II*, 11th ed. Washington, D.C.: CQ Press, 1988.

Spicer, Nick. "France States They Are Not Prepared to Support Any UN Security Council Resolution That Would Authorize War with Iraq." *National Public Radio Morning Edition*, January 21, 2003.

"Statement on Kosovo Genocide," http//www.glypx.com/balkanwitness/genocide.htm.

Stent, Angela. *Russia and Germany Reborn: Unification, the Soviet Collapse, and the New Europe*. Princeton, N.J.: Princeton University Press, 1999.

Stowell, Ellery. *Intervention in International Law*. Washington, D.C.: John Byrne and Co., 1921.

Strategy and Force Planning, 3rd ed. Newport, R.I.: U.S. Naval War College Press, 2000.

Straw, Jack. "Strategic Priorities for British Foreign Policy," http://www:fco.gov.uk.

Stroebele, Hans Christian. March 26, 1999, Bundestag proceedings, http://www.bundestag.de/aktuell/bp/1999/bp9901/9901034b.html.

"Surveys Show Overwhelming Majority of French Oppose War with Iraq." *Deutsche Presse-Agentur*, January 9, 2003.

Sylva, Doulas A., and Susan Yoshihara. "Rights by Stealth: The Role of UN Human Rights Treaty Bodies in the Campaign for an International Right to Abortion." *National Catholic Bioethics Quarterly* 7, no. 1 (Spring 2007): 97–128. http://www.c-fam.org/docLib/20080425_Number_8_Rights_By_Stealth.pdf.

"That Awkward Relationship,"*The Economist*, May 14, 1998, http://www.economist.com.

Thatcher, Margaret. Interview with London Weekend Television *Weekend World*, January 6, 1980.

Thucydides. *History of the Peloponnesian War*. London: Penguin, 1972.

Transatlantic Trends 2003, http://www.transatlantictrends.org/trends/.

Travers, David. "The UN: Squaring the Circle." *The Kosovo Crisis: The Last American War in Europe?*, ed. Tony Weymouth and Stanley Henig. London: Reuters, 2001, 246–77.

United Nations Press Release, "Secretary General Presents His Annual Report to the General Assembly," September 20, 1999, http://www.un.org/News/Press/docs/1999/19990920.sgsm7136.html.

United Nations Security Council Resolution 1441 (8 November 2002), S/RES/1441 (2002).

Urban, Andrei. "Germany to Fulfil Obligations in Case of War with Iraq—Minister," *TASS*, December 13, 2002.

U.S. Code; Chapter 50A; Section 1091. Genocide, http://www.preventgenocide.org/law/domestic/uscode.htm.

"U.S. Congress Gives Bush Authority to Go to War against Iraq,"*Agence France Presse*, October 11, 2002.

Van Eekelen, Willem. *The Security Agenda for 1996: Background and Proposals*. CEPS Paper No. 64. Brussels: Centre for European Policy Studies, 1995.

Vasagar, Jeevan. "Schroeder Makes U-Turn on Iraq: Chancellor Will Allow US to Use German Bases in Event of War." *The Guardian London*, November 28, 2002.

Vedrine, Hubert. *Le Monde Diplomatique,* December 2000. http://mondediplo.com/2000/12/14foreignpolicy.

Vincour, John. "Going it Alone, U.S. Upsets France; So Paris Begins a Campaign to Strengthen Multilateral Institutions." *International Herald Tribune,* February 3, 1999, 1.

Viotti, Paul R. and Mark V. Kauppi. *International Relations Theory: Realism, Pluralism, Globalism and Beyond.* Boston: Allyn and Bacon, 1999.

"Volmer: Milosevic Counts on Greens' Pacifism against NATO," *Main Frankfurter Rundschau,* March 27, 1999, FBIS-WEU-1999–0327.

Von Clausewitz, Carl. *On War.* Princeton, N.J.: Princeton University Press, 1976.

Vrazo, Fawn. "Blair Manages a Vote of Support: A House of Commons Majority Backed a War Role. But Blair's Own Party Signaled Distaste." *The Philadelphia Inquirer,* March 19, 2003, A19.

Wallace, William. "Foreign Policy and National Identity in the United Kingdom." *International Affairs* 67, no. 1 (1991): 65–80.

———. "What Price Interdependence? Sovereignty and Interdependence in British Politics." *International Affairs* 62, no. 3 (Summer 1986): 382–85.

Walsh, Thomas F. III. "Operation Allied Force: Setting a New Precedent for Humanitarian Intervention?"Masters thesis, Naval Postgraduate School, Monterey, Calif., 2000.

Walzer, Michael. *Just and Unjust Wars: A Moral Argument with Historical Illustrations.* New York: Basic Books, 1977.

"War in Europe." *PBS Frontline,* http://www.pbs.org/wgbh/pages/frontline/shows/kosovo/etc/cron.html.

"War with Iraq" (poll). *MORI Social Research Institute,* http://www.mori.com/polls/2003/iraq2.shtml.

Warner, John. Interview with PBS *NewsHour* Online, October 1, 1998.

Weed, Perry L. *The White Ethnic Movement and Ethnic Politics.* New York: Praeger, 1973.

Weigel, David, "Obama's Wars." *Reason* 40, no. 5 (October 2008): 16.

Weigel, George. "The Just War Case for the War." *America.* March 31, 2003. http://www.americamagazine.org/content/article.cfm?article_id=2879.

———. "Iraq and Just War, Revisited."*The Catholic Difference.* April 21, 2004, http://www.catholicexchange.com/vm/PFarticle.asp?vm_id=2&art_id=23364&sec_id=44806.

Weigley, Russel Frank. *The American Way of War: A History of United States Military Strategy and Policy.* Bloomington: Indiana University Press, 1977.

Weinlein, Alexander. "Friedliche Losung mit militarischen Mitteln 24 Marz 1999: Erster Kampfeinsatz der Bundeswehr," http://www.das-parlament.de/2001/10/Titelseite/2001_10_001_4751.html.

Weiss, Thomas G. *Humanitarian Intervention: War and Conflict in the Modern World.* Malden, Mass.: Polity, 2007.

Wells, Bowen. *Hansard,* March 25, 1999. http://www.publications.parliament.uk/cgi-bin/semaphoreserver?DB=semukparl&FILE=search.

Weymouth, Anthony. "Why War, Why NATO." In *The Kosovo Crisis: The Last American War in Europe?,* ed. Tony Weymouth and Stanley Henig. London: Reuters, 2001, 1–14.

Wheeler, Nicholas. *Saving Strangers: Humanitarian Intervention in International Society.* Oxford: Oxford University Press, 2000.

"When You've a Moment, Bill." *The Economist,* September 24, 1998, http://www.economist.com.

White, N. D. *Keeping the Peace.* Manchester, UK: Manchester University Press, 1997.

Whitney, Craig R. "French Are Gearing Up to Join in Dousing the Flames in Kosovo." *The New York Times,* January 25, 1999, A6.

———. "Western Officials Say Accord on Kosovo Seems Uncertain," *The New York Times,* July 4, 1998, A6.

Wight, Martin. *Four Seminal Thinkers in International Theory: Machiavelli, Grotius, Kant, & Mazzini,* ed. Gabrielle Wight and Brian Porter. Oxford: Oxford University Press, 2005.

———. *International Theory: The Three Traditions.* London: Holmes & Meier, 1991.

———. *Power Politics,* ed. Hedley Bull and Carsten Holbraad. New York: Holmes & Meier Publishers, 1978.

———. *Systems of States,* ed. Hedley Bull. London: Leicester University Press, 1977.

———. "Western Values in International Relations." In *Diplomatic Investigations: Essays in the Theory of International Politics.* Cambridge, Mass.: Harvard University Press, 1966, 89–131.

Worldviews 2002 Survey of American and European Attitudes and Public Opinion on Foreign Policy, http://www.worldviews.org/key_findings/us_911_report.htm.

York, Byron. "President of the World." *National Review Online,* July 25, 3008. http://article.nationalreview.com/?q=ZTJkNzIwZWQ5MTU3OWY2ODM2OWRkZjczYjVjMGU4Yjg=.

Yoshihara, Susan. "The Quest for Happiness: How the UN's Advocacy of Economic, Social, and Cultural Rights Undermines Liberty and Opportunity." In *ConUNdrum: The Limits of the United Nations and the Search for Alternatives.* ed. Brett D. Schaefer. New York: Rowman & Littlefield, 2009, 169–208. http://www.c-fam.org/docLib/20091020_ConUNdrum.pdf.

Yost, David. *NATO and International Organizations.* Rome: NATO Defense College, 2007.

———. *NATO Transformed: The Alliance's New Roles in International Security.* Washington, D.C.: United States Institute for Peace, 1998.

Younger, Kenneth. "Britain in Europe: The Impact on Foreign Policy." *International Affairs* 48, no. 4 (1972): 579–92.

Zeman, Zybnek. *Selling the War: Art and Propaganda in World War II.* New York: Exeter, 1982.

Zumach, Andreas. "Rambouillet, ein Jahr danach," http://www.blaetter.de/kommenta/zuma0300.htm.

Index

About the Author

SUSAN YOSHIHARA is vice president for research at Catholic Family & Human Rights Institute. She previously served on the faculty at the Naval War College, where she taught national security affairs. She is a retired U.S. Navy helicopter pilot and Gulf War veteran. She is the author of numerous articles on human rights and development issues at the United Nations.

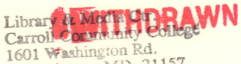